HIPS FROM REVAL TO TSUSHIM

P9-EDO-108

——————— Rozhdestvensky

—— —— —— Nebogatov

•••••••••• Folkersham

La Perouse Strait

Vladivostok
Port Arthur
Tsugaru Strait

Shanghai
Tsushima Strait

Hong Kong
FORMOSA

PHILIPPINES

Van Phong
Camranh
Bay

Malacca Strait

Singapore

By the Same Author

MY UNCONSIDERED JUDGEMENT
WHAT MANNER OF MAN
LOST CONTINENT
FALLEN SUN
BRITON HADDEN, CO-FOUNDER OF *Time*
ADLAI STEVENSON OF ILLINOIS
THAILAND, AN INTRODUCTION TO MODERN SIAM
TWO MINUTES TO NOON
T. R. AND HIS INFLUENCE ON OUR TIMES

THE
EMPEROR'S
SWORD

Togo and his officers on the forebridge of the *Mikasa*. In this punctilious representation by a Japanese painter, the Commander in Chief is holding his Zeiss binoculars and wearing the Emperor's sword. On his right hand stands Chief of Staff Kato. Behind the compass, bound in hammocks to impede the ricochet of shell splinters, is Chief Gunnery Officer Abo. Operations Officer Akiyama stands behind the sword. Zed Flag, on its way up the halyard at the left, shows that the battle is about to start.

THE EMPEROR'S SWORD

JAPAN vs. RUSSIA
IN THE BATTLE OF
TSUSHIMA

NOEL F. BUSCH

FUNK & WAGNALLS | NEW YORK

Copyright © 1969 by Noel F. Busch

All Rights Reserved.

Library of Congress Catalog Card Number: 69–15900

Published by Funk & Wagnalls,
   A *Division of* Reader's Digest Books, Inc.

Credit is due to The Illustrated London News for permission
to reproduce the photograph facing page 80.

BOSTON PUBLIC LIBRARY

Printed in the United States of America

TO MARY, WITH LOVE

Contents

THE
EMPEROR'S
SWORD

Prologue

Shortly before noon on the 21st of October, 1805, proceeding on his flagship, *Victory*, toward the battle of Trafalgar and his death a few hours later, Admiral Horatio Lord Nelson ordered his flag lieutenant, John Pasco, to signal a message to the fleet: "England confides that every man will do his duty."

"You must be quick," added the Admiral, "for I have one more to make, which is for 'Close Action.'"

Pasco had a helpful suggestion: "confides," he pointed out, was an unusual word that would have to be spelled out letter by letter. By replacing it with "expects," for which there was a single flag in the code book, he could save many precious moments.

"That will do, Pasco," exclaimed Lord Nelson, "but do it directly!"

Hasty improvisations like this were not at all in the style of Japan's Admiral Heihachiro Togo, who in Trafalgar's anniversary year of 1905 was proceeding, on the morning of May 27th, toward a naval encounter of at least comparable importance. A longtime admirer of Nelson, Togo had studied his career in detail some thirty years earlier, during a three-year stint on board the British training ship *Worcester,* anchored in Portsmouth harbor within sight of the famous *Victory,* and he was now about to signal his own fleet a message that amounted in large part to a Japanese paraphrase of Nelson's. There was, however, one noteworthy and characteristic difference between the two. Far from making his up on the spur of the moment, Togo had composed it months ahead of time and then had it committed to the navy code book, so that the whole thing could be conveyed by a single flag. The flag was the one representing the letter Z—or "zed," as Togo had learned to call it—which in the book was a spare letter to which the fleet commander could assign any significance he chose.

British pronunciation of the last letter in the alphabet and the splendid example of Lord Nelson were only two of several noteworthy contributions that the island kingdom off Europe had made to its counterpart off Asia in the critical occasion just then developing. Another was Togo's flagship itself, now heading southwest across the straits of Tsushima between Japan and Korea, against a stiff breeze that flung spray across her foredeck. Named for a hallowed Japanese mountain, the *Mikasa* had been built by the world-renowned firm of Vickers Sons and Maxim, Ltd., and launched at Barrow-in-Furness on November 8, 1900. Four hundred feet long, 76 feet wide, and displacing over 15,000 tons, she had a top speed of 18 knots. With her four 12-inch, fourteen 16-inch, and thirty-two smaller guns, she was rated by the editor of *Jane's Fighting Ships* at the time of her launching as the biggest and most powerful vessel in the world.

Mikasa, along with three sister ships and six armored cruisers, of which four were products of Britain and one each of Germany and France, had been completed just in time for the outbreak of the Russo-Japanese War in 1904. This coincidence was by no means accidental; and Togo was now leading his fleet into the climactic engagement in that war. His adversary was Russia's tall, bewhiskered Vice Admiral Zinovy Petrovich Rozhdestvensky, at the head of a vast armada of thirty-eight warships that were now on the last leg of an epic eighteen-thousand mile voyage from the Baltic Sea to Russia's Far East base of Vladivostok.

On the bridge of the *Mikasa* Togo stood in his accustomed position near the forward rail, one foot slightly advanced and his body thrust forward in the determined stance of some classic Japanese war-god. A tiny, Napoleonic figure —barely five feet, three inches tall and weighing less than 130 pounds—the Admiral somehow dominated the taller officers who surrounded him. These included Rear Admiral Tomosaburo Kato, his seasoned Chief of Staff; Commander Masayuki Akiyama, the brilliant and eccentric officer in charge of plans and operations, who had studied naval tactics for two years under the great Alfred Thayer Mahan at Newport, Rhode Island; and Captain Hikojiro Ijichi, Togo's boyhood friend, who was in command of the flagship itself.

The Commander in Chief was distinguishable from the rest of the group not only by his diminutive size but also by two items of equipment that he carried as a matter of inflexible habit. One was a pair of high-powered Zeiss binoculars, of which there were only four others in all of Japan. The other was a magnificent ceremonial sword in a gold-encrusted scabbard that hung at his left side, nearly touching the deck.

Togo's insistence on wearing this sword was a puzzle to some of his officers. They knew that it was a present from the Emperor but they also knew that the *Mikasa's* magnetic compass—today wrapped in tarpaulin to impede the ricochet of shell splinters—was such a delicate instrument that no one else on the bridge was allowed to carry so much as a penknife, lest it deflect the needle. The clue to this apparent contradiction lay in Togo's mystic devotion to swords generally and to the one he was wearing in particular.

For Togo a sword was far more than a mere weapon; it was also, in some occult way, a living part of its owner, an outward manifestation of his inward spirit. The blade given to Togo by the deified ruler was almost equivalent to the actual presence of its donor. When he wore it, as Togo had explained to Kato and one or two others, he felt as though the Mikado himself were standing at his side to ward off danger and strengthen his spirit.

The combination of prudent foresight on the one hand and reckless intuition on the other that characterized the complex mind of the Commander in Chief was soon to be displayed to maximum effect. Searching the horizon through his powerful glasses, Togo at 1:45 caught sight at last of the long smudge of smoke on the Southern sky that signified the approach of the Russian fleet. The moment to hoist the Zed flag had now arrived, and the order, at a sign from the Admiral, went from Togo to Captain Ijichi to a young signalman named Jinzaemon Takizawa, who stood at the flag locker. A moment later there shot up the slanting line to the yard-arm a four-foot square of Japanese cotton whose converging triangles of yellow, blue, red and black expressed Togo's message to his fleet: ON THIS ONE BATTLE RESTS THE FATE OF OUR NATION. LET EVERY MAN DO HIS UTMOST.

If the second part of this message was a paraphrase of Nelson's, the first half was to some degree an understatement. In tonnage of ships lost, the Battle of Tsushima, which was to begin a very few minutes later, was not only bigger than Trafalgar or any other previous sea fight. It was also, in all probability—since the great naval battles of World War II were, and those of the future presumably will be, decided by air-power—the biggest sea-battle, in the true sense of the term, that ever will be fought. On it depended not only the immediate fate of Japan but much more besides; and it had correspondingly deep and remote historical causes.

PART ONE

Preparation

Bushi wa kuwanedo taka yoji—
Samurai, when starving: long toothpick.

I

In exploring the historical origins of any event, the best place to start is no doubt at the very beginning. In the case of the battle of Tsushima, this involves the Sun Goddess Amaterasu and her grandson, Ninigi, who descended from a cloud in 660 B.C. to found the Imperial family that has indubitably ruled Japan ever since without noticeable break. The part of Japan on which Ninigi is supposed to have landed is not the main island of Honshu but the southernmost island of Kyushu; and on this point Japanese mythology is confirmed by the findings of modern anthropologists who agree that the earliest migrants to Japan, whether from the mainland of Asia or the islands to the south, landed on Kyushu before proceeding northward to displace the aboriginal Ainu. In any case, whether Ninigi or some less august personages began it, Kyushu's subsequent role in Japan's history has been fully commensurate with its importance as the nation's starting point.

One of the things that helps to account for Kyushu's peculiar role in Japanese history is the character of its people. Owing doubtless in part to the region's topography, which is mountainous and infertile, Kyushu's residents are traditionally even more hard-working and diligent than their descendants on the more moderately inhospitable islands to the north. Likewise, whether because of their agricultural disadvantages or because of their migratory heritage, Kyushu's denizens, making a virtue of their craggy and irregular coastline, have always been seafarers. In addition to heading north to populate the islands of Honshu, Shikoku, and Hokkaido, early settlers of Kyushu, especially those in its extreme southwestern province of Satsuma, ventured even further south. Around A.D. 1600 they took partial possession of the island chain that the Chinese call Liu-Ch'iu, and the Japanese, Ryukyu, whose residents also paid tribute to the emperors of China. This mobility required ocean-going warships at a time when the rest of Japan had only fishing boats; and the salty traditions of Satsuma, as maintained to the present day, have always been not merely nautical but naval.

Owing to its accessibility from the south, Kyushu was always, until recent times, the part of Japan where strangers, divine or otherwise, were most likely to land first. After Ninigi the most notable of these was the great Jesuit missionary St. Francis Xavier, who in the year 1549 spent some months in Satsuma before moving on to the more populous, and hence for his purposes more productive, metropolis of Nagasaki. In both areas the hardy character of Kyushu's inhabitants had deep appeal for the bold and austere Jesuit saint, and he paid them a memorable tribute: "These people are the delight of my heart."

Fortunately for his own peace of mind St. Francis could not foresee, and did not live to witness, the unhappy results of his attachment. Shortly after relieving the Emperor of the responsibility for governing Japan early in the following century, the shoguns, or hereditary chief executives, of the Tokugawa family reached the conclusion that

Kyushu's growing Christian minority constituted a subversive element in the population and should be ruthlessly eliminated. To this end they first closed the country to all outsiders except a few docile and non-Catholic Dutch traders and then launched the most bloodthirsty persecution of Christians since the days of Imperial Rome, climaxed in 1638 by the slaughter of thirty-seven thousand who had taken refuge in a Kyushu fortress. For the next two hundred and forty years all four islands—Kyushu, Shikoku, Honshu, and Hokkaido—remained *terra incognita* to all foreigners and entirely isolated from the rest of the world except for the two ships a year with which the Dutch were allowed to carry on a minuscule trade from a bleak little island in Nagasaki harbor.

During the period of Japan's self-imposed isolation, numerous changes occurred in the rest of the world. By the middle of the nineteenth century these included the American and French Revolutions, the development of the steam engine, and the European colonization of Asia. To the U.S., which had only recently acquired its own shore frontage on the Pacific, the rapid expansion of English, French, Portuguese, and Dutch outposts in India, the East Indies, and along the coast of China suggested the distasteful possibility that European powers might attempt to help themselves also to the Japanese islands. By this time, moreover, U.S. clipper ships were conducting a brisk trade with China, and six hundred U.S. whalers a year were operating in the North Pacific. Both types of vessels would often have found it convenient to take on supplies and water in Japan. Instead, on the rare occasions when they were wrecked or otherwise forced to put ashore on any of its islands, their occupants were either rudely ejected or—apparently in conformity with the Japanese law governing such contingencies—summarily done away with.

U.S. efforts to remedy this unsatisfactory state of affairs started in the 1840s, when two U.S. vessels put in at Japanese ports and politely suggested that the shogunal government moderate its xenophobia to the extent of letting occasional visitors drop in to replenish supplies. When these suggestions were ignored, President Millard Fillmore took the step that perhaps chiefly qualifies his term in the White House for historical attention, although he had already moved out by the time it became effective. This was to draft a strong letter to the shogun, demanding not only that U.S. ships be allowed to land in Japan but also that Japan open at least one of its ports to international trade. The President's somewhat peremptory message called for a prompt reply and implied that an unfavorable one would be regarded as an invitation to use more coercive measures. For delivery to the shogunal government, the letter was entrusted to a stern, dignified, and widely traveled commodore of the U.S. Navy whose name was Matthew Calbraith Perry and whose nickname was "Old Bruin." On July 8, 1853, Old Bruin sailed into what was then called Edo Bay at the head of a flotilla of four warships.

Under the Tokugawa shoguns, Japanese shipyards had been forbidden to build anything much bigger than fishing smacks or coastal junks, all of which, like Japanese houses, were constructed of unpainted wood bleached by the weather to a light, faded gray. Foreign vessels—usually painted some color that showed up dark against the distant horizon—were customarily referred to as "black ships"; and this term, which the islanders naturally applied to Perry's, was mistakenly supposed by later foreign commentators to impute to them some evil purpose or character. But if the hue of Perry's squadron did not particularly surprise the Japanese who first saw them, both their armament and their method of propulsion did.

Two of Perry's black ships were paddle-wheel steamers,

and these towed the two others, their sails furled, into the harbor against the wind. The four vessels bristled with more than a hundred guns of various sizes, and the Japanese had learned enough about cannon from the Dutch to be well aware that they had no weapons to match them. When Perry, before departing for the Ryukyus to pass the typhoon season and the winter, announced that he would return the next spring for the answer to his letter, the shogun's emissaries asked whether he meant to bring all his ships back with him.

"Probably more," growled Old Bruin.

When, true to his word, Perry returned with seven ships the following February, the answer he had sought was speedily forthcoming in the form of an agreement to permit the establishment of a U.S. Consulate and the opening of trade relations. News of Perry's accomplishment soon reached Europe, and within two years more or less similar trade agreements had been reached with England, France, and Germany, bringing Japan's long era of isolation to an astonishingly abrupt conclusion. While the results for the foreign powers were generally satisfactory, the consequences within Japan were, to put it mildly, most unsettling.

According to widely accepted Western theory, feudal Japan at the time of Perry's arrival was a nation whose development, already retarded by the geographical handicap of being so far away from Europe, had been impeded even more drastically by its long period of intentional isolation. Japan's emergence from "feudalism"—a word that for Westerners is likely to connote crossbows, forelock-tugging yeomen, and King Alfred watching a batch of pancakes—accordingly seemed little short of miraculous. In fact, while Japan's rapid readjustment to the rest of the world may well have been miraculous, the miracle was of a somewhat different sort which, all the more for that reason, deserves to be better understood.

In the first place, Japanese feudalism differed from the medieval version in Europe so markedly that the use of the same term for both may well be misleading. In the second, the progress made by Europe during the period of Japan's isolation had perhaps been less prodigious than many Western observers are inclined to suppose. To be sure, by 1853 the industrial revolution was well under way and steam transportation—as Perry's own mode of arrival amply suggested—was about to usher in a new era of commerce. On the other hand, the steam engines of the mid-nineteenth century were still relatively primitive contrivances and the mass production era of the twentieth century still lay far in the future. In short, Japan had much less distance to make up than would have been the case a few decades later; and the rigidly compartmentalized nature of its social order perhaps made it more, rather than less, capable of coping with changes engendered by industrialization than were the societies of Europe.

Under the Tokugawa shoguns, Japan had in fact managed to do quite well without outside assistance; relieved of the burden of foreign entanglements, bellicose or otherwise, the nation had developed a serene and harmonious culture that was in many ways further advanced than any produced in the more gregarious West. In Japan, local administration was provided by two hundred or so hereditary *daimio,* or princes, each with his own private army of *samurai,* or hereditary warriors, paid in bags of rice contributed by the peasants who worked the daimio's land holdings.

Each daimio also maintained, along with the rural castle from which he governed his province, another resi-

dence in the shogunal capital of Edo. Here he was expected to dwell for part of each year, and to leave his
family as hostages the rest of the time so that, through
them, the shogun could exert effective supervision and influence. Meanwhile, the figurehead Emperor maintained
his traditional court at Kyoto, where a small band of noble
families devoted their ample leisure to the pleasures of art,
erudition, and amorous frivolities.

Abruptly confronted by the question of how to deal
with a gross invasion of national privacy, the shogunal
government, or *Bakufu,* reacted with praiseworthy resili-
ence. Obviously, the West had gotten far ahead of Japan
in regard to the instruments of transportation and combat,
in both of which it behooved Japan to catch up before she
was subjected to the ignominious fate of her more accessible neighbors. Obviously, also, the best way to do so was
by sending emissaries abroad to look into the matter as
rapidly and exhaustively as possible. The first of these missions came to the U.S. in 1860 for the express purpose of
signing a trade treaty in Washington and the diary kept by
its diligent reporting officer, Muragaku Awaji-no-kami, still
makes engaging reading.

On arriving in San Francisco aboard the *Powhatan,*
which had been Perry's flagship six years before, the
ninety-three members of the group, wearing kimono and
geta, or wooden clogs, were a source of considerable
wonder to the ten thousand residents of what was then
still not much more than an outsize mining camp. Quartered at the Matheson International Hotel, the members
of the mission found their first glimpse of Western civiliza-
tion equally astonishing and gasped with amazement at
such innovations as beds, newspapers, and chamber-pots.
Concerning the latter, the diarist reported understandable
confusion: "One of my friends, who could not find his pil-

low though he searched the room, found a clean white jar under the bed which he used as a pillow and was very happy."

From San Francisco, whose energetic Chinese immigrants had not yet completed its rail link with the rest of the nation, the mission proceeded by steamship to Panama, where the railroad train that took them across the Isthmus was the first they had ever seen. The ride made a profound impression:

> The train was released and started. As it sped like an arrow we could not distinguish the trees and plants on either side of the road. The noise sounded like a thousand peals of thunder over one's head and no matter with how loud a voice one spoke he still could not be understood. But the cars did not rock and they went very fast. . . . The distance of 57 miles . . . was covered in three hours. The reader will please consider this great speed. . . .

In due course, the mission found itself at Washington, where the members attended a ball given by Secretary of State Lewis Cass. "Officers in uniform with epaulets and swords and ladies dressed in gowns of light white material began, couple by couple, moving around the room, walking on tiptoe to the tune of the music. They went round and round as nimbly as so many white mice on their monotonous walk, without making fluttering gestures with their hands even. . . . Upon our enquiring, we were told that this was what is called a 'waltz'. . . ."

In Philadelphia they visited the Mint, among other places of interest, and in New York attended a performance by a professional magician which also elicited favorable comment. Catching sight of them as they moved up Broadway, Walt Whitman felt inspired to start his poem entitled "A Broadway Pageant" with the resounding lines:

Over sea, hither from Niphon,
Courteous, the Princes of Asia, swart cheek'd princes,
First-comers, guests, two-sworded princes,
Lesson-giving princes, leaning back in their open barouches, bare-headed, impassive,
This day they ride through Manhattan. . . .

When the time came for their return, around Cape Horn on the *Niagara,* they passed the 675-foot *Great Eastern* coming up the harbor on its maiden voyage from England, powered by five masts of sail, five smokestacks, two paddle wheels, and a screw propeller.

Perhaps even more significant than the things that dazzled the mission, however, were those that failed to surprise its more sophisticated members. Among the most observant of these was a twenty-five-year-old student named Yukichi Fukuzawa, who had come along as an aide to one of the senior dignitaries on the Japanese steamship *Kanrin Maru,* recently purchased from the Dutch to accompany the *Powhatan* for face-saving purposes.

To Fukuzawa, his cramped quarters on the voyage were suggestive of being in jail during a marathon earthquake. In San Francisco he was astounded by "the valuable carpets which in Japan only the more wealthy could buy from importers' shops at so much a square inch to make purses and tobacco pouches . . . laid over an entire room." On being served champagne "we noticed strange fragments floating in them. . . . Some of the party swallowed these floating particles; others expelled them suddenly; others bravely chewed them. This was an adventure—finding out that they were ice. . . ."

Much less astounding to Fukuzawa than such questionable amenities as ice in champagne was, as he later recalled, the absence of some others that he had been led to expect.

There was as yet no railway laid to the city. . . . But the telegraph system and also Galvani's electroplating were already in use. . . . We were taken to a sugar refinery and had the principle of the operation explained to us quite minutely. I am sure that our hosts thought they were showing us something entirely new, naturally looking for our surprise at each new device of modern engineering. But, on the contrary, there was nothing really new, at least to me. . . . I had been studying nothing else but such scientific principles ever since I had entered Ogata's school. . . .

The Japanese mission that visited the U.S. was only the first of many such groups that were shortly thereafter dispatched to England, France, and Germany, to study not only the industrial, educational, and political systems in those lands but also, and more especially, the composition, training, and equipment of their armed forces. Meanwhile, at the tiny fishing village of Yokohama, which had been designated by the shogun as the appropriate residence for Western diplomats and traders, a lively foreign colony soon appeared on the scene. Dean of the diplomatic community was U.S. Consul Townsend Harris, who, with his Dutch amanuensis, Henricus Heusken, had arrived in 1856 to spend his first two years in a converted temple at the even more remote hamlet of Shimoda. The community's most conspicuous member was naturally the British Minister, Sir Rutherford Alcock, who, soon after his appearance two years later, assembled a staff of six, several members of which accompanied him when in 1861 he attracted national attention by climbing Japan's sacred 12,365-foot Mount Fuji.

It was activities like this, far more than the fact-finding missions dispatched abroad, that led to serious unrest in Japan in the years just after Perry's arrival. Despite the best efforts of the shogunal government, the foreigners

tended to behave themselves with an apparently incorrigible nonchalance. This caused serious misunderstandings
for reasons that the visitors could hardly be expected to
grasp.

While the shogunal system had conferred on Japan the
blessings of domestic tranquillity for more than two centuries, it had never been wholly acceptable to some of the
more powerful daimio, especially those whose fiefs lay fur-
thest away from the capital. By the mid-nineteenth century, even before the arrival of Perry, some of these dissat-
isfied nobles were murmuring that, after nearly two and a
half centuries of Tokugawa rule, the time might have come
for a change. Had things gone on as usual these murmurs,
like others in the past, might well have died down without
noteworthy consequences. Instead, the arrival of Perry
and the influx of Europeans that followed provoked an internal crisis.

While the shogun's advisors at Edo, having seen Perry's
ships, quickly realized what damage they could inflict, the
imperial court at Kyoto, three hundred miles inland to the
southwest, had not had this opportunity. There the opinion prevailed that the shogun had simply been frightened
into an overly hasty compliance with Perry's demands.
Led by the great daimio of the southwestern regions, who
had long envied the Tokugawa their political preemi-
nence, there arose a faction whose slogan was "Honor the
Emperor and expel the barbarians."

Even more wholehearted supporters of this policy than
the daimio themselves were their loyal samurai followers,
who sensed that, so far as they were concerned, admitting
strangers and opening Japan to such plebeian pursuits as
commerce might well have disastrous consequences. How
deep these feelings ran was dramatically revealed from
time to time in gory episodes such as the murder of two
Russian sailors in a Yokohama side street in 1860, and that

of the good natured, happy-go-lucky Henricus Heusken after a New Year's Eve party in Edo a year later. More alarming than either was an incident in the following year which had more immediate consequences—as well as an indirect bearing on the battle of Tsushima, still almost half a century in the future.

Of all the powerful daimio whose fiefs were remote from the shogunal capital of Edo, the most remote and the most powerful was probably Saburo Shimazu, lord of Satsuma. While not actually an independent nation, his domain was closest of any in Japan to being just that. Satsuma had its own dialect, its own music, and its own pottery (the nation's finest), of which examples were to be sent to the Paris World Fair of 1871 as though from a sovereign state. Satsuma not only had its own crest—a cross inside a circle—but even its own flag—a red sun against a white background—which was presently to become that of the entire nation. The flag already flew on the six ships of Satsuma's private navy, of which, by 1861, three were steamers recently purchased from Holland. These ships were based at the Satsuma capital of Kagoshima, a picturesque little port notched into the lush semi-tropical hills surrounding a bay whose most noteworthy feature was a smoky, three-thousand-foot volcano.

To the Shimazu clan of Satsuma, whose lineage naturally went back to the dawn of history, the Tokugawa shoguns had never seemed much more than insolent parvenus. Supported by the bravest and most skillful samurai in the land, the former were inevitably prime proponents of the new policy of "Honor the Emperor and expel the barbarians." Hence, when, in the summer of 1862, the Emperor was persuaded to step out of his role of figurehead and call a council of nobles at Kyoto, requesting the shogun to attend it—a request unprecedented for over two centuries—it was naturally Saburo Shimazu, acting as regent on behalf of his small son, who volunteered to deliver the invitation.

Accompanied by his top general and political adviser, the renowned Takamori Saigo, along with six hundred other retainers, Saburo Shimazu delivered his invitation at Edo with due ceremony. The result—since the aging shogun was not yet prepared for sudden demotion to the role of a mere member of a court council—was a curt refusal. Left with no recourse but to report this snub to the Mikado, the lord of Satsuma set out on his return journey on September 13th, in a far from festive state of mind. The next morning he and his great procession reached the small hamlet of Namamugi, where the famous Tokaido highway from Edo to Kyoto turned inland from the shoreline of Edo Bay.

The morning of the 14th was cool and clear, an ideal day for outdoor diversions. Hence, it was by no means surprising that a party of four blithe British sightseers who had set out from Yokohama on horseback an hour or so earlier arrived at Namamugi at about the same time. One member of this party was an out-of-town visitor named Charles Lennox Richardson, a thirty-five-year-old trader from Shanghai who on his way back to England had stopped off in Japan to see some old friends from China who had just settled down there. The others were his two local acquaintances, William Marshall and Woodthorpe Clarke, and Marshall's sister-in-law, a Mrs. Borrodaile.

Hoping to witness some picturesque Tokaido doings, such as formed the subject of Hiroshige's famous series of prints, the four excursionists were understandably gratified when they encountered what seemed to them to be just such a spectacle. This was a procession of armed warriors whose uniforms were adorned with a crest in the form of a circle around a cross and whose flags showed a red ball against a white background. Where the roadway grew narrow, the British party reined in their horses and prepared to enjoy the colorful scene. Shouts by the advance guard of something that sounded like "*Sh'ta ni, sh'ta ni!*" did not in the least disturb them; they did not know what the words meant, and, had they done so, would doubtless have considered them applicable only to "natives." This was unfortunate, for they were the traditional cry with which members of the local population along the line of march were warned when a major lord and his retinue passed by. The words meant "Show respect!" or, more literally, "Kneel down!"

As to precisely what happened next, accounts understandably differ. According to the Shimazu version of the affair, the British party, displaying arrogance of a sort that might have been acceptable in China or India, not only failed to dismount but actually tried to ride directly across the Shimazu line of march. According to Marshall, Clarke, and Mrs. Borrodaile, the four visitors paired off to squeeze out of the way and then sat their horses quietly at the edge of the roadway. In any event, even the latter procedure might well have seemed—to the followers of a princely daimio whose already keen distaste for foreign intruders had just been honed to a fine edge by his cold reception from the shogun—to call for a sharp reprisal.

What all except Richardson—who did not live to report —agreed was that several members of the daimio's guard drew their swords and rushed at the foreigners. Clarke and Marshall were both painfully slashed, the former so severely that he later lost an arm. Both wheeled their mounts and retired, calling the others to follow. Mrs. Borrodaile and Richardson, who were closer to the line of the procession, bore the brunt of the attack, but although the former had her hat knocked off and her hair disarranged, she managed to make her escape. Richardson was cut and mauled so severely that he fell from his horse and was then slashed at again on the ground.

When the procession went on, leaving Richardson prostrate and almost helpless, he managed to drag himself as far as a nearby tea shop, where he asked for water. A few minutes later retainers of a lesser Satsuma nobleman whose palanquin was following that of the daimio himself, discovered him and administered a gruesome *coup de grâce*. Later that afternoon Richardson's partly disemboweled body, with one severed hand lying beside it, was found by a party of his Yokohama compatriots who rode out to look for him after the return of his three companions.

That evening a meeting of Yokohama's horrified foreigners convened to debate setting off in a body to overtake the Shimazu army, by this time quartered for the night in nearby Hodogaya. There, reinforced by seamen from all the ships in the harbor, they could administer appropriate vengeance. Cooler council eventually prevailed, specifically that of the British Chargé d'Affaires, a sensible and seasoned little man called Colonel Neale, who persuaded the foreign community that the matter could be handled more effectively through diplomacy than by direct action. Since the nearest cable-head was in India, arrangements to this end took time, but the British Embassy was eventually instructed by the Foreign Office in London to exact an indemnity of £100,000 from the Shogun and an additional payment of £25,000 from the lord of Satsuma, the latter amount to be distributed to Richardson's heirs and to the three friends who had accompanied him. In addition, the actual assassins of Richardson were to be apprehended and executed in the presence of British officers.

Confronted by these demands, the shogun in due course agreed to pay his £100,000 but stated that he had no means whatsoever of compelling Satsuma to contribute its share of the indemnity, let alone of forcing its daimio to produce the samurai actually guilty of Richardson's murder. The inference to be drawn was that the British would have to attend to these details for themselves; and perhaps also that, from the shogun's viewpoint, a direct confrontation with the barbarians might be a salutary experience for the haughty and heretofore unmolested lords of Satsuma. For the British, situations of this sort were far from a novelty. Similar occurrences in India, Hong Kong, and elsewhere had served as convenient pretexts for corrective measures that sometimes led to outright foreclosure. In this instance the results were predictable.

On the 14th of August, 1863, just eleven months to the day after the encounter at Namamugi and an even decade after Perry's arrival at Edo, Britain's 101-gun China squadron, with Rear Admiral Augustus Leopold Kuper commanding and Colonel Neale aboard his flagship, the *Euryalus,* which was leading the *Pearl, Perseus, Argus, Racehorse, Coquette,* and *Havoc,* sailed into Kagoshima Bay to demand payment of the indemnity and surrender of Richardson's murderer. Informed that the daimio was out of town at the moment, enjoying the hot springs at a mountain resort several days' travel away, the British authorities were invited to await his return or, if they preferred, to go ashore to parley with his highest-ranking retainers. Kuper refused to do either. Instead, to ensure prompt compliance with his demands, he seized the three Satsuma steamships that were at anchor in one corner of the harbor and had them towed into the center of the British squadron, to serve as hostages.

In Japan's colorful history *kamikaze,* or divine winds, have come to her rescue so dramatically at moments of threatened invasion that an opportune typhoon on such occasions is almost a prerequisite. The Kagoshima crisis of

1863 was no exception and when the barometer, after a rapid rise in exceptionally dry air, suddenly began falling as the sky clouded over and the breeze freshened, the citizens of Kagoshima knew just what to expect. Meanwhile, the Satsuma army rushed to man the harbor fortifications— a dozen or so batteries ringing the bay from the hillsides with eighty-seven smooth-bore muzzle-loading cannon trained on the harbor below. At midday on the 15th the first shot was fired—not from one of the warships of the punitive expedition but from one of the Japanese forts.

What followed was a lively ship-to-shore engagement in which, as the typhoon gathered force, the British squadron first set fire to the three Satsuma hostage ships and then cruised along the shoreline, pouring broadsides into the town. The British shells, exploding as they landed, set fire to the flimsy wooden houses and soon the whole city was in flames. Nonetheless, at such close range even the antiquated guns of the harbor batteries were able to provide effective retaliation.

Firing from fixed platforms that supplied better footing than the increasingly unsteady decks of the warships, the smooth-bore harbor guns, though they used only nonexplosive cannon balls, could be aimed accurately at the ships below them. Manned by some of the ablest gunners in Japan, they found their mark frequently—most notably one forty-pound shot that neatly decapitated both the *Euryalus*'s Captain Josling and his executive officer, Commander Wilmot, as they stood beside Admiral Kuper, who happened at the moment to be bending over a chart, on the bridge of the flagship. "Boy, have that mess wiped up!" said the Admiral after a quick backward glance at the two headless bodies, and then resumed the study of his chart.

As the typhoon reached maximum fury, the warships withdrew to shelter behind the volcano. The next morning, after a few more rounds directed toward the now si-

lent shore batteries, the squadron sailed back to Yokohama. The battle of Kagoshima Bay thus ended with both
sides claiming victory. The British basis for the claim was
that they had in fact demolished a large part of the town
and that, a month or so later, the indemnity was finally
paid. Satsuma, however, preferred to regard the indemnity as more in the nature of a charitable contribution, motivated by *noblesse oblige;* and it could point to
the fact that the British forces had been repulsed after
suffering damage and casualties, without effecting a land-
ing, and leaving the harbor forts still effective. Most important of all, the swordsman chiefly guilty of Richardson's death, later well known to have been a particularly
hot-tempered samurai named Kizaemon Narabara, had
never been even arrested, let alone surrendered or executed—in strict accord with the samurai code of loyalty
from master to warrior.

Whatever its outcome, the battle of Kagoshima also had
other claims to historical recognition, one of which was
ably set forth in a speech delivered on the lawn of the
Shimazu residence there, forty-three years later. The
speech was made by a Japanese dignitary in the course of
welcoming a mission sent by Britain's King Edward VII to
award the Order of the Garter to Kagoshima's most famous citizen. One member of the British Mission was
Lord Redesdale, who, as the Hon. Algernon Mitford, had
served in the Tokyo Embassy under Sir Richard Alcock.
Redesdale quoted the Japanese speaker as saying that the
Kagoshima engagement had been "largely instrumental in
bringing about the reformation . . . in Japan" and showing its recalcitrant isolationists that "no country in these
days could hope to stand alone."

Listening to these worthy sentiments with a slight, enigmatic smile was the guest of honor and actual recipient of
the Garter: Heihachiro Togo, by that time one of the

world's most celebrated admirals. The ceremony was taking place at Kagoshima because it was there, according to his official biographer, that Togo, at the age of fifteen, wearing "a tight sleeved *haori* and short *hakama,* with a round hat adorned with the family crest" and "with two swords at his side and a match-lock on his shoulder," had received his baptism of fire while serving one of the city's hillside guns.

II

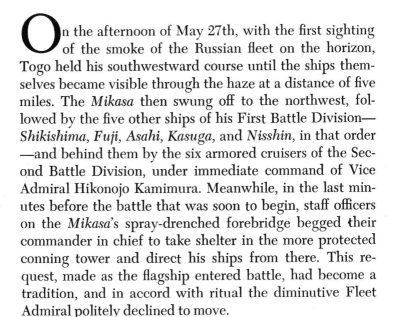

On the afternoon of May 27th, with the first sighting of the smoke of the Russian fleet on the horizon, Togo held his southwestward course until the ships themselves became visible through the haze at a distance of five miles. The *Mikasa* then swung off to the northwest, followed by the five other ships of his First Battle Division—*Shikishima, Fuji, Asahi, Kasuga,* and *Nisshin,* in that order—and behind them by the six armored cruisers of the Second Battle Division, under immediate command of Vice Admiral Hikonojo Kamimura. Meanwhile, in the last minutes before the battle that was soon to begin, staff officers on the *Mikasa's* spray-drenched forebridge begged their commander in chief to take shelter in the more protected conning tower and direct his ships from there. This request, made as the flagship entered battle, had become a tradition, and in accord with ritual the diminutive Fleet Admiral politely declined to move.

"I am getting on for sixty," he said, "and this old body of mine is no longer worth caring for. But you are all young men with your futures before you, so take care of yourselves and continue living in order to serve your country."

The colloquy pointed up a noteworthy distinction between war on sea and war on land. In a land battle the commanding general normally and quite properly occupies a central headquarters far behind the lines, from which, entirely protected from shot and shell, he can communicate readily with all his subordinate field officers. At sea the conditions are reversed. Communications between the commander in chief and his subordinates, all of them in motion, are precarious at best and the commander in chief, far from occupying a safe headquarters, is not merely on the firing line but—since his flagship traditionally leads the line of battle—the bull's-eye of the target.

Among the items of decor in Togo's cabin on the *Mikasa* were an unexploded Russian shell that had landed on the bridge, where it would have killed the Admiral if it had gone off, and a torpedo whisker found in the *Mikasa*'s net. These grim reminders of the hazards of his profession were to Togo merely encouraging evidence that he had now remained almost magically untouched by them for upward of forty years. In his case, indeed, the dangers of his present exposed position on the bridge of his flagship as she went into battle might well have seemed trivial compared to many others of widely diverse nature which he had been fortunate enough to survive in the long decades since the precocious start of his career.

That the future naval hero of Japan should have made his martial debut at the age of fifteen was actually not especially surprising, in view of the circumstances in general and of his family background in particular. While the social structure of Japan, beneath the ruling oligarchy, was rigidly stratified into samurai, artisans, and merchants, the samurai aristocracy itself was even more sharply divided into upper-class members, who might become advisers to their lord or even to the Emperor, and lower-class ones,

who were little more than patrician foot soldiers. Heihachiro Togo's father, whose lineage dated back to a fifteenth
century daimio of Togo (whence he derived his surname
meaning "Eastern Village"), had held the post of *kori
bugyo,* or district magistrate, for thirteen years, though
the normal tenure was only three. That he belonged well
up in the upper half of the samurai order could be deduced
from the locale of this district, which also contained the
family residence. Quite separate from the seaside residen-
tial palace in which the daimio of Satsuma lived—and
where Togo was later to be awarded the Order of the
Garter—was the castle in downtown Kagoshima from
which Saburo Shimazu administered his province. This
castle stood on a hill not far from the little Kotsuki
River, flowing through the center of the town. The resi-
dential section of town, reserved for the samurai, lay between the castle and the river and in this enclave the status
of each resident could be roughly inferred from the proxim-
ity of his house to that of the castle. The block from which
Togo came, close enough to suggest considerable eminence,
also contributed several other celebrated citizens to
Japanese history. These included Toshimichi Okubo, the
distinguished statesman who was assassinated in 1878,
Iwao Oyama, the renowned general who helped found
Japan's national army, and, most famous of all, Oyama's
cousin, the great Takamori Saigo, who by 1863 was the
daimio's principle adviser. Saigo's younger brother lived
nearby, and during young Togo's childhood tutored him
in calligraphy.

Togo's schooling followed conventional Satsuma patterns. After going to the younger Saigo's house for his calligraphy lesson at six A.M., he came home for breakfast at
eight and then spent the rest of the morning studying Chinese classics. The afternoons were devoted to lessons in
such practical pursuits as fencing and wrestling, or else to

games and swimming in the nearby river. At the age of twelve, along with his primary-school classmates, Togo entered the *Goju*, or Village Association of Young Men, where the schedule of instruction, like many other things in Japan, was digitally subdivided. One morning in five was spent on writing, one on military history, one on tactics, and one each on two other subjects of presumptive relevance to a future career as a warrior. The afternoons were assigned to similarly appropriate physical exercise.

The object of all this training was not merely to enable its recipients to read, write, and take care of themselves in a quarrel. Even more important was to instill in them the spirit of *bushido*—the samurai code based on courage, endurance, and unswerving loyalty to one's parents, prince, and Emperor. In demonstrating these qualities a samurai was expected to take pride in ignoring all forms of hardship or trouble. His disdain for poverty occasioned the popular saying *"Bushi wa kuwanedo taka yoji,"* of which a literal English translation might be "Samurai, when starving: long toothpick." Even more characteristic than the long toothpick was the short sword that every samurai wore at his side, next to the long one normally employed in combat. The dirk was for use in close fighting and also, in the event that this proved unsuccessful or other circumstances made it seem appropriate, for the act of *seppuku* (more vulgarly called *hara kiri*), or ceremonial suicide by disembowelment.

According to Togo's semiofficial biographer, Nagayo Ogasawara, a friend and fellow officer who was later to become a vice admiral, Togo's first display of aptitude for swordplay took place at the age of nine, when, at a family picnic, he spied some carp in a pool and astonished grown-up onlookers by his ability to slice their heads off as they swam about. Another incident related by Ogasawara concerns Togo's reaction when one of his older brothers rather too brusquely commanded him to fetch a glass of water. Togo brought the water, but not until he had poured enough red pepper into it to cause its recipient to splutter and choke. This was a relatively minor offense, but when Togo's father, with full magisterial authority, ordered him to apologize, Togo committed a much graver offense by refusing to do so. Rather than back down, he accepted the unusual chastisement of being sent away from home for ten days.

In his *Life of Admiral Togo*, of which a partial English translation was published in Tokyo in 1934, Ogasawara, with no doubt commendable adherence to the Weemsian tradition, relates such incidents to illustrate his hero's early possession of such praiseworthy traits as resolution, fearlessness, and manual dexterity. Actually—like some of those, including the cherry-tree episode, that were cited by the renowned parson himself—these may, when studied in the light of modern psychiatric insight, reveal even more significant substrata of the subject's personality. Especially relevant in this respect may be an item omitted in the translated version of the Ogasawara opus, concerning Togo and his father's favorite riding horse.

Playing about in the stable one day, Togo contrived to annoy this high-tempered animal to such an extent that it knocked him down with its front leg and then bit him on the head. Enraged at such untoward treatment, Togo seized a stick and gave the horse a beating for which—when he related the incident to his mother in response to her questions about the cut on his scalp—he received a sharp rebuke for losing his temper. Feeling even more aggrieved with the horse for causing him this additional humiliation, Togo responded by administering a second caning for which Ogasawara fails to record the penalty.

What lay behind Togo's disproportionate concern with his father's favorite mount may well have been some sort of childish transference involving fear of, or resentment toward, paternal authority. In any event, like many other nautically inclined characters, Togo retained a lifelong uneasiness about equine association of all kinds, and the only occasion on which as an adult he appears to have confessed to experiencing genuine fright was that of a horseback ride with some fellow officers many years later. Togo had just succeeded in slowing his spirited mount down to a walk when one of his companions, attributing its gait to the animal's laziness rather than its rider's prudence, gave it what was meant to be a helpful whack on the rump. Togo's trepidation during the ensuing gallop may be deduced from his own description: "I managed to hang on, like a man at the helm in stormy weather . . . and I could not complain. But I was very much worried."

According to a thesis advanced by the distinguished Dr. Karl Menninger in *Man Against Himself*, an ax-murderer, a butcher, and a successful surgeon may all be motivated by a basically similar, if not indeed identical, neurotic propensity for sanguinary slicing. By analogy, the "killer instinct" that society abhors in the perpetrators of capital crimes may well be applauded when expressed in socially acceptable or even beneficial forms by pugilists, champion golfers, and martial celebrities from Miltiades or Caesar to such recent notables as Generals Montgomery or Patton. Togo's possession of an ample quota of this interesting characteristic is suggested not only by the streak of ruthlessness discernible in his childhood antics but in his entire behavior pattern as an adult, including his profound affinity for all sorts of instruments of discipline or destruction, from battleships to gardening shears.

The major objective of all samurai parents in rearing their offspring was not to eradicate the "killer instinct" but to enhance it and to encourage its fullest possible expression in ways not merely permissible but generally recognized as actively advantageous to the national interest. When Admiral Kuper and the ships of his China squadron sailed into Kagoshima Bay it was entirely *de rigueur* for Togo, as well as both his older brothers, to help their father man the forts. Under somewhat similar circumstances a Spartan mother achieved a niche in legend by telling her son to come back with his shield or on it. Togo's mother, when she sent her sons off to war for the first time, is said to have given even more laconic instructions: "Don't lose!"

The lesson that Admiral Kuper was trying to teach the daimio of Satsuma by bombarding his city was, of course, that his followers had no business trifling with the lives of British subjects. Togo, however, drew a different conclusion—that, just as a navy had long been essential to Satsuma for dealing with the Ryukyu islanders, a navy had now become even more essential to Japan as a whole for dealing with the world's other nations. Such a navy presumably would be an extension or projection of its Satsuma nucleus; in any case, it promised him a congenial career. After the battle of Kagoshima Bay, Togo went back to his books for three years. On graduation at eighteen, in the summer of 1866, he started his life-work by joining the Satsuma navy as a junior sub-lieutenant.

The year in which Togo joined the provincial navy was an important one in the protracted struggle between the political factions representing the Emperor and the shogun. By this time the daimio of Satsuma, along with the lords of the neighboring fiefs of Chosu and Tosa, had formed what consequently became known as the *Sa-cho-to* Party, in opposition to the Bakufu, or shogunal, government. In December of 1866 the reigning shogun died, to be succeeded by his son, an amiable young Tokugawa named Yoshinobu, who had no particular aptitude for politics or leadership. Less than four months later, in February of 1867, the shogun's death was followed by that of the 121st Emperor, Komei, who was succeeded by his son, fifteen-year-old Mutsuhito. Japanese emperors are known historically by a name given to the era of their reign after their demise. Thus, Mutsuhito, one of the most energetic and illustrious sovereigns in Japan's entire twenty-five hundred year line, has been known since 1912 by his posthumous title of Meiji, meaning "Enlightened Rule."

With this dramatically sudden change in the identity of its protagonists, the rivalry between Emperor and shogun entered a new and climactic phase. When, in December of 1867, a gang of anti-Sa-cho-to followers set fire to the Edo residence of Satsuma's Saburo Shimazu, open warfare broke out, in which the land forces of the Sa-cho-to, composed mostly of peasantry led by Takamori Saigo, routed the shogunal armies. Having already tried to abdicate once before, young Yoshinobu hastily seized the opportunity to do so again, and, after handing over all his possessions to the Crown, retired to a private life that eventually outlasted even that of Meiji. Meanwhile, the latter, in a move known to history as the "Meiji Restoration," transferred his court from Kyoto, or Capital City, to Edo, which was renamed Tokyo, or Eastern Capital. Here he took up residence in the shogunal castle located in a wide park at the center of town where Japan's emperors have lived ever since.

After the capitulation of Yoshinobu Tokugawa, the only serious obstacle to national unity that remained was the shogunal navy, started a few years before on the Satsuma model, Its most energetic commander was a dashing young captain named Enomoto, recently returned from training in the Netherlands, where he had acquired Dutch textbooks on tactics and a pair of long sideburns. Rounding up nine of the shogunal ships, Enomoto set off with them for the port of Hakodate in southern Hokkaido, where he proposed to establish an independent republic. There the Satsuma navy, now representing the Emperor Meiji, found and defeated him in what proved to be one of the liveliest fights of Togo's entire career.

Serving on board the warship *Kasuga*, Togo was assigned to the crew of a 40-pound gun on the port side. In the thick of the fighting throughout, the *Kasuga* got off a total of 170 shots and took 18 hits, causing numerous casualties—among whom Togo was not included. Enomoto also survived uninjured and, having surrendered his person and two ponderous Dutch tomes that he said might be useful to the nation in future, prepared for seppuku. In a generous response to this loyal gesture, which set the precedent for his treatment of many other reformed political adversaries later on, the Emperor thereupon not only pardoned Enomoto but also presented him with five casks of sake with which to mitigate the hardships of a brief *pro-forma* sojourn in prison. After serving his term, Enomoto rejoined the national government, in which he became Minister of the Navy in 1880.

While the Battle of Hakodate ended the strife between the forces of the shogun and the Emperor, of whose navy the remnants of the shogunal fleet now became part, it did not altogether terminate the civil unrest in Japan. This was mainly because, on their accession to power, it became as clear to the Sa-cho-to leaders as it had been before to the Bakufu that the policy of expelling the barbarians, however inviting it sounded, was one that they sadly lacked means to enforce. Instead, they soon came to see that merely to keep the foreigners at bay would require further profound alterations in Japan's whole social and political structure.

In 1869, by handing over their domains to the Crown, the Sa-cho-to leaders set a national example which the rest of the nation's public-spirited peers presently followed. In the new order devised by the alert and intelligent group of top-level samurai who were now advising their able young ruler, the daimio were to hold office for two years as governors of their old fiefs, drawing personal salaries equal to one-tenth of their former revenues. Thereafter each would receive a lump sum from the Crown and the boundaries of their fiefs would be re-drawn into prefectures, or *ken*. As a further compensation for accepting this change, designed to convert Japan from a confederation of loosely allied principalities into a strongly unified nation, each of the former daimio would receive a title. Derived from the European nobility, these ranged downward from Prince to Baron, in accord with the extent of the recipient's former holdings.

While this plan assured the loyalty of the former daimio to the new regime and enabled a clique of a hundred or so influential samurai to function as an efficient corps of advisers to the young Meiji, it also left most of the rest of the samurai poorly provided for. All they stood to receive were pensions even more modest than the salaries previously paid them in rice bags by their feudal lords, which had been none too generous to start with. From the viewpoint of the samurai, worse yet was to come. In the winter of 1873 the government introduced universal military service based on the model of Germany—which had established its right to such emulation by its victory over France two years before—thus depriving the samurai of their previous status as a warrior aristocracy. Finally, in 1876 the government converted the samurai pensions into even more niggardly lump-sum settlements and added sartorial insult to financial injury by depriving them of their immemorial privilege of wearing two swords.

Abruptly reduced from an armed aristocracy to the low social level of mere artisans or merchants, the samurai, still loyal to the Emperor, tried hard to adjust to their new situation. Some, by doing as Togo had already done, set out to make new careers for themselves in the national army or navy. Others joined the police force, where they could at least wear some kind of weapons with which to exact a modicum of public respect. Still others, notably those of the Mitsubishi clan, used their government settlements to get a foothold in business. A substantial remainder, on finding themselves through no fault of their own deprived of both livelihood and social standing, sought a leader who could help to restore at least part of their former status.

Opposed to many such government policies, which were largely promulgated by his onetime neighbor and former colleague, Toshimichi Okubo, Takamori Saigo, after leading the army whose victory restored Meiji to power, had returned to Kagoshima. There he had founded a sort of local West Point in which to train young officer-candidates in the use of the new weapons destined to replace their traditional swords. Thus cast in the role of the only leader to whom the dispossessed samurai could now turn for help in redressing their grievances, Saigo felt obliged by loyalty to his own followers to accept it. A national hero whose six-foot stature and military bearing made him an impressive as well as appealing figure, he presently found himself at the head of a rapidly growing samurai army.

To Okubo and other Meiji advisers it seemed clear that Saigo's Satsuma forces constituted a threat to the newly forged national unity under the Emperor. In the brief but bloody civil war that resulted, elements of the national army, one of them under Saigo's own cousin, Iwao Oyama, eventually surrounded Saigo and his samurai followers on a high hill just outside Kagoshima. Here, after a gallant but candidly suicidal last stand, most of them were slaughtered. Saigo himself, after spending his last hours playing *go* against one of his captains in a hillside cave, coolly committed seppuku. After his death, in posthumous accord with the Imperial policy of amnesty toward loyal opponents clearly motivated by their own concept of the national interest, Meiji restored all Saigo's previous honors and titles, thus assuring him a position in Japan's history analogous to Robert E. Lee's in that of the U.S.

By 1877 Togo's father and one of his three brothers had already died, of natural causes. The other two brothers were Saigo adherents and one was among those slain in the tragic last stand at Kagoshima. When he was buried in a mass grave with hundreds of others, his mother dug up his corpse with her fingers—since the touch of a metal spade would have been defiling—for re-interment in the family cemetery.

That Togo himself was not likewise committed to the lost cause of his father's good friend and neighbor was due to the fortunate chance that he heard about the Saigo rebellion only when it was practically over. Soon after the Meiji Restoration, the Emperor's government had borrowed the shogunal procedure of sending clever young men to Europe for military instruction. As a promising Navy officer with friends at the imperial court, Togo had naturally been among those chosen. In February 1871, after a cram course in English, he set off, to spend the next six years first as a cadet on the Marine Officers' training ship *Worcester*, anchored at Portsmouth near Nelson's *Victory*, and later at Cambridge, where he studied mathematics and navigation. Between the two, Togo—known to his mates on the *Worcester*, who were careless about fine Oriental distinctions, as "Johnny Chinaman"—took a training cruise to Australia aboard the cargo ship *Hampshire*.

News of the Saigo rebellion, when it finally reached Togo at Cambridge, caused a serious conflict in his personal loyalties. On the one hand, since his first obligation was to his family, he should perhaps hurry home to fight for Saigo. On the other, since his ultimate duty was to the Emperor, in whose service he had come to England, perhaps he should stay there. To Togo's dilemma in deciding which course to take, modern doctors might well ascribe the psychosomatic element in a severe case of eyestrain that he experienced at the same time, and which threatened to end his naval career before it had fairly begun.

At Cambridge, Togo lived for some two years in the house of a clergyman named A. D. Capel, along with Mrs. Capel and their three daughters. Interviewed during the Russo-Japanese War, after Togo had become famous, the Rev. Capel remembered the stoicism that his young lodger had shown under painful treatment for his ocular difficulties, and said: "Had I not had this personal acquaintance with the way in which Japanese can endure and bear, I should almost have doubted the truth of many of the stories told of them during this present war."

Togo's final decision was to stay on and complete his training in England. For this the Emperor Meiji, with characteristic magnanimity gave him good marks instead of the bad ones Togo might have incurred on account of the conduct of his brothers. Thus were sown the seeds of the deep reciprocal attachment that was to develop later on between Togo and his ruler, and that was to have profound consequences for the nation.

According to Britain's renowned naval authority, Frederick Thomas Jane, there was one salient difference between Japan's method of building up sea power and that of China under the Manchu dynasty at about the same time. This was that "Japan's energies were concentrated on training personnel, China's on acquiring matériel." Nonetheless, while Togo's presence in England confirmed Jane's conclusion, this by no means implied that Japan had overlooked the importance of acquiring weapons as well as officers well trained to use them.

While Togo was at Cambridge, three warships were being built for Japan in English yards, the first she had ever ordered made to her own specifications. Togo's last months in England were spent in supervising the construction of the biggest of the three, named the *Fuso*. When the ships were finished, his orders were to come home on one of the others, the *Hiei*.

The Japan to which Togo returned on the *Hiei* in 1878 had changed substantially from that in which he had started his naval career fifteen years before. Far more astounding, for example, than the speed of the train that had carried members of Japan's first foreign mission across the Isthmus of Panama was that with which Japan had imported locomotives and cars of its own from the U.S. and Britain, along with engineers to build tracks and set the locomotives in motion. On September 9, 1872, the Emperor Meiji was able to attend the gala opening of the rail link between Tokyo and Yokohama, where by this time over a thousand Europeans were in more or less agreeable residence.

While foreigners elsewhere were confined to a few seaboard cities, their influence was pervading the rest of the nation to an extent perhaps most readily discernable from the columns of the *Mainichi*, or "Daily News," another cultural importation, which had started in 1866. In June of the next year the cost of setting up a telegraph line between Tokyo and Yokohama was estimated at two thousand yen—then roughly the equivalent of half that many dollars. November 1868 marked the publication of the first really serviceable English-Japanese dictionary. In 1869 postal service was started, and Japan sent displays to the

London World's Fair. In 1871, a banner year for progress, five upper-class girls were packed off to study in U.S. schools and colleges, while some of their less affluent sisters were perhaps cheered by the news that houses of pleasure in Tokyo's Yoshiwara District were to be built in Western style the next spring.

The next year, also, the number of Tokyo's rickshaws—two-wheeled, man-powered passenger vehicles, modeled on those used in Hong Kong—had reached a total of forty thousand. On November 14 the first full-sized ocean-going ship built in Japan for over two centuries reached San Francisco on its maiden voyage. The eating of meat, long forbidden by the Tokugawa, had by 1873 become so fashionable that a score of cows was slaughtered daily in Tokyo, providing portions of beef for an estimated five thousand newly carnivorous citizens. In that year also the First National Bank was formed, with a capital of three million yen, and geisha in the Shinagawa district of Tokyo threw the capital's night-life into the doldrums by going on strike for ten days.

By 1876 the tide of Westernization reached a crest, when the first ice-cream freezer was purchased by a government office and overseas mails began to be exchanged between Japan and the U.S., with service to Europe promised for the near future. Sulfur matches were being produced in Yokohama for 30 yen a gross, against 36 yen for the imported product, and factory girls were getting paid as much as two yen a day, with even twelve-year-olds earning as much as a yen and a half, a situation that some felt might lead to dangerous self-indulgence. Meanwhile, though foreign dress was still such a novelty as to cause dogs to bark in the street, the governor of Akita felt bold enough to go for a drive in a carriage. "A rickshaw drawn by a horse!" screamed the amazed crowds in the streets of his provincial capital.

Shortly after his return Togo received his Imperial commission as a junior lieutenant and transferred from the *Hiei* back to the *Fuso*, where one of his fellow officers was a jolly young fellow-Satsuman named Gombei Yamamoto, who became his close friend. Later to be a Minister of the Navy and twice a Prime Minister, the future Admiral Count Yamamoto at this time had more romantic concerns. These involved a fisherman's daughter, sold into servitude, whom he fell in love with and presently married.

More prudent in such matters, Togo attained matrimonial status by wholly conventional methods. His bride was Tetsu Kaieda, the daughter of a Satsuma noble whose younger brother was later to become a viscount. Brought up like himself in the thrifty Satsuma tradition, his bride had acquired a modest dowry by the ingeniously novel procedure of painting decorative matchboxes, which she then sold to friends and neighbors. This enabled the young couple to acquire an unpretentious town house not far from Tokyo's Yasukuni shrine, in which they lived for the rest of their lives, raising two sons and a daughter.

That Japan's emergence from her long isolation coincided, not altogether by chance, with the switch from sail to steam in nautical transportation had several advantages. One of these was that her young naval officers, unlike those of some older sea powers, were not handicapped by obsolescent notions surviving from the age of sail. Another was that Togo, Yamamoto, and their juniors who were now emerging from the new Naval Academy, founded by Imperial Edict in 1869 and staffed largely by British officers, were assured of rapid promotion and found full play for their talents in the ships that Japan was soon buying up all over the world and starting to build at home.

From the *Fuso*, Togo was sent to the *Jingei*, a paddle-wheel steamer on which he was to serve for the next two years. The prime importance of this berth was that the *Jingei* was the Imperial yacht, and his post as her executive officer brought him to the personal notice of the Emperor for the first time. Just when Togo and his ruler first met, and what occured to cement the bond of loyalty formed by Togo's decision to stay on in England a few years before, remains unrecorded, but Togo thereafter was to enjoy frequent signs of Imperial favor, which culminated during the Russo-Japanese war. At a court banquet shortly before the battle of Tsushima, someone hinted to Meiji that there were other candidates who might also deserve consideration for the post of commander in chief. The Emperor dismissed the suggestion with an impatient wave of his hand. "Togo," he said, "will stay on."

One of the earliest indications that Togo had attracted the attention of his ruler as well as that of his naval superiors was the rate at which his responsibilities as well as his rank increased soon after the period of his service on the *Jingei.* Promoted to full lieutenant and then to lieutenant-commander in the first year after his return from England, he became a full commander in 1885 and a captain in 1886, while still under forty. For Togo the years of rapid promotion were markedly peripatetic ones. During the Franco-Chinese war, as a result of which France substantially enlarged her holdings in what were later to be known as Laos, Cambodia, and Vietnam, Togo was sent to inspect the Formosan port of Keelung shortly after its capture by the French. Here he was guided about the fortifications by a young army officer he was to meet again in Japan after World War I. At this second meeting he learned that his guide at Keelung had been the future general Joffre, hero of the Marne.

On his return from Keelung, Togo received further marks of Imperial favor. One was an invitation to report

on his travels directly to the Emperor, who had been favorably impressed by his record. Another was a court banquet in his honor. The third was an advance in court rank,
which to Japanese officers counted for more than the
pseudo-European titles of which Togo later acquired his
quota also.

Some indication that Togo was regarded as favorably by
his naval superiors as he was by his ruler was provided by
the wide range of his assignments. These included not
only sea duty in a variety of ships but also service on shore
in posts calculated to give him encyclopedic knowledge of
the service as a whole. Most important among the latter
was that of deputy commander of the new base at Kure,
on Japan's Inland Sea, which, during his tenure, received a
ceremonial visit from China's top Admiral Ting Ju-Ch'ang
in his handsome new flagship, the *Ting-Yuen.* One of two
splendid battleships built for China in Stettin, weighing
nearly 7500 tons each and carrying four Krupp 12-inch
guns, these vessels were the envy of most of the Japanese
officers invited by Admiral Ting to the lavish receptions
that he enjoyed giving on board. Looking over the *Ting-
Yuen* at Kure, Togo noted that her seamen had hung out
their laundry to dry over the long barrels of the twelve-
inch guns. Later on, when asked his opinion of the Chinese warships, he entered a characteristic dissent:

"In the Japanese Navy guns are considered the most important things on board our ships. The Chinese seem more
concerned about their wash. I am not much impressed . . ."

Togo's assignment to Kure took place in 1890 and followed a period of four years spent not only on shore but
mostly on sick leave. Afflicted by what appeared to be a
virulent form of rheumatic fever that failed to respond to
medical treatment, Togo had begun to fear, even more
than when his eyesight failed him at Cambridge, that he

might never be able to go back to sea. During his illness, however, he did what he could to make a virtue of necessity by spending his sick leaves on the study of international law. A taciturn, conscientious, and methodical young officer, he was subsequently to find this so profitable that in the years before Tsushima he often advised ambitious juniors to follow the same procedure.

The importance to a naval officer of a thorough grounding in international law was brought home to Togo soon after he was rewarded for recovering his health by being given command of one of the finest fighting ships in the Japanese navy or, for that matter, any other. In 1884 Chile had acquired a cruiser named the *Esmerelda* that compiled such an impressive record in the 1891 war between Chile and Argentina that Japan not only bought her as soon as that war ended but also in the meantime ordered a glorified copy built at Elswick and named the *Naniwa*. Both the *Naniwa* and the *Esmerelda,* renamed *Izumi,* were still in service at the time of Tsushima, in which the latter did especially noteworthy duty. It was, however, during his own period in command of the *Naniwa,* starting in 1890, that Togo's newly acquired erudition in international law enabled him to justify the confidence of his superiors, royal and nautical. From then on his fate was, while no less fraught with personal and political dangers than it had been previously, to be inextricably bound up with that of the nation as a whole, until both were subjected to final simultaneous jeopardy in the climactic engagement of the Russo-Japanese war.

III

"The Pacific Ocean, its shores, its islands, and the vast regions beyond, will become the chief theatre of events in the world's great hereafter." This resounding prophecy, then considerably more far-fetched than it may seem a century later, was advanced by U.S. Secretary of State William H. Seward in 1867 as one of the premises for his purchase of Alaska from Russia for $7,200,000. According to historian Edwin A. Falk, in *Togo and the Rise of Japanese Sea Power*, the *Times* of London added a commendably precise corollary: "The Maritime Power that holds Pearl River, and moors its fleet there, possesses the key to the Northern Pacific."

The Hawaiian archipelago, of which the Pearl River port of Honolulu was the capital, represents the mid-point on an arc, drawn with San Francisco as its hub, from the Aleutian Islands to the Isthmus of Panama. Britain's Captain Cook had staked the first claim to what he called the Sandwich Islands in honor of his patron, after his brief visit in 1778, and both Russia and France had claimed them since then, but the maritime power most interested by 1887 was naturally the United States. U.S. whaling ships in the North Pacific had long used Hawaii as a supply port, and numerous U.S. missionaries, starting as early as 1820, had braved the climate to confer upon the untutored natives the blessings of Christianity and the *mumu,* for which their energetic descendants later on received the more mundane rewards attendant upon the cultivation of pineapples and sugar cane.

By the late 1880s seeds of dissension had begun to germinate in this tropical paradise. First, an inept Hawaiian monarch called Kalakaua distressed both alien residents and his own subjects by the clumsiness of his efforts to govern it. Then, in 1891, he was succeeded by a sister called Mrs. Lydia Dominis, whose reign, under the even more euphonious name of Queen Liliuokalani, reached even more impressive levels of incompetence. In 1891 influential Hawaiian residents of mainland origin launched a movement to have the islands annexed by the United States and formed a "Committee of Safety" to achieve this end. In January of 1893, encouraged by the presence of a pro-annexation U.S. Minister and a U.S. warship carrying a complement of Marines, the Committee installed a provisional government headed by a prosperous pineapple squire named Judge Sanford B. Dole.

During the eighties the expansion of Hawaii's pineapple groves and cane fields had led to the importation of a Japanese labor force that by 1892 had reached a total of 15,000. Had this growth—which by 1896 was to reach 24,000 out of a total island population of 109,000—continued under the native monarchy, Japan might eventually have become a serious rival to the United States for possession of the islands, but even under the existing conditions the Meiji government took an understandable interest in them. In late February of 1893 a fast Japanese warship with the Rising Sun at her masthead flashed around Diamond Head and dropped anchor in the harbor off Waikiki Beach. This was the splendid cruiser *Naniwa*, whose Captain Togo had three weeks earlier received orders to take her to Honolulu and keep an eye on developments there.

Togo's opportunely acquired skills in international law were to be tested twice during his Hawaiian visit. The first test arose when the provisional government's dignified and bewhiskered president came aboard a U.S. warship anchored near the *Naniwa*. Its guns accorded Judge Dole the salute appropriate for a head of state which, under normal circumstances, the *Naniwa* would have been obliged to acknowledge by a similar salvo, accompanied by the hoisting of appropriate flags. Restrained from so doing by the knowledge that Japan had not recognized the provisional government, Togo instead deemed it proper to ignore the commotion and to stand on his bridge, gazing ostentatiously out to sea.

This ceremonial snub implied no personal animosity between Togo and Dole, who had already met each other amicably at social events on shore. By an odd coincidence, however, it was to be echoed eighteen years later when, visiting London as a world-famous admiral and Japan's representative at the coronation of King George V, Togo was warmly greeted by a gray-bearded American whom he encountered at the door of the British Museum. When Togo failed to return the greeting, a knowledgable aide hastened to save the situation by helping to identify the stranger as Judge Dole, now retired from public life but nonetheless of a fame commensurate with Togo's, as the top tycoon of the canned pineapple industry. The two elderly foreigners then shook hands cordially and engaged in a reminiscent chat about old times in the islands.

One subject of their recollections might well have been the second test of Togo's recently acquired legal sophistication. This was a somewhat macabre incident involving a Japanese field-hand named Yasaka Imada, who, accused of murdering one of his compatriots with a hatchet, had been convicted of manslaughter, sentenced to twenty years' hard labor, and confined at Oahu Prison, on a reef in the harbor. On the morning of March 15th, 1893, a detail of Oahu prisoners including Imada was taken from the prison under armed guard to work on the shorefront Quarantine Station. Possibly emboldened by the recent example of two white convicts who had escaped from Oahu to a vessel in the harbor, Imada suddenly made a dash for the water, plunged in, and swam out to the *Naniwa* so fast that a pursuing outrigger canoe failed to catch up before he reached the ship's ladder. Hauled aboard by sympathetic sailors to whom he gasped out his story, Imada begged for asylum, which, when the incident was reported to him, Togo promptly agreed to grant. To the astonished police officers who came aboard to demand their prisoner's return, the *Naniwa*'s diminutive captain courteously but coolly replied: "I cannot deliver to you this subject of Japan."

In fact, the altercation about Imada that developed thereafter hinged on a nice point of maritime law. As pointed out by Edwin Falk, himself a lawyer, the issue was well summed up in the next day's edition of the *Daily Pacific Commercial Advertiser:* "As there is no extradition treaty between this country and Japan, doubtless the Japanese authorities are in no way bound to comply with the request of this government for the return of the prisoner. If the *Naniwa* were a merchantman, she would be under Hawaiian jurisdiction, but the case is different with vessels of war, which carry their national sovereignty with them. The *Naniwa* is as it were a piece of Japanese territory, subject to Japanese laws, and merely set down in Honolulu harbor."

While Honolulu newspapers wrote angry editorials, threatening the use of Marines from one of the U.S. warships in the harbor to retrieve the prisoner, the vice president of the provisional government apologized for their bellicose tone and politely requested the refugee's return as a matter of international courtesy. The *Naniwa's* captain smiled calmly but persisted in his refusals until, apparently at the request of the somewhat less resolute Japanese consul, a cable from Tokyo ordered Togo to turn the prisoner over to him. Togo then reluctantly complied but only after punctilious exposition to the consul of his reasons:

"As a naval officer, I cannot but obey the orders I have just received. . . . The police officers of the provisional government are no doubt waiting to seize him as soon as he is brought to shore. I am not delivering the man to them, but to you. Do as you please with him; only do it where I cannot see."

Owing to the exigencies of party politics in the United States, the sovereignty of Hawaii thereafter oscillated between the provisional government and the native monarchy until annexation by the U.S. finally became permanently effective in 1895. Meanwhile, Togo and the *Naniwa* returned to the Far East, to become involved in a third and climactic test of the captain's forensic aplomb that was to make headlines not merely in local gazettes but all over the world. This was the sensational sinking of the *Kowshing,* a Chinese troop transport flying the British flag, and it constituted the curtain raiser to the Sino-Japanese War, which in turn proved to be merely the prelude to Japan's 1905 war with Russia.

Among the numerous causes of the outbreak of war between Japan and China in 1894, the most important, if not the most immediate, was no doubt that Japan's population was increasing out of all proportion to her national resources. By 1892 the population had reached 41 million and was still growing at the rate of seven hundred thousand a year. To sustain all these lively and philoprogenitive citizens, the home islands provided an area smaller than that of Montana, of which only one-fifteenth could be used for farming and which contained no natural resources worth mentioning except the annual rainfall. If Britain, with inexhaustible mines of top-quality coal and several times as much arable acreage, required foreign colonies all over the globe to support far fewer subjects, Japan's case for acquiring a more modest colonial empire seemed a reasonably sound one.)

To the Meiji government it seemed equally clear that a neat solution for this vexing dilemma lay ready to hand. It consisted of Korea, the so called "Hermit Kingdom," a lavishly endowed and relatively underpopulated peninsula whose southern tip lay a scant sixty miles away, across Tsushima Strait. If Japan had remained isolated from Western progress for two centuries and a half, the Hermit Kingdom, separated from China by a barrier of mountains, had during the same period remained isolated from Eastern progress as well. Now presided over by a feeble monarchy that was patently incapable of maintaining domestic order let alone of conducting a rational foreign policy, Korea seemed much more urgently in need of a prod from her neighbor to the west than had Japan herself a few years before, from a neighbor some six thousand miles further away. Indeed, as early as 1876 Japan had dispatched a naval mission, composed along much the same lines as Perry's, to inform the Koreans that it was high time for them to open up the hermitage to international commerce generally and trade with Japan in particular.

Japan's attention to Korea was by no means a complete

novelty; in the last decade of the sixteenth century she had made strenuous though eventually unavailing efforts to conquer the entire peninsula. During the period of Japanese isolation under the Tokugawa shoguns, China had languidly undertaken to fill up the power vacuum by adopting Korea as a "tributary state" from which occasional levies were extracted in exchange for the privilege of allowing the Koreans to mismanage their own domestic affairs. This arrangement obviously constituted an obstacle to Japan's more ambitious plans for the hermit kingdom's future, but it was not one that the Meiji regime was prepared to regard as insurmountable. Meanwhile, the situation had been temporarily stabilized by an 1885 agreement whereby both China and Japan agreed that neither would move troops into Korea without giving the other appropriate advance notice.

In the summer of 1894 the ruling queen of Korea had asked her matriarchal Manchu colleague in Peking to send some troops to suppress internal disorders caused by the increasing influx of Japanese. When the Chinese Minister in Tokyo informed the Japanese Government that his country meant to accede to this request by sending two thousand soldiers to Chemulpo, it provided the opportunity that Japan had been awaiting for several years to settle the Korean question along very different lines. Announcing that it, too, would send troops, the Meiji government promptly dispatched a force of four thousand to occupy the Korean capital of Seoul. It was at this tense moment in the situation that, on the misty morning of July 25, the *Naniwa,* as one of three fast cruisers comprising a "Flying Squadron" whose mission was to prevent the transportation of additional Chinese troops across the Yellow Sea, sighted two Chinese warships off the coast of Korea and promptly opened fire.

The lively engagement that followed ended when both

Chinese ships—one of them after hoisting a white flag of surrender—vanished into the haze. Then, as the *Naniwa* set off to join the pursuit, she sighted a new arrival on the scene. This was the steamer *Kowshing,* apparently heading for Chemulpo with what looked like a whole shipload of Chinese soldiers crowding her decks and the British merchant flag at her masthead.

When Togo signaled the merchantman to stop, the *Kowshing* obediently dropped anchor, and Togo sent Lieutenant Zengoro Hitomi by cutter to inspect her cargo. Hitomi learned from the British captain, whose name was Thomas Ryder Galsworthy, that the *Kowshing* was indeed carrying Chinese troops—eleven hundred of them, under the command of a German major traveling as "an ordinary passenger." According to Captain Galsworthy, since the war that Togo himself had just opened had not yet been officially declared, the *Kowshing* was not subject to seizure and search. Nonetheless, to Hitomi's pointed question as to what action he would take if ordered to follow the *Naniwa,* Galsworthy's reply was that he would obey under protest.

On receiving Hitomi's report Togo, as Captain Galsworthy had expected, signaled the *Kowshing* to follow him, planning to take her back to the naval base at Sasebo, where she could be interned and the Chinese troops made prisoners. Instead of complying, her captain signaled a request for furthur parley. When Lieutenant Hitomi came aboard for the second time, Galsworthy explained that his cargo of soldiers, who had been growing increasingly restive during their previous conference, now threatened to shoot down the ship's officers, whom they vastly outnumbered, if the *Kowshing* obeyed Togo's instructions or if the officers tried to leave the ship.

By the time Hitomi reported back to the *Naniwa* once more, four hours had elapsed since the beginning of the encounter and Togo was in no mood for further haggling. Inferring from the *Kowshing*'s dilatory behavior that she might be expecting aid from the main body of the Chinese fleet, which could well be near at hand, he signaled her captain to quit the ship immediately. When Galsworthy failed to do so Togo hoisted a red danger signal and opened fire. Five shells from the *Naniwa*'s main batteries at close range crashed into the *Kowshing*'s side. Half an hour later she sank stern first, leaving most of her crew and many of the soldiers struggling to stay afloat in the sea around her.

The *Naniwa*'s boats picked up Captain Galsworthy, his chief officer, and one other member of the crew. The German major and a hundred and sixty Chinese crewmen and soldiers managed to swim two miles to the offshore island of Shopaioul. The rest either drowned or were killed by gunfire directed at them first from the enraged soldiers, who, unable to swim, had stayed on board the sinking transport, and later from both the *Naniwa* and her cutters, which sank two of the three lifeboats that the *Kowshing* had contrived to launch in the moments before her submersion.

That in firing on defenseless Chinese crewmen and soldiers, in life boats or struggling in the water, the *Naniwa* had displayed far less than exemplary chivalry neither Togo nor anyone else concerned was ever able successfully to deny. The only excuses for his conduct—one of two noteworthy occasions in his career when the "killer instinct" found expression in a form that was, to put it mildly, open to question—was that the soldiers had brought about their own predicament and that if later rescued by the ships of their own navy—as they might well have been after the *Naniwa*'s departure—they would have lived to fight against, and perhaps to kill, some soldiers of Japan.

Much more diplomatically urgent than the question of Togo's lack of chivalry was the question of whether or not he had behaved in accord with the dictates of international law. If not, it might well develop that to the enmity already incurred of China, whose fleet vastly outnumbered Japan's, and of Russia, which was known to be strongly partial to China's side of the Korean dispute and thus a potential Chinese ally, he had added that of the strongest maritime power in the world. In the latter case the price of destroying one insignificant merchantman and her pitiful human cargo could easily prove to be an overwhelming defeat for Japan even before the war had officially started.

Togo, who had weighed these eventualities with characteristic caution before opening fire, was, of course, prepared for conventional atonement in case he were found to be in the wrong. "I knew," he was to say years later, "that upon my action depended the future of my country—perhaps its very life. And I was quite ready to answer with my own."

As was to have been expected, first press reactions to the sinking of the *Kowshing* in London were that it was "an act of piracy" and an "insult to the British flag," calling for the "condign punishment of the Japanese commander." Presently, however, Britain's top expert on international law, Thomas Erskine Holland, dispatched to the *Times,* as was his wont in moments of comparable crisis, a letter from his club, the Athenaeum, proposing a contrary view. This was that in view of Togo's conduct on first meeting the *Kowshing* and of the laborious steps he had taken to inform her commander that a state of war, declared or otherwise, in fact existed between China and Japan, the *Kowshing* had been legitimately liable to seizure, just as Togo had thought.

Holland also found the degree of force employed when the *Kowshing* refused to obey Togo's command to follow the *Naniwa* "not to have been in excess of what might lawfully be used." Other legal authorities concurred with Holland, and the British government allowed itself to be guided by their view, as did Vice Admiral E. R. Freemantle, in command of Britain's Far East Squadron, whose first response to the sinking had been a sharp note to Togo's superior, forbidding further interference with ships of the British merchant marine. The net result of the *Kowshing* episode was that far from being obliged to perform seppuku, Togo became a world figure and in due course the outstanding naval personage of the war that was finally declared a week later.

Among the funds allocated to the development of the Chinese navy shortly before the outbreak of hostilities with Japan was an item of $40 million, which, in an era when top-notch battleships cost $3 million apiece, would have sufficed to pay for the ships of a first-class fleet, along with the crews and the foreign tutors to train them. Like most of her more aristocratic subjects, China's Dowager Empress Tzu-Hsi regarded war as a vulgar distraction from more important objectives, such as gracious living and spiritual serenity. The nautical improvement on which the $40 million was spent consequently took the form of a magnificent marble pier shaped in the form of a double-decked sailing ship, to adorn a small pond near her summer palace outside Peking, where it presumably still stands.

Actually, the Empress Tzu-Hsi's belief that the navy already had plenty of genuine warships to get along with was by no means wholly unfounded. On paper her fleet outnumbered Japan's by almost four to one, and the real difficulty was not so much its lack of war vessels as the fact that, owing to their geographical distribution and the rivalries among provincial authorities, it seemed impracticable to gather them all together in one place. The result was that China found itself forced to fight Japan with about a quarter of the naval armament nominally at its disposal, thus in effect cancelling out its numerical superiority. The naval force involved consisted of the Peiyang, or North Pacific, squadron, of which the major elements were the German-built battleships *Ting-Yuen* and *Chen-Yuen,* whose reassuring resemblance to Chinese laundries Togo had noted after inspecting them at Kure a few years before.

In addition to these two battleships, whose guns were actually considerably heavier than anything in Japan's line of battle, the Peiyang squadron included three smaller armored ships, ten unarmored light cruisers, nine 1000-ton "sloops," and thirty torpedo boats. To oppose these Japan's battle fleet comprised thirty-eight torpedo boats, twelve sloops, seven cruisers (including the *Naniwa*) of varying size, age, and armament, and three armored battleships of which no one was individually quite a match for either of China's two best. Where Japan held an immeasurable advantage, however, was in the capability of the crews that manned her ships, starting with the two fleet commanders. Japan's was Vice Admiral Yuko Ito, whose flagship was the *Matsushima,* and whose naval debut had taken place, like Togo's, at the battle of Kagoshima, where he had served as a drummer-boy. His adversary in the *Ting-Yuen* was the brave and gregarious Admiral Ting Ju-Ch'ang whose early military training as a cavalry officer had been only partially offset by later coaching under British naval tutors and by the immediate assistance of an American captain named Philo N. McGiffin on the *Chen-Yuen.*

(According to traditional naval doctrine of the period, the best way for a fleet to fight was from a "line-ahead" formation in which the ships of the main body, known for that reason as "ships of the line," proceeded single file, usually in the wake of the flagship. When so aligned, each ship could bring to bear against the enemy the full firepower of all guns mounted along the side nearest him. One accepted way of achieving a line-ahead formation was to proceed toward battle in "line-abreast," from which, when steaming ahead with their bows in line with each other, the ships could readily switch to a line-ahead in either direction by making a simultaneous "eight-point," or right-angle, turn to either port or starboard.

If, as quite often turned out to be the case, this resulted in both fleets forming parallel line-ahead formations headed in the same direction, the two lines customarily fired salvos at each other until one or the other had achieved a decisive advantage. One way for a fleet to achieve such an advantage was to "cross the T" of its adversary—that is, to get far enough ahead to steam directly across the course of the leading ship in the enemy's column. Under these circumstances the fleet that did the crossing could bring at least half of its guns to bear on the adversary, while the "capped" fleet could use only its bow guns and even these guns, for most of its ships, would be blocked, or "masked," by the ships ahead in the column.

The first and, as it turned out, most decisive naval engagement of the Sino-Japanese War, fought on the sunny afternoon of September 17, provided an interesting demonstration of these basic tactics. Surprised by the approach of the Japanese fleet while riding at anchor in the mouth of the Yalu River, Ting hurried his ships out in line-abreast formation to offer battle. Meanwhile, the Japanese main body approached his port side in a line-ahead led by the four ships of the "Flying Squadron" under Admiral Kozo Tsuboi. What Tsuboi expected Ting to do was to make an eight-point, turn-together to starboard, thus forming his fleet into a similar line-ahead proceeding in the same direction. Whether because his line-abreast was so uneven that this seemed impractical or for some other reason, Admiral Ting continued to advance without doing it. This gave Ito a chance first to cross his bows and then, having turned to starboard around Ting's starboard flank, to cross astern of his formation, meanwhile ordering the Flying Squadron to separate from the main body and engage Ting's ships from the front.

(In the engagement that developed from these opening moves the Japanese won a resounding victory, sinking five of Ting's larger ships and causing the battered remainder, including the two thick-skinned battleships, *Ting-Yuen* and *Chen-Yuen*, to flee under cover of darkness to refuge at Port Arthur.) A month later, while Admiral Ito's attention was engrossed in convoying troop transports, Ting managed to withdraw his ships, now more or less repaired, to the seemingly safer harbor of Wei-Hai-Wei, and it was in and near this harbor that the second and final naval engagement of the war took place. In it Ito's torpedo boats sank the *Ting-Yuen* and most of Ting's remaining larger ships, while the Flying Squadron, including the *Naniwa*, demolished the Chinese torpedo boats as they attempted to race off to refuge at Chephu.

Ito, who had become Ting's close friend during the period of the latter's pleasure-cruising before the war, fully realized the degree to which bureaucratic graft and autocratic whimsy had handicapped his colleague's efforts to turn China's fleet into an effective fighting force. As the moment of final victory approached he wrote Ting an amazing letter, inviting him first to capitulate and then seek asylum in Japan whose magnanimous ruler would not only provide this but would also see to it that his professional talents were more appropriately rewarded than they had been by the corrupt and frivolous regime in Peking. Ting felt compelled to accept the first part of Ito's invitation but not the second. After returning a case of champagne and other consolatory gifts sent by his adversary, he surrendered Wei-Hai-Wei and then committed suicide by downing an overdose of opium.

While the battle of Wei-Hai-Wei helped to decide the war's outcome by giving Japan undisputed command of the Yellow Sea, its main prize was won not by the Navy but by the Army, commanded by Marquis Iwao Oyama. Cousin of the great Takamori Saigo and offspring of the Togo family's close neighbors in the samurai section of Kagoshima, Oyama had landed his men on the Liaotung Peninsula on October 24, eighty-five miles north of the splendid harbor and fleet base of Port Arthur. Four weeks later, after a campaign in which the outstanding personal hero was a young major general named Maresuke Nogi, they had taken possession of this valuable objective in a breath-taking victory achieved at the cost of only eighteen men killed in action.

Whatever its effects upon the haughty Chinese—one of whose more flattering epithets for their off-shore neighbors was "the Island Dwarfs"—the enlightening influence of the Japanese accomplishment at Port Arthur was even more noticeable in Europe. There it was felt that the army's mastery of up-to-date tactics and intelligence would have done credit to its Prussian models and gave even more convincing proof than did the élan of the Japanese navy that the Island Dwarfs rated full honors for completion of their quarter-century of discipline in modern military methods. The net effect on the Western world was well summarized by Italy's historian Zenome Volpicelli in his authoritative account of the war:

> The fall of Port Arthur caused an immense sensation. The foreigners in the Far East had been inclined to discount the Japanese victories. These had been won in ob-

scure corners of Korea and the Chinese frontier, and they suspected exaggeration in the Japanese accounts. They also considered that China had not had time to put forth her whole strength, and imagined that with a few months preparation the Chinese could repulse any Japanese attack on such a formidable fortress as Port Arthur. All these surmises were refuted by a day's fighting. . . .

By the same token, the fall of Port Arthur also encouraged the inviting conjecture that, while the ease and celerity of the Japanese victory might testify to the quality of the army that had achieved it, they might also to some extent bespeak a considerable degree of incompetence on the part of the opposition. (The combined consequence of a new European respect for Japan's rising military power and a fresh realization of the deterioration of that representing the vast Empire of China were soon to have the ironic result of depriving the agent of this enlightenment of the fruits of the victory by which it had been effected)

By the time the Chinese were prepared to start discussing an armistice with Japan on April Fool's Day of 1895, the Japanese fleet had already topped off its earlier achievements by taking possession of Formosa and the Pescadores Islands between it and the mainland after a brief campaign, during which Togo, who played a major part in it, received promotion to Rear Admiral. By the Treaty of Shimonoseki that followed, China agreed to recognize Korea's independence (in effect allowing Japan the privilege of subsequent annexation); undertook to pay a $25 million indemnity over a period of seven years, during which Japan would hold the port of Wei-Hai-Wei as security; and ceded to Japan the entire Liaotung Peninsula, including not only Port Arthur at its tip but also the adjoining portion of Southern Manchuria between the Yalu and Liao Rivers.

It was the latter expropriation that caused an understandable flurry of alarm in the chancelleries of Europe. While the major powers were quite prepared to accept the Japanese view that Formosa and the Pescadores made a logical extension of the Ryukyu chain along the coast of the mainland, the transfer of title to Liaotung and Port Arthur was another matter entirely. These were properties in an area that had already attracted the attention of the other side of the world and for which it had made plans which Japan's easy victory over China seemed to prove capable of unexpectedly prompt realization.

The tangible result of this situation was that, as soon as the terms of the Treaty of Shimonoseki were published to the world, Russia, France, and Germany together protested strongly and in horrified tones. Thereupon, Japan, as yet in no position to incur the enmity of such a powerful coalition, "yielded to the dictates of humanity and accepted the advice of the three powers" by restoring the Liaotung Peninsula to China. Within three years, ostensibly in consideration of financial assistance in paying her indemnity, China granted Russia a twenty-five-year lease on Port Arthur, along with the right to fortify the port and connect it with Vladivostok by means of a railroad line across Manchuria. With Russia's cards thus placed in plain view on the table it became painfully obvious to Japan that the main result of a smashing victory in her first foray into nineteenth-century colonial competition had been to advance the interests of a far more dangerous adversary than the one she had just defeated.

IV

During the latter half of the nineteenth century, while Japan was engaged first in emerging from her centuries of seclusion and then in catching up with the Western world, her neighbor to the northwest was completing a gradual process of expansion that had been going on for half a millenium. Starting out in the fourteenth century as a minute duchy at the most remote corner of the Baltic Sea, Russia, under Ivan the Terrible, Peter the Great, and Catharine I, had gradually edged eastward across the vast wastes of Siberia until, by the middle of the nineteenth century, she had acquired the maritime province of Usuri, giving her a substantial frontage on the Pacific that included the splendid harbor of Vladivostok at the northernmost extremity of the Japan Sea. In 1902 the completion of the trans-Siberian Railroad, save for a forty-mile stretch of tunnels along the south shore of Lake Baikal, the world's largest body of fresh water, linked this new acquisition with the capital at St. Petersburg, five thousand miles to the East. Japan's first adversary on her return to international altercations had been the most populous nation on the surface of the globe, but China was at least a familiar Asian opponent with which she had cultural and racial ties predating history. Her second was to be an empire which, covering one sixth of the earth's land surface, was not only by far the world's largest but also a European power with which Japan had never before experienced any dealings whatsoever.

As the Japanese were not slow to perceive, Russia's geographical immensity tended to conceal important spiritual and physical defects. Among the latter was the noteworthy fact that despite its enormous breadth her territory lay so far north that most of its seacoast fronted the Arctic Ocean and all Russian ports, except those on the Caspian and Black Seas, were icebound for at least one third of the year. It was Russia's defeat in the Crimean War,—of which one objective had been to acquire the warm water port of Constantinople—that had led to her compensatory interest in the Far East generally and, since even Vladivostok was icebound for three months every year, in Port Arthur most particularly. Shortly after Russia set up shop in that splendid and ice-free harbor, there occurred the Boxer Rebellion of 1900, during which the European colony in Peking found itself imprisoned in its own embassies, with the Manchu Government apparently powerless to protect them. Russia used this as a welcome pretext for taking outright possession of most of Manchuria, as a preliminary to turning it into an additional Russian province.

More conspicuous than Russia's geographical shortcomings was a less material defect whereby her very size tended to become a liability rather than an asset. This was a high degree of internal dissension between a corrupt and ineffectual ruling autocracy on the one hand and a surly and ignorant peasantry on the other, which the shrill complaints of an overly-articulate intelligentsia did more to accentuate than to relieve. The unexpectedly early death of Czar Alexander III in 1897 had brought to the throne his son Nicholas II, who, though conscientious, well-mannered, and benevolent, was woefully lacking in both aptitude and training for his job. In 1903 Nicholas appointed his half-brother, Alexander's natural son, Vice Admiral Eugene Alexeyev, as his viceroy in the Far East.

Resigned to relinquishing her own strong claims on Port Arthur and its environs, Japan was by no means prepared to see the same territories and much more blandly annexed by Russia. By the turn of the century, however, Japan had become much too conversant with the ways of the West to betray her chagrin in useless lamentations. Instead, she set about making plans of her own to redress her grievances by a combination of martial and diplomatic means as soon as circumstances should permit.

The diplomatic foundation of Japan's new foreign policy, laid down in 1902, was an alliance with Britain ostensibly intended to "maintain the status quo and general peace in the extreme East." By its terms each nation was obliged to come to the aid of the other in the event that either one were to become involved in hostilities against more than one opponent, thus assuring Japan that if she fought Russia, France and Germany would stay on the sidelines. What gave this treaty its immense value was that, by the time it was signed, Japan had already put herself in a position to capitalize on it through military expenditures which had risen from the level of $10 million in 1893 to $65 million in 1900, an increase spent mostly on major additions to the navy.)

In addition to the *Mikasa,* later to become Togo's flagship, these included her sister ships the *Shikishima, Asahi* and *Hatuse,* and two other slightly smaller battleships, the *Fuji* and the *Yashima,* along with six armored cruisers, the *Izumi, Azuma, Asama, Yakumo, Tokiwa,* and *Iwate.* When two smaller armored cruisers built by Italy for Argentina (which later cancelled its order) were also offered to her after Russia had scornfully declined them, Japan promptly bought these as well.

Thus, by 1903, when Russia's own belated naval construction program in preparation for war in the Far East was still far from complete, Japan had acquired a total of twelve capital ships all built since 1899—late enough to be of the most up-to-date design but early enough to have enabled their crews to be completely used to them. These comprised the nucleus of a fleet quite strong enough to handle the Russian Far East Squadron already based at Port Arthur—so long as the opportunity to do so arrived before Russia could reinforce the Far East Squadron by the ships still under construction in her Baltic yards.

Meanwhile, still understandably reluctant to take on what would at best be an extremely risky war, Japan made efforts to reach an acceptable compromise by diplomatic means. These took the form first of requests that Russia honor her promise, extracted under pressure from Great Britain and the U.S., to remove her armies from Manchuria. When Russia, having reiterated her intention of doing so, still allowed the troops to remain, Japan proposed an agreement whereby she would waive her objections to Russian acquisition of Manchuria in return for Russian recognition of Japan's special interests in Korea.

Instead of the hasty acceptance that might have been prudent in view of her own unreadiness for war, Russia's response to this proposal consisted of disdainful delay followed by rude rejection. Meanwhile, far from reducing her Manchurian military commitments, which now ran to some fifty thousand men, she undertook to introduce a new irritant into the situation. This took the form of a lumber company launched by an adventurous entrepreneur and former cavalry officer named Bezobrazov, which proposed to develop the timber resources on the Korean side of the Yalu River boundary between Korea and Manchuria. Bezobrazov's backers included a lengthy roster of St. Petersburg plutocrats of whom one was the Czar himself, and Viceroy Alexeyev soon came to feel that to withdraw from Korea in response to Japanese demands, let alone to evacuate Manchuria, would be inexcusable. Japan's protests on the subject of the Bezobrazov lumber company, like all her earlier ones, were pointedly ignored.

As the war clouds gathered, a few Russians in posts of authority expressed appropriate alarm, based on an educated respect for Japan's martial potential as exemplified in her recent naval acquisitions as well as her previous accomplishments. One of these was the Finance Minister, Sergius Witte, who resigned in 1903. Another was the Czar's outspoken cousin, the energetic Grand Duke Alexander, who knew something about naval affairs and who had spent two informative years in Japan. A third was the War Minister, General Alexei Nikolaevich Kuropatkin, who was presently to have the responsibility for waging the war as the Russian Commander in Chief in Manchuria. Most Russians, however,—and especially those stationed in the Far East—had, by some sort of contagion, acquired in an even more acute form the same optical deficiency that had previously caused the Chinese to dismiss the Japanese as mere "Island Dwarfs." In Vladivostok and Port Arthur the fashionable witticism was that the Japanese were as harmless as butterflies and that if it came to war, "we'll pin one on a postcard and send him home for a souvenir."

Japan's military preparations for the trial of strength that the Czarist government seemed so clearly to be inviting were by no means confined to the purchase of battleships in Europe. Under Field Marshal Oyama, the army had experienced a seven-year program of reorganization and enlargement to a total of some million and a half men. In the process a top field command had been conferred upon the able Maresuke Nogi in reward for his accomplishments at Port Arthur.

Like Togo, Nogi carried a special *on,* or obligation, to his Emperor, which also dated back to the Saigo Rebellion. In his case, however, the burden of the debt—for which he was only much later to show what he considered an adequate repayment—had a totally different origin. Fighting against Saigo, as a young officer at the siege of Kagoshima, Nogi had been in command of a battalion that lost its standard in battle, a disgrace for which his responsibility made it traditionally encumbent upon him to perform seppuku. By a special dispensation that took into account both the circumstances affecting the loss and Nogi's conspicuous capacities and personal courage, the Emperor had exonerated him from all blame, thus obliging him to devote the remainder of his unexpectedly renewed lease on life to the service of the nation.

Organizational changes in the Japanese Army were paralleled by comparable changes in the Navy. By 1903 the Navy Minister was Gombei Yamamoto, the fellow Satsuman whom Togo had known as his romantically inclined messmate in the *Fuso,* just after his own return from training in England; and Yamamoto had recalled Admiral Yuko Ito from sea duty to serve as Chief of Staff. The fleet's Commander in Chief was Yamamoto's classmate and equally good friend, Sonojo Hidaka, who, however, suffered from an intermittent digestive ailment that made it seem prudent to appoint a successor. Confronted with the painful necessity of breaking the news to Hidaka, Yamamoto's only satisfaction was the knowledge that the name of his successor, chosen with the explicit approval of the Emperor, was one that even Hidaka himself would be sure to endorse: Heihachiro Togo.

What was to astonish Yamamoto was that of the two interviews that followed, the first was the longer. Hidaka first asked to know the reason for his removal. Even when this had been explained as tactfully as possible he still seemed to find it adequate grounds for seppuku. Given the name of his successor, however, Hidaka finally recovered his equanimity and congratulated his superior on a wise choice.

During the two years before the Russo-Japanese war Togo's assignment had been to supervise the construction of, and then to command, the new naval base at Maizuru on the Japan Sea, a port that left him considerable spare time for his favorite pastime of bird-shooting. Now, summoned from Maizuru to receive the highest honor that it was in the power of his old friend to bestow, Togo listened in absolute silence while Yamamoto gave him a complete briefing on diplomatic background, outlined the Ministry's war plan, and at last conferred upon him his promotion to the top command of the greatest fleet in Japan's history. When Yamamoto had finished outlining the Ministry plan for the war and the commander in chief's role in it Togo, instead of trying to express his satisfaction or asking any questions, merely replied: "I shall execute your orders." A long silence ensued, after which Togo bowed and withdrew without further comment.

Togo's distrust of language at moments of intense emotion or major decision was to be displayed again a few weeks later, when, having assumed command of his ships at Sasebo, he got word of the final break with Russia. A visit to St. Petersburg by Japan's leading statesman, Prince Ito, to seek a peaceful solution had met with a scornful reception in 1903. Japan's final conciliatory proposal to the Russian Foreign Office had been dispatched in January 1904, calling for a reply by February 4. When no reply arrived by that date, Ambassador Kurino packed his bags

and departed from St. Petersburg signifying the formal
severance of diplomatic relations, which took place two
days later. When Togo received word of the impending
break on the night of February 5, he summoned the top
officers of the fleet to his staff room on the *Mikasa*. On the
long table in front of him there lay an unlacquered tray
and on the tray a short bright blade whose significance
required no explanation.

"We sail tomorrow, and our enemy flies the Russian
flag," said Togo, and paused to let the words sink in. He
then read the Emperor's command to vanquish the enemy
fleet and the meeting ended.

The war plans that Navy Minister Yamamoto had read
to Togo in awarding him command of the combined fleet
were based upon a rigid schedule imposed by the related
factors of time, space, and money. Though generous loans
were later on to be raised from private bankers abroad—
chiefly King Edward's good friend Sir Ernest Cassell, and
Sir Ernest's good friend Jacob H. Schiff of Kuhn, Loeb &
Company in New York, who together underwrote a total of
almost half a billion dollars—none of this was on hand or
even in sight when hositilities started. On the contrary,
Japan's resources had been worn exceedingly thin by her
intensive preparations, whereas Russia appeared to have
almost limitless natural advantages, including a superiority of at least four to one in man power. What Japan
needed was a victory so rapid and decisive that Russia's
superior resources could never be brought into play.

That a victory, if it were to be gained at all, would have
to be gained quickly was even more clearly underlined by
the inherent logistic problems. For supplying her Far East
garrison, Russia was wholly dependent on the trans-Siberian railway, but this five-thousand-mile, single-track ar-
tery, with the gap at Lake Baikal, could at best produce
only a thin trickle of men and supplies. Japan, on the con-

trary, had broad avenues of water across which to ferry her army the short distance to the scene of the struggle—but these were available only so long as she possessed complete control of the intervening seas.)

While Japan's twelve new battleships and cruisers were more than a match for the seven battleships and nine cruisers of Russia's Pacific Squadron as presently constituted—and especially when this squadron was divided, as it now was, between Port Arthur and Vladivostok—they could hardly expect to handle both the Pacific Squadron and Russia's Baltic Fleet, especially with the latter reinforced by the new ships now nearing completion in the Baltic Sea yards. Consequently, Togo had a dual assignment of which the first part would be to destroy the Pacific Squadron, or at least keep it bottled up, while ferrying across to the mainland an army of which one wing would move inland to attack Mukden while the other would turn south to capture the Squadron's base at Port Arthur. With the Pacific Squadron thus eliminated, the second part of the assignment was to demolish whatever new naval force Russia might be able to send out to replace it.

Plans for an opening gambit appropriate to such a tight schedule had naturally been drafted far in advance. They consisted primarily of a surprise night attack by torpedo boats on the Russian ships based at Port Arthur, to take place immediately after notification to Russia of the termination of diplomatic relations. Like the similar airborne attack on Pearl Harbor thirty-six years later, the purpose of this attack was to cripple, and if possible to destroy, the enemy's sea power so as to assure the army of unimpeded access to Japan's main objective—in this case, the mainland of Manchuria and the fleet base at Port Arthur itself.

Togo's fleet reached the southwestern coast of Korea on February 8th. Late that afternoon his torpedo-boat cap-

tains gathered in Togo's spacious staff cabin on the *Mikasa*
to receive orders, shake hands with their Commander in
Chief, and drink a toast to victory. As dusk fell the tiny
vessels, weighing less than a hundred tons each, set off on
their desperate mission.

While aware that a severance of diplomatic relations
may, and often does, mean the immediate start of hostilities, Viceroy Alexeyev had chosen to assume that on this
occasion it had no such significance. That evening the
warships in the harbor were fully lighted while most of
their officers attended a reception on shore in honor of
Fleet Commander Stark's wife and daughter, who were
celebrating their name day. Shortly before ten o'clock, the
hour of moonrise, ten torpedo boats slid quietly into the
harbor, where they were at first mistaken for Russian craft
returning from patrol. Eighteen torpedos were released, of
which three found their targets. These severely damaged
the cruiser *Pallada* and the battleships *Czarevich* and *Retvisan*, causing the latter to run aground in the channel between the outer harbor and the open sea.

Reluctant to bring his capital ships within range of land-
based artillery, Togo did not approach the scene of action
until almost noon the next day, when an hour-long gun
duel at four-mile range ensued between them and the Russian ships in the outer harbor. The result was further damage to the Russians, at the cost of a few scattered hits,
including one near the *Mikasa*'s afterbridge, to the Japanese. Not until long afterward did Togo learn that had he
used his whole fleet in the attack the evening before, the
state of the port's total unpreparedness might well have
enabled him to sink every ship in the squadron, silence the
forts, and thus perhaps end the war literally before it had
begun.

If Viceroy Eugene Alexeyev was less than an inspiring commander in chief for all the Russian forces in the Far East, the same could not be said of the man who was soon to replace Stark in command of the fleet. This was Admiral Stepan Ossipovich Makarov, who was not only Russia's top naval personage but probably one of the half-dozen best-known and most-respected naval officers in the world. A hero of the Turkish War of 1877–78, author of a widely translated treatise on strategy that was familiar not only to most of Togo's officers but to many of his seamen as well and a huge bear of a man whose two-point, twelve-inch set of chin whiskers fully justified his nickname of "Old Beardy," Makarov arrived in Port Arthur on March 7th. The immediate change in the morale and efficiency of the Pacific Squadron was noticeable not only to his own subordinates—one of whom, Captain Vladimir Semenoff, was to record it for posterity in his memoirs—but even to the attacking fleet.

Though in many respects ideal as a major fleet base, (Port Arthur had one grave disadvantage in that the channel between the outer port and the roadstead, or harbormouth outside, was so shallow that it was passable for deep-draft vessels only at high tide and even then for only one ship at a time. This had always meant that to go to sea the fleet required two high tides, or at least twelve hours, and it also suggested that if some obstruction could be sunk in the channel so as to block it, the Pacific Squadron would either be closed up in the harbor as securely as a model frigate in a corked bottle or else just as securely locked out.)

During the first months of the war, Togo made three attempts to provide such an obstruction by sending heavily ballasted old hulks into the channel and having them sunk there by skeleton crews who were then picked up by torpedo boats. For various reasons, including mine fields and

heavy fire from the guns of the stranded but later refloated
Retvisan as well as those on the hills around the harbor, all
three attempts failed. After losing scores of men and seventeen old ships, of which some use could have been
made as transports, Togo was obliged to conclude that
the scheme was unworkable. So, too, were his efforts to
sink the Russian ships in the harbor by long-range bombardment from outside, and Togo had no intention of risking
his own fleet by getting within range of the land-based
guns. Meanwhile, to make sure the Russian Squadron did
not emulate Ting's escape from the same harbor a decade
before, he settled down to watch the entrance like a cat
at a mouse-hole, ready to pounce on the Squadron if it
showed the least signs of venturing out of range of the
hilltop cannon at the harbor's mouth.

One of Makarov's first accomplishments after his arrival was to show that by careful timing and skillful maneuvering it was actually possible to get the whole fleet
out on a single tide; and this change alone, which quickly
became apparent to the besiegers, was enough to enliven
their task considerably. When it became clear that, unlike
Stark, Makarov was ready to venture out for purposes of
reconnaissance, Togo saw in his boldness a chance to introduce a new tactic that had been relatively useless so
long as the Russians stayed inside their port. This was to
lay mines along the unmarked channel used by the Russian ships, to make such sorties as costly as possible.

Just how costly they were to prove not even Togo would
have dared to hope before the morning of April 12, hardly
more than a month after his famous adversary's arrival.
On the snowy night of the 11th Togo's destroyers, accompanied by a mine-layer, had laid a field of thirty mines
around the harbor entrance, and the next morning a flotilla
of his torpedo boats showed themselves just beyond it, as
bait to entice the Russian ships out. Sure enough, four

cruisers soon appeared and, having negotiated the mine field safely, were attacked by Togo's cruiser division under Admiral Dewa which presently drove them in again.

Shortly after this, on the report that survivors from a Russian destroyer sunk earlier while on patrol duty might still be afloat, and also perhaps in the hopes of catching up with Dewa's cruisers, Makarov's flagship, the *Petropavlovsk*, accompanied by another battleship and an armored cruiser, emerged in their place. Dewa drew away, hoping to lure Makarov's big ships within striking distance of Togo's battleships further offshore but the Russian admiral was too clever to fall into the trap. After an hour's running fight with Dewa, in which no major damage was inflicted by either side, he turned back toward Port Arthur.

Makarov had been warned about the possibility of a new mine field by patrols that had sighted the Japanese destroyers through the snow the night before but in the ensuing excitement this danger had apparently slipped his mind. In any case, as the *Petropavlovsk* turned to enter the channel Togo, watching from afar with his Zeiss glasses, saw a sudden huge cloud of smoke envelop the Russian flagship. The sound of a muffled explosion followed, and then two other louder explosions as the ship's magazines were touched off by the first blast. When the smoke cleared after several minutes, all that was visible of the *Petropavlovsk* was some floating debris, from which eighty survivors, seven of them officers, were eventually picked up. "Old Beardy" was not among those rescued, nor was his guest, the internationally famous Russian war artist Vasili Vereshchagin, on his way home from a U.S. tour during which he had painted the best-known battle scene of San Juan Hill, with Theodore Roosevelt leading the charge.

If Makarov's loss—which one expert rated as roughly equivalent to that of five battleships—was convincing proof of the risks to which a commander in chief may be exposed in a sea battle, an even more dramatic example in support of the same principle was to be provided not long afterward by his successor, Rear Admiral Vitgeft. That Vitgeft should have been the agent of such a demonstration was in itself one of the ironies of combat. Unlike Makarov, he belonged essentially to the breed of officers more accustomed to desks than to decks and to making comment upon battles than to taking command in them. Pushed into the unaccustomed and uncongenial task of leading the fleet so brilliantly revitalized by Makarov, Vitgeft understandably found, in the tragic death of the former, a justifiable pretext for resuming the policy of keeping his six remaining battleships safe inside the harbor. By late July, however, Japanese army artillery, creeping up on the outer ring of the Russian fortifications, began to impair the security of this haven, and its shells soon damaged the ships enough to suggest that their only alternative to destruction might be departure.

A message, signed by the Czar himself and brought in by a torpedo boat on August 7th, ordered Vitgeft to take the fleet to Vladivostok. Vitgeft's caution had been less the result of timidity than of indecision; now, given a firm directive from the top, he lost no time complying with it. On the early morning of August 10th, the Far East Squadron stood out to sea. Togo's whole fleet, except for Kamimura's six cruisers, which had been dispatched to Vladivostok to mount guard on the three Russian armored cruisers based there, was lying in wait for it.

The ensuing Battle of the Yellow Sea was the closest and—except for Tshushima—the most decisive naval engagement of the war. Encountering Vitgeft's squadron in the early afternoon, Togo's first moves were designed to put himself between it and Port Arthur, so as to prevent its return and force a major fleet action. However, when it had become clear that the Russians this time had no intention of going back but were making for their alternate Far Eastern base, Togo was so far behind his opponent that he had to waste precious hours in detouring Vitgeft's weaker elements so as to catch up with the battleships at the head of the Russian line. It was 5:43 in the afternoon when he opened fire on the leading Russian ships. From then until dusk Togo's First Division and the six Russian battleships, steaming on parallel southeasterly courses four miles apart banged away at each other on almost even terms, with the flagships *Mikasa* and *Czarevich* sharing the brunt of the punishment.

What decided the issue, just as it was beginning to look as though the Russians would be able to hold their course until darkness enabled them to escape, was a double hit by two Japanese shells that at almost the same instant chanced to land on the exact center of the bull's-eye—the *Czarevich's* forward bridge. The result was not merely the death of Vitgeft—of whom all that was later found was a part of one leg—but the death or incapacitation of everyone else on the bridge or in the conning tower beneath it. These included the helmsman, whose loss proved to be of even more immediate significance than that of the commander in chief.

In addition to killing the helmsman, the effect of the explosion—actually a premature one, since the Japanese were using armor-piercing shells designed to penetrate the target rather than to explode on impact—was to wedge the wheel itself into the position of a port turn. An instant later the turn began, so sharply that the *Czarevich* heeled over 12 degrees; and the *Retvisan,* which had detected nothing about the latest hit on the flagship to distinguish it from earlier ones—followed in her wake. By the time the third ship arrived at the turning point, the *Czarevich* had swung around more than 180 degrees and was heading back into her own line, making it apparent at last that something was seriously wrong. Nonetheless, in the absence of any signal to indicate what had happened, there was no way for the other ships to deduce that in fact the *Czarevich* was not only out of control and without an admiral but actually without any one at all in command.

By the time an officer from another part of the flagship had been found to take charge, and by the time this officer had managed to signal Rear Admiral Prince Uktomsky, Vitgeft's second in command on the *Peresviet,* that responsibility for the fleet now rested with him, most of the cruisers stationed to port of the battleships had copied the 180-degree turn of the leading *Czarevich* and the *Retvisan,* with the result that the entire squadron was in total disarray. There was little left for Uktomsky to do but give up the attempt to reach Vladivostok, and order the squadron to follow him back to Port Arthur. Even this—since the *Peresviet* was too damaged to hoist intelligible signals—was not clearly understood, and many of the cruisers wandered off on their own, to eventual internment, capture, or destruction.

What Togo had to decide at this critical point was whether to leave it to his torpedo boats and destroyers to try to prevent the Squadron from regaining its home port or to risk trying to finish it off himself by a night-fleet action at short range. The latter effort, if successful, would end the threat of the Squadron once and for all, but it had serious drawbacks. The *Mikasa* had already taken more than twenty hits in the course of the battle, and his other three battleships were damaged to a comparable degree. To risk losing one or more of these irreplaceable vessels without the chance of at least a proportionate gain seemed to Togo unjustifiable, and it also seemed to him doubtful that the present circumstances provided any such chance.

The Russian squadron had been turned back from its objective and the torpedo boats and destroyers might well be able to damage it further during the night. Even if the Squadron did get back to Port Arthur, the ships would remain subject to Japanese artillery fire; and any that survived would become Japanese prizes when Port Arthur finally fell, as in due course it was bound to do. Togo choose the prudent course, with the result that five of the six Russian battleships,—on which the Japanese torpedo boats proved unable to score any hits at all—found their way home by dawn the next day. The *Czarevich,* unable to keep up with the others, eventually put in at the German port of Chingtao, where she was interned.

Togo has been sharply criticized by students of the Port Arthur campaign for over-caution in not seizing his chance to annihilate the remainder of the Russian squadron on the afternoon of August 10th. In fact, while caution did in fact prove costly to him on at least two occasions during the blockade of Port Arthur, he was later to demonstrate that he was entirely ready to gamble for the highest stakes possible when he felt that the odds warranted it. One reason, not apparent at the time, that he was averse to risking the four battleships he had with him on August 10 was that these four were all he had left out of the six with which he had started the campaign.

On May 15th, two of his battleships, the *Hatuse,* of the *Mikasa* class, and the *Fuji's* sister ship *Yashima,* had both been sunk by mines on the same afternoon—the former with the loss of two thirds of her crew. Since the entire complement of the *Yashima* had been taken off before she went down, Togo was able to conceal the loss of this ship, which was not announced until after the war. Nonetheless, the reduction of his battleship force by 33 percent in the course of a few hours had naturally increased his reluctance to jeopardize the four that he had left.

In the interim, grounds for caution on Togo's part had been increased by the announcement in St. Petersburg that Russia was now planning, however belatedly, to reinforce the Far Eastern Squadron by sending out the entire Baltic Fleet, including four new battleships as strong as or stronger than his own *Mikasa.* Togo assumed that to meet this fleet when it arrived he would need every ship, every gun, and every man he could assemble. Why risk all his major assets in a preliminary engagement against the already battered Port Arthur squadron when there was every reason to think that this could be demolished from land by the Japanese army without such a risk?

It was perhaps in part the need for making more or less instantaneous decisions such as this, on which Japan's fate might well depend, that had helped turn Togo's close-cropped black hair to sandy gray during the first year of the war. What his staff officers found even more remarkable than the change in their Commander in Chief's appearance, however, was his taciturn but always calm and even-tempered confrontation of the fortunes of war. The loss of two capital ships on the same afternoon—and during a disastrous week when mishaps rather than enemy action had claimed four smaller warships as well—might have moved any other commander to aggrieved complaint. Togo, wrote one of his young officers, calmly dismissed all his losses as "incidents of the campaign."

During the months of patrol duty before Port Arthur, Togo spent much of his time alone in his cabin, just aft of the much larger conference room spanning the width of the ship, where he took his meals with Kato, Akiyama, and the half-dozen other officers on his staff. This cabin, whose porthole looked out on the afterdeck, was furnished in a style that owed more to the British taste of the period, which he had picked up during his sojourn on the *Worcester* and at Cambridge, than to traditional Japanese decor, which might well have seemed incongruous on a warship. A roll-top desk faced the afterdeck port-holes and two couches had been specially built to fit the slanting partitions to port and starboard. In the center of the room was a round, cloth-covered table and on the walls hung two pictures, one showing a bombardment of Port Arthur done by his devoted steward and the other a training ship that Togo had commanded before the Chinese war, braving a typhoon off Australia.

Other decorative items were two *bonsai*, one a five-hundred-year-old dwarf cedar and the other a fir, given to him by his good friend Baron Okura; a basket of artificial flowers made out of feathers, presented to him by citizens of Kobe; and, of course, those grimly appropriate reminders of the uncertain fortunes of war, the unexploded Russian shell that had landed on the *Mikasa*'s bridge and the torpedo whisker found in the *Mikasa*'s net.

In his cabin, usually puffing on one of his several briar pipes, Togo received his immediate subordinates and occasional foreign visitors. Of the latter, the most frequent was Captain William C. Pakenham of the British Embassy, who, as one of two naval attachés assigned to the fleet, stayed with it throughout the entire campaign. Togo slept, always at least partially in uniform, in a cubicle adjoining a bathroom with a Japanese-style wooden tub on one side and the wireless room on the other. Over his narrow wooden bunk there hung the portrait of his Emperor.

As late summer turned to fall, and it became clear that the Far East Squadron was resigned to meeting its fate without again venturing outside the harbor, the problem confronting Togo in his hours of pipe-smoking cogitation was how to hasten its end. In October news came that the Baltic Fleet had actually left the Russian port of Libau on the eighteen-thousand-mile voyage that might bring it to the Japan Sea as early as January. Meanwhile, the Army was still bogged down around the outer defenses of the citadel at Port Arthur that Viceroy Alexeyev had described

—it now began to seem with some justification—as impregnable.

In order to meet the coming test with the Baltic Fleet, Togo felt, it was imperative to give his ships a thorough refit to restore them to full fighting efficiency after their arduous duty during the ten months' siege. A few could be sent back to the Sasebo docks in relays but by no means all—and this still left the urgent problem of sinking and disabling the Russian ships still afloat in the harbor which otherwise, if added to the new squadron on the way, would give the Russians a substantial superiority in the battle that would surely decide the outcome of the war. To ensure himself an even chance in this, Togo estimated that the ships at Port Arthur would have to be destroyed by the first of the year at the latest. And—since it was unthinkable to risk his own vessels against shore-based Russian artillery—the job would have to be done by the army.

The key to the whole tactical situation at Port Arthur was a single eminence known as Hill 203 (its height in meters), from which cannon could pinpoint their fire on targets within either the town or the harbor. Nogi's efforts to gain this peak were in bitter contrast to the easy triumph against Port Arthur's Chinese defenders a decade earlier. His soldiers this time inched forward against machine-gun fire in suicidal waves, ousting the defenders from carefully constructed trenches and redoubts at bayonet or dagger point. Casualties mounted to a rate never previously attained in human warfare, to be matched again only in the trenches of World War I, but no accusation of careless bloodletting, such as was made against some later field officers in Europe, was ever brought against General Count Maresuke Nogi. One reason was that, fully conscious of the significance of their objective, his men died in their attempt to gain it with the same fatalistic patriotism to be displayed by the kamikaze pilots and cave defenders of a later generation. Another was that among those killed in the autumn offensive were the commander in chief's two sons.

When it finally came, the fall of Port Arthur did so with breath-taking suddenness. As early as September Nogi had sent its defending Russian commander, Major General Anatoly Stoessel, a summons to surrender which had been contemptuously rejected. Now, on New Year's Day, though the town still had supplies enough to keep the besiegers at bay, Stoessel, who was later to be court-martialed for an action that most of his officers disapproved, concluded that further resistance was useless and sent emissaries under a flag of truce to propose a meeting, at which terms of surrender were agreed upon.

In fact, since the main value of Port Arthur had been that of a haven for the Far East Squadron, Stoessel's conclusion was by no means an unreasonable one. Hill 203, which alone had cost the attackers eleven thousand in killed and wounded, had fallen on December 6. That same evening an observation post had been established on its peak and for the next three days 11-inch shells poured down on the five great battleships in the inner basin until all except the *Sevastopol,* which managed to crawl to the outer harbor, where she was scuttled in deep water, were lying submerged in the mud. Only then did the gunners turn their attention to the town itself. By this time Togo's ships had already withdrawn. He and they were hurrying back to Sasebo to use every available moment to prepare for the arrival of the Baltic Fleet and for the final test that Togo well knew would determine the war's outcome.

PART TWO

Encounter

Nanji no katana mijikakeraba, ippo susunde—
If your sword is too short, take one step forward.

Vice Admiral Zinovy Petrovich Rozhdestvensky

V

Whatever else may be said of the voyage of Russia's Second Pacific Squadron from the Baltic Sea to the Sea of Japan, it is at least sure that few nautical adventures since the Odyssey can have been more thoroughly reported. Occurring when the Russo-Japanese War had, in orderly sequence and with short intermissions, replaced the Spanish-American and Boer Wars as the main event in the international arena, the progress of the fleet received extensive if not always reliable coverage in the world's press. The orders and tactics of the admirals involved later became the subject of erudite inquiry and study. And at least three members of the expedition wrote voluminous accounts of it that received wide attention at the time of their original publication and later provided rich source material for such able historians as Edwin A. Falk in the U.S., Frank Thiess in Germany, and Richard Hough in England.

One of these books consists of the almost daily letters addressed to his wife by the fleet's nimble and industrious engineer, Eugene Sigismondovich Politovsky, forming what amounts to a diary focused on one of the most significant aspects of the voyage. Another is the account of the journey and its termination by Captain Vladimir Semenoff, who, as a member of the commander in chief's staff, was at his side throughout and had the further advantage of having served, since soon after the start of the war, in the First Far East Squadron under Admirals Stark, Makarov, and Vitgeft as executive officer of the cruiser *Diana*, which had been interned at Saigon after the battle of August 10. By many years the last but by no means least interesting of the three memoirs is an extraordinary volume published thirty years after the event by one of the ordinary seamen involved, a paymaster's steward named A. Novikoff-Priboy.

An outspoken revolutionary whose account of the voyage doubtless reflects the viewpoint of many of his fellow malcontents among the ten thousand or so deckhands, stokers, and miscellaneous ratings who served on the Russian ships, Novikoff-Priboy, according to his introduction, compiled his story in a Japanese prison camp shortly after the war, from his own notes and those of comrades on other ships. After two versions of the manuscript had been destroyed by fire, a third version, concealed by his brother in a hiding place that he later forgot during the last days of the Czarist regime, was finally rediscovered in a beehive on the family farm in 1928. The author thereupon revised his narrative for the fourth time in a semifictional form so well-calculated to enlist the approval of the regime then at the peak of its power in the U.S.S.R. that on March 15th, 1941, it received a Stalin Prize in the Soviet Military Novel series.

While numerous disparities may be detected in these accounts, and consequently in their later derivatives, the basic facts of the extraordinary eighteen thousand mile passage are readily ascertainable and have been superbly

related by Hough in *The Fleet that Had to Die.* The back-
bone of the Second Pacific Squadron consisted of four
brand-new and substantially identical 13,500-ton 16,300-
horse-power battleships named *Alexander III, Borodino,
Orel,* and *Kniaz Suvorov,* the last serving as flagship for the
Commander in Chief, Vice Admiral Zinovy Petrovich
Rozhdestvensky. Each of these formidable vessels carried
four 12-inch guns, mounted in pairs in well-protected turrets fore and aft, whose 650-pound projectiles had an
effective range of ten miles. For further offensive purposes
each had a dozen 6-inch and forty-six smaller guns, along
with four torpedo tubes and the bow rams then still customary for battleships. Defensively, each had strips of
steel armor-plating ten inches thick around the waterline,
four-inch deck armor, and heavy steel canopies over the
conning tower. Their estimated speed was 18 knots.

Built with an eye to offsetting the *Mikasa*-class battleships acquired by Japan at about the same time, these four
ships, had they been incorporated in the First Pacific
Squadron at the start of the war, might well have given
Russia command of the Japan Sea and thus have made the
ferrying of Japanese armies to the mainland wholly impractical. Delays in construction, along with Japan's decision to inaugurate hostilities before the new ships were
ready, had combined to prevent this. It was not until
June of 1904 that the Czar's government even concluded
that the original squadron, by that time effectively bottled
up inside Port Arthur, would really need reinforcement at
all.

By the time the new battleships were completed, after-
thoughts for improving the officers' quarters, which tended
to make the ships top-heavy, and profiteering on the
material involved had considerably diminished their
book-value effectiveness. A much more serious deficiency
in the new fleet, however, was the inclusion in it of

inferior elements, starting with the Second Battle Division, composed of two older and slower battleships, the *Sissoi Veliky* and the *Navarin;* an even more ancient armored cruiser, the *Admiral Nakhimov;* and a slab-sided monstrosity called the *Oslyabya* that served as flagship for the elderly and ailing Rear Admiral Baron Dimitri von Folkersham. The Squadron included four fast new cruisers, the *Oleg, Aurora, Zhemchug,* and *Izumrud,* but their usefulness, like that of the new battleships, was compromised by markedly inferior specimens of the same class, including the *Dmitri Donskoi,* originally designed for sail, and the fast but inadequately gunned *Svetlana.* The rest of the armada, which totaled some forty-two vessels, consisted of nine 350-ton "torpedo-boat destroyers" and non-combatant auxiliaries such as ocean-going tugs, repair vessels, and miscellaneous transports of which two were especially to distinguish themselves by various misdemeanors en route. One of these was the *Kamchatka,* a floating workshop loaded with spare parts and gear, which caused more trouble than the vessels she was supposed to assist. The other was a hospital ship whose name, identical with that of the battleship, was *Orel* (meaning "Eagle") but which carried a very different type of complement: a score of patrician Muscovite Florence Nightingales of whom one was the niece of the commander in chief.

The hulls of all the ships, except for the *Orel* and another hospital ship, which were white with a Red Cross on their funnels, were painted black, but since the art of camouflage was not yet then even in its infancy this choice of hue was less remarkable than that picked for their towering smokestacks. With a genius for nautical ineptitude bordering on the clairvoyant, these had been painted bright yellow with a black stripe at the top, a color combination that was to be recognized only decades later as the most eye-catching in the entire spectrum. But the bright hues of its chimneys were among the fleet's more trivial defects.

Measuring the effectiveness of a fleet by the number of its guns is rather like estimating that of a football team by the number of players on its roster or that of a prize-fighter by the number of his fists. Nonetheless, this a method often employed by naval statisticians, and in the case of the Russian fleet it showed an advantage in long-range guns of forty-three against seventeen, which seemed more than enough to compensate for a relative weakness in guns of 6 inches or less of some 300 to 200. But what such calculations failed to include were the disparities in the quality of the man power available to handle both the ships and their weapons. It was here that the discrepancy between the two fleets was perhaps most marked. Recruited mainly from the farming peasantry of the Baltic provinces, whose inhabitants had limited seagoing traditions to start with, the crews of the Russian Navy as a whole were inevitably handicapped by being restricted to six months of training a year owing to the ice that immobilized their ships the rest of the time. However, by the summer of 1904 most of the best-trained seamen in the fleet had long since been assigned to the First Far East Squadron and Rozhdestvensky had to depend for his crews upon reservists, merchant-marine seamen, and totally inexperienced conscripts from the lowest strata of the urban and agricultural proletariat. In the words of the senior gunnery lieutenant on the *Suvorov:* "Some of them know nothing and the rest can remember only what is obsolete and useless!"

Since time in which to train the new crews was severely limited, and since many of the officers were almost as lacking in experience as the men under them, it was not surprising that the standard of proficiency on even the best of the ships was low. With a round-the-world voyage for a shakedown cruise, prospects for remedying this fault might have been reasonably bright had it not been for another one much less susceptible to such treatment. This was that many of the seamen and even some of their officers were already sufficiently disaffected with the Czarist regime to be hopeful less of victory that would bring glory to the fleet than of a defeat that would bring discredit to the monarchy. While Novikoff-Priboy's emotional bias may make him factually unreliable on some counts, there is little reason to distrust his appraisal of the revolutinary temper of his comrades and superiors. According to this, many if not most of the seamen were bitterly hostile to those of their officers who—unlike the engineer of the battleship *Orel*, whom Novikoff-Priboy credits with maintaining an informal lending library of seditious literature— were not themselves in active sympathy with the rebellious elements under their command.

Given such crews and such ships, Rozhdestvensky might well have had a hard time even getting to the Far East had there been no other obstacles for him to overcome, but in fact, even without counting the Japanese, there were several. Most formidable of these was that of coaling en route —a feat that no other fleet in history had ever even considered on a comparable scale. Unlike Great Britain, which had built up a world-wide network of fuel depots since the start of the age of steam, Russia had not a single outpost of any sort between the Baltic Sea and Vladivostok; and the punctilious neutrality of the powers who controlled most of the internationally used ports between—not to mention England, with her open alliance with the enemy—left small hope that they could be counted on for assistance.

Since Rozhdestvensky's ships would burn five hundred tons a day just for heat and light while in harbor, more than three thousand tons a day at their most economical cruising speed, and more than ten thousand a day when travelling at their fastest, a rough estimate of their needs for the whole voyage was half a million tons. The means devised to provide them with this formidable load was a contract with Germany's Hamburg-Amerika Line whereby the Line agreed to furnish a fleet of colliers to accompany the Squadron and provision it en route. When harbors were available, the coaling would be done therein. When they were not, the ships would have to heave-to on the open sea so that the fuel could be carried from the colliers to the ships' bunkers in sacks by the already overworked and unwilling crews.

According to an ancient recipe sometimes attributed to Themistocles, the Athenian hero of the battle of Salamis, the secret of success in sea warfare is: "Providence—and a good admiral." Never was this prescription to be put to a more severe test than by the voyage of Russia's Second Pacific Squadron, but at least, whatever the Squadron's other drawbacks, there could be little doubt about its commander in chief's qualifications for his task. One of the few top-ranking officers in the Russian Navy who had made his way up by merit rather than birth or connections, Rozhdestvensky was, like Togo, primarily a specialist in weapons, a gunnery officer who had crowned a reputation founded as a youth during the 1870 war with Turkey by a brilliant performance at a fleet review in Reval in 1902. There, in the presence of both the Czar and the German Kaiser, Captain Rozhdestvensky's Baltic Fleet gunners put on a three-hour display of marksmanship so spectacular that it caused Wilhelm II to exclaim, within hearing of his own Fleet Admiral Alfred von Tirpitz, "I wish I had such splendid admirals as your Captain Rozhdestvensky in my fleet!"

Generally considered the ablest officer in the Russian Navy since the demise of Makarov (under whom he had served in the Far East during the nineties), Rozhdestvensky, at fifty-six, was a tall, imposing man with a spade-shaped beard, deep-set black eyes, a bald head, and a habit of grinding his jaws together at moments of tension or excitement. Quick to rage and quick to praise, a commander who spared himself even less than he did the men under him, he was the kind of admiral whose temperament Russians could understand and whose leadership they could welcome. For his own part, Rozhdestvensky was under no illusions about the appalling difficulties of his assignment. He meant to overcome them all, using every means that came to hand. At the end of August 1904 he boarded the *Suvorov* and took command of the squadron. "Safe voyage and success against the enemy," signaled Admiral Birilev, Chief of Defense for the Baltic Sea.

The first target practice for 6-inch and 12-pounder guns was held a few days later and resulted in none of the ships' scoring a single hit. Early in September a surprise alarm drill was held, with comparable results: few crew members even woke up, and those who did stood about on the decks with no notion of what to do. On October 3 the Squadron was scheduled to leave Kronstadt for final assembly and formal departure from Reval. Kronstadt was bedecked with flowers, and the bells chimed gaily as the ships moved proudly out to sea—until the already overloaded battleship *Orel* came slowly to rest upon a sand bar.

In order to extricate her from this predicament, Admiral Birilev himself, wearing full dress uniform and medals, came hurrying on board. A wily, waggish personage, who liked to refer to himself as "a fighting admiral" although he had never actually witnessed a naval engagement, he ordered tugs into action and then, to augment their efforts, had the crew race from side to side in an effort to rock the 15,000-ton monster off the sand. This exercise gave rise to considerable hilarity, but the ship was not freed until a

day and a half later, after dredges had deepened the channel by five feet.

At Reval, the formal send-off took place on October 9th,
a cool, gusty day with rain-squalls broken by intervals of
bright autumnal sun. Standing on the deck of the Imperial
yacht, the *Shtandart,* from which he had watched Rozhdestvensky's gunners distinguish themselves in the same
harbor in 1902, the Czar, whose hemophilic Crown Prince
had been born less than two months before, took the salute
in the early afternoon. Later he boarded each of the battleships whose sailors, in new blue jumpers and black
trousers, lined the rails, to greet the officers and deliver a
brief speech from the forebridge. His diary for that day
contains a prayerful entry: "Bless its voyage, Lord. Permit
that it arrive safe and sound at its destination, that it succeed in its terrible mission for the safety and happiness of
Russia."

That evening after the Czar's return to his winter palace
at Czarskoe Selo, his uncle, Grand Duke Alexis, the Grand
Admiral of the Navy, gave a banquet for the fleet officers,
followed by innumerable champagne toasts and speeches.
A somber note was struck in one of the latter by the
Alexander III's outspoken Captain Bukhvostov, who said,
"You have all wished us a happy voyage. You feel sure
our brave sailors will smash the Japanese. We thank
you for your good opinion, but it only shows that you
know nothing about this squadron. We do. We know
that Russia is no sea power and that government funds
were wasted on these ships. You have wished us victory
but there will be no victory. Probably half our squadron
will be lost on the way. Perhaps I am too pessimistic, and
all our ships will arrive in the Yellow Sea. If they do, Togo
will blow them to bits. His fleet is infinitely better than
ours and the Japanese are real sailors. I can promise you
one thing, however. All of us here, the officers of the Sec-

ond Pacific Squadron, shall at least know how to die. We shall not surrender."

Thirty-six hours later the squadron put out to sea, with the four splendid battleships bringing up the rear. A strong southwest wind that sprang up suddenly in the late afternoon made it hard for them to gain headway against the tide. When the tide turned, they finally cleared the harbor around 4 P.M. Two days later the ships stopped at the last home port of Libau, to top off bunkers and take on additional supplies. This time, as she led the fleet toward the open sea, it was the flagship herself that went aground. When the *Suvorov* was finally freed, the fleet steamed slowly into the Baltic to start a voyage that was to make the Odyssey look like a Cook's Tour.

Trouble started promptly when, on the 21st of October, a heavy fog blanketed the North Sea as the squadron moved slowly southward, sirens screaming at maximum decibel, with the cruisers under Rear Admiral Oscar Enquist sent far ahead to scout for signs of the enemy. The possibility that the Japanese might surreptitiously have sent ships around the world to attack the Second Pacific Squadron at the outset of its voyage had been brought sharply to mind the day before, when, during the first real coaling stop at Skagen, lookouts had reported sighting two observation balloons and four enemy cruisers. Lest hostile destroyers attempt to lay mines in the ships' course or launch a suicide torpedo attack, Admiral Rozhdestvensky's orders to his captains were that "no vessel of any sort whatever be allowed to get in amongst the fleet," and each commander was instructed to train his guns on any vessel that refused to show its flag when hailed.

Now, with the crews of all the ships at general quarters as dusk began to fall, a wireless message came to the flag-

ship from the *Kamchatka,* which, supposedly ahead of the
main body with the cruisers, had experienced an engine
failure during the night and was somewhere astern. The
message, couched in a dramatic vein later to become all
too familiar, seemed to confirm these suspicions: "Chased
by torpedoes" it stated, and then, after a pause, "Foreign
torpedo boats are attacking me from every side."

"How many and from which side?" asked the *Suvorov.*

"About eight, from all directions."

"Have they discharged any torpedoes?"

"We haven't seen any," replied the *Kamchatka.*

Requests from the *Kamchatka* that the flagship turn on
her searchlights were declined, lest these reveal her position to the enemy. Requests from the *Suvorov* that the
Kamchatka identify her position by wireless were likewise
ignored for the same reason but, in response to later inquiry as to whether the torpedo boats were still in sight,
the repair ship reported back somewhat more reassur-
ingly: "We can't see any."

A tense calm was thus restored until well after midnight
on the early morning of the 22nd, when someone on the
Suvorov sighted unfamiliar lights ahead and swung searchlights in their direction. The other ships followed the flagship's example and soon the whole sky was bright with
beams that wove huge patterns through the fog and
caused strange shadows to dance across the waves. In
their uncertain glare, the shapes of many small ships and a
few larger ones could be discerned in the adjacent waters.
"Engage the enemy," signaled the *Suvorov* and instantly
the night became hideous with detonations as first the
6-inch broadsides and then the huge 12-inch turret guns
boomed into action. The scene on board the flagship was
vividly described by Commander Semenoff, who, having
arrived from Saigon after a breathless train journey across
Europe just in time to catch up with the Second Squadron

at Libau, had retired to his cabin to enjoy a well-earned night's sleep after the excitements caused by the *Kamchatka.*

> I was awakened, as it seemed to me, by the sound of the bugle "Action!" . . . "Am I awake or asleep?" was my first thought. The trampling of men's feet, who were running up the ladders, the rattle of the ammunition carriers in the hoists, dispelled any doubts . . . and now the first gun had been fired! . . . I rushed up to the afterbridge and nearly knocked down Lieutenant B—— and Dr. N——. "What's the meaning of this? What are they firing at?"
>
> "Torpedo boats! A torpedo attack!" they both shouted. "There! There!"
>
> I now ran to the forebridge where the Admiral, Captain and staff were sure to be . . . To the starboard of us and ahead I saw, several miles off, a number of lights amongst which, from time to time, signals flashed out. Someone (I don't remember to whom I addressed myself) explained to me that this was Admiral Folkersham's division.

An even more colorful version of the night action as witnessed on board the *Orel* was produced by the busy pen of Paymaster Steward Novikoff-Priboy:

> The *Orel* was humming like a hive of angry bees. Bugles blared; drums rumbled; rails rattled under the weight of hand-trucks laden with shells; heavy guns fired from the starboard and port turrets, lighting the darkness with flashes as they discharged and stirring the night with echoing thunder. Men swarmed onto decks and bridges. Discipline went west. Men yelled:
>
> "Destroyers. The destroyers!"
>
> "Where are they? How many?"
>
> "A dozen, at least!"

"We're done for!"
"It's all up with us!"

On the night of October 21, the Gamecock Fleet of 100-ton, single-screw fishing trawlers, having left Hull two days before, was on its regular fishing ground, known as the Dogger Bank, 220 miles northeast of Spurn Head, along with a hundred or so other trawlers from other ports along England's east coast. On first sighting the Second Pacific Squadron the boats of the Gamecock Fleet, each manned by a crew of eight or nine, had mistaken it for the Channel Fleet under Admiral Lord Charles Beresford, and they counted on their red, white, and green lanterns to establish their own identity. When the warships began using searchlights and then firing off their guns, the fishermen took it for some sort of night gunnery drill but, to be on the safe side, sent up some green flares. Then, as the first shells began to fall among their boats, they hurried to cut their nets and put on full steam to get out of the way.

Only when the warships' searchlights were beamed directly upon them and when the hail of shells, instead of ceasing, simultaneously increased did the terrified fishermen on the three trawlers receiving the most concentrated fire rush on deck in a panic comparable to that of their assailants, waving their arms and shouting as loudly as they could. Since their shouts were inaudible and the trawlers lacked wireless or signal flags with which to establish their identity, they were driven to improvise appropriate novelties in nautical communication. "To show what we were, I held a big plaice up," one skipper stated later. "My mate, Jim Tozier, showed a haddock."

No more intelligible than the efforts of the fishermen to establish their character by displaying specimens of their catch were those of Rear Admiral Oscar Enquist's cruisers, which by this time, attracted by the lights and the sound of the gunfire, had fallen back on the scene of action and were exchanging salvos with the battleships as fast as they could load and reload. That none of them managed to sink one another was due primarily to the fact that their marksmanship had not noticeably improved since their first practice trials six weeks before. Nonetheless by the time that Enquist's interrogatory searchlight signals were finally recognized as being in a code known as *Tabulevich*, used only by the Russian Navy, it was too late to save the trawler *Crane*. At point-blank range of a hundred yards the *Suvorov*'s guns had decapitated both the *Crane*'s skipper and her third mate, while wounding several other members of the crew. Shortly after one o'clock in the morning, twenty minutes after the engagement had started, the *Suvorov* sent her searchlight beam straight up into the sky, a signal meaning "Discontinue action." Making no effort to rescue the victims of its fury, the Russian Squadron resumed formation and proceeded on its way.

In the wardrooms of the Russian warships, where the officers exchanged their reminiscences of the battle in the hours before dawn, the consensus was that a flotilla of Japanese torpedo boats had somehow made its way into the Hull fishing fleet and tried to use the trawlers as a disguise to launch their treacherous attack, until the Russian fire drove them off. It became known that the battleship *Orel* alone had fired seventeen 6-inch shells, and five hundred of smaller caliber. Some of these had apparently found the cruiser *Aurora*, which reported four hits by 6- and 12-pound shells, and hits had also been reported by the cruiser *Dmitri Donskoi*. Russian casualties were only two, both on the *Aurora*—a chief gunner who had been slightly injured and the ship's chaplain, who had lost a hand when a .45-mm shell went through his cabin. "Not bad for a beginning," said a cynical young gunnery lieutenant on the *Suvorov*.

The next afternoon, when the *Suvorov* and her sister ships stopped to take on coal within sight of the board-walk at Brighton, the Dogger Bank Incident, as it later became known to the world, had not yet been reported, and a crowd of admiring sight-seers watched the operation from the Palace Pier. Not until its diminutive flagship, the *Moulmein,* led the battered remnants of the Gamecock Fleet, two of whose trawlers had eventually sunk, into their home port the next day did the full story reach the press to create an international storm of indignation. The consequences of the night action became known to Admiral Rozhdestvensky only when the squadron put in at the Spanish port of Vigo, almost a week later. There he learned that, after several days when it looked as though Britain and Russia might go to war about the matter, it had been tentatively referred for settlement to an International Court of Enquiry to be convened at Paris. Instructed to send witnesses to testify before it, Rozhdestvensky chose three young officers from the other ships and, as the senior member of the delegation, a Staff Captain from the *Suvorov* named Nicholas Klado. The latter, a naval theorist and tactician whose overly-developed loquacity Rozhdestvensky had already begun to find exasperating, was an obvious choice but one that the Admiral would later have good cause to regret.

On departing from Vigo, where it had refueled over the protests of the local authorities, the squadron—now referred to in the British press as "the mad-dog fleet"—found itself being escorted somewhat ostentatiously by Admiral Lord Beresford's powerful cruisers. For the next three days, on the way to Tangier, these formed a sort of quarantine patrol, while at the same time providing the Russians with a demonstration of fleet maneuvering that might have served as a sort of premature postgraduate course in this field of naval discipline.

At Tangier, the Bey offered a hearty welcome to his Russian visitors and the fleet enjoyed a deceptively refreshing pause, perhaps comparable to that of Ulysses at the Isle of the Lotus Eaters. On their departure—of which the only untoward incident was the tearing asunder of Tangier's cable connection with Europe—Admiral Folkersham's division parted company with the rest, to proceed through the Mediterranean Sea and the Suez Canal. This shorter route was judged too risky for the larger ships, whose propensity for going aground had already been amply demonstrated, but the two divisions planned to rejoin at the French Island of Madagascar, there to rest and refit before completing their journey.

For the main body of the squadron under Admiral Rozhdestvensky, the cruise down the East Coast of Africa was a painfully slow and laborious one, broken only by short stops at Dakar, Gabon, and Great Fish Bay for repairs and coaling. Loading coal by the bagful in equatorial heat involved not only hideous labor for the deck hands but intense and lasting discomfort for all, since the supplies taken on were not limited to bunker-capacity but were stored on the decks, in cabins, and everywhere else that a spare cranny could be found, much to the detriment of both the ships' stability and their sanitation. Under these conditions, the always risky passage around the Cape of Good Hope was rendered especially precarious, and no sooner had this been safely accomplished than the squadron encountered a storm of gale force as it entered the Indian Ocean. Somehow or other, the overloaded vessels survived it, including a Christmas Eve crisis involving the *Kamchatka* which, when asked why it had again fallen behind, replied: "Bad Coal," and requested permission to throw 150 tons overboard. Aware that the *Kamchatka's* coal was identical with that used by the other ships, Rozhdestvensky irritably signaled back: "Only the culprits to be thrown overboard."

At his last coaling stop on the African West Coast, the German port of Angra Pequeña, the Commander in Chief had learned on December 15th that the Japanese, at a hideous cost of life, had finally taken Hill 203 but he was not sufficiently informed on the land phases of the battle for Port Arthur to grasp the full significance of this news. It was only after he had rounded the Cape that the hospital ship *Orel*—as a noncombatant, she had been able to call in at Capetown—brought word of the fall of Port Arthur and the destruction of the remaining ships of the First Pacific Squadron. This meant that the fleet he was being sent out to reinforce no longer existed, a situation foreseen months before by Admiral Viren, Vitgeft's successor. In a message to Viceroy Alexeyev on September 15, Viren had pointed out that if his own squadron were to be destroyed, "the Second Pacific Squadron would be too weak to fight the whole Japanese fleet. In that case, it would be better if the Baltic Squadron did not come here at all."

Among the supporters of this viewpoint on board the *Suvorov* was Commander Semenoff, who like many fellow officers who shared his misgivings, felt constrained to conceal them.

> To declare ourselves to be incompetent, to turn back and run the risk of being branded as cowards—these ideas never entered my head. If, however, (and I mean to be ruthlessly candid about this) St. Petersburg had realized how utterly hopeless—not to say criminal—our venture was, and had sent us categorical orders to come back, I should have said, "The Lord be praised."

Had Rozhdestvensky reached the same conclusions, which would have been quite understandable, he was even less appropriately placed than Semenoff to voice them. On the contrary, for him the news of the destruction of the Port Arthur Squadron merely meant that it was now more urgent than ever to get to the Japan Sea as soon as possible. After a year of strenuous duty Togo's ships must be in acute need of repairs and refitting. If the Second Pacific Squadron could reach Japanese waters before the Japanese fleet had been restored to full fighting efficiency, its chances would be to that extent improved. In view of this, the most discouraging news that reached him on his arrival at the Madagascan harbor of Nossi Bé, where he was to meet Folkersham, was a new development in St. Petersburg resulting indirectly from the hasty decision to send Captain Nicholas Klado to Paris to testify about the Dogger Bank Incident.

After giving his testimony at the Court of Enquiry—at which the majority of the judges soon concluded that there had been no torpedo boats concealed among the trawlers of the Gamecock Fleet and assessed damages of $300,000 against the Russian Government—Captain Klado had returned to the capitol, where his characteristic verbosity took the form of a series of articles in the newspaper *Novoye Vremya*. In his role as a journalist Klado appeared to combine the stylistic eloquence of a latter-day Gibbon with the technical authority of a Muscovite Mahan, basing the latter on his service both on Rozhdestvensky's flagship and previously as an aid to Viceroy Alexeyev at Vladivostok. The theme of his articles was that instead of letting Rozhdestvensky dash off for Vladivostok with his present squadron, the defeat at Port Arthur made it imperative that he be given substantial reinforcements. While perhaps sound in principle, what rendered this argument totally specious was that the only reinforcements available were a few vessels of even poorer quality than the poorest that Rozhdestvensky's command already included.

Klado was well aware that Rozhdestvensky had previously been urged to include these dregs of the Baltic Fleet in his original armada and had declined on the ground that their inability to keep up with the rest would make them a liability rather than an asset. In his articles for *Novoye Vremya* he gracefully implied that the Commander in Chief's reluctance to take the additional overage vessels had been due not to plain common sense but to a praiseworthy excess of impetuous gallantry. "All these old ships," Klado urged, "could be used to attract the enemy's fire and consequently diminish the number of projectiles that might otherwise strike the modern ships."

Whether Klado was dutifully trying to enlist public support for a viewpoint favored by Birilev at the instigation of the latter, or merely trying to ingratiate himself with his chief by advocating a procedure that the latter was well-known to favor, the result soon became apparent. A message that reached him at Nossi Bé shortly before Christmas informed the Commander in Chief that the Admiralty had now finally decided to send out an addition to the present Second Squadron, under the command of Rear Admiral Nicholas Nebogatov. This addition, composed of the 1888 battleship, *Emperor Nikolai I*, the 1882 armored cruiser *Vladimir Monomakh*, and three ten-year-old Coast Defense ships named the *General Admiral Apraxin*, the *Admiral Seniavin*, and the *Admiral Ushakov*, along with seven transports and auxiliaries, was now being assembled at Libau and would be sent out to join him in eight or ten weeks.

The news that, under circumstances making it essential to get to the Far East with all possible speed, he was now to await the arrival at Madagascar of reinforcements

that would impair rather than enhance his fleet's effectiveness by slowing it down even further, was more than Rozhdestvensky was prepared to accept. Ordering his chief of
staff, Captain Clapier de Colongue, to cable St. Petersburg
that he wished to be relieved of his command, the Admiral
retired to his cabin and took to his bunk.

During the first days after their arrival at Nossi Bé the
crews of the Second Pacific Squadron had experienced a
sudden lift in spirits, owing to their success in completing
the first half of their journey, the triumph over the elements while rounding the Cape, and their first shore leave
since leaving home. The picturesque little harbor town
called Hellville, after the French Admiral who had
founded it, provided hastily improvised attractions, including bars, bordellos, and gambling dens, that made its
odd name appropriate. The Christmas holidays were celebrated in a blaze of good humor that reached its peak
when the resilient Admiral, still thought to be ill, emerged
from his cabin to make a stirring speech and raise a glass
to his men in a toast to their valor and determination
which caused them to cheer and wave caps in the air.

As the holidays ended, this mood of exhiliration subsided rapidly, and the Admiral's good humor with it. As
was to have been expected, his request to be relieved had
been summarily refused. Now, on top of this, he found that
the implied instructions to await the arrival of Nebogatov,
which he had intended to ignore, had been reinforced by a
new cause of delay that was much less readily brushed
aside.This was the announcement by a representative of
the Hamburg-Amerika Line that in view of a threat by
Togo to sink any colliers accompanying the Russian Fleet
the German company regretted that it would be unable to
coal the squadron on its way across the Indian Ocean. On
hearing this news, and on finding that the Admiralty in
St. Petersburg seemed to feel that there was no particular

hurry about breaking the impasse, Rozhdestvensky retired to his cabin for the second time, now suffering from severe neuralgia for which he needed ice packs. The refrigeration machinery on the supply ships had by this time ceased to function, necessitating the destruction of several hundred tons of meat, and no ice could be found.

As the days lengthened into weeks and the weeks to one month and then two, the charms of Hellville as a winter resort began to wear exceedingly thin. Temperatures of 90 degrees accompanied by a humidity of 90 percent encouraged heat rash, lethargy, and miscellaneous tropical diseases, a surprising number of them fatal. Dissipations in the town—where the proprietor of one ramshackle resort called the Café de Paris said he had chosen this name because he meant to depart for that capital with his profits as soon as the fleet left—became so boisterous that shore leaves had to be canceled. Boredom thereafter was alleviated mainly by collecting exotic animals that were kept on board the ships and taught to perform tricks or pitted against each other in rings improvised on the decks. Copies of *Novoye Vremya* containing articles in which Klado drew disheartening comparisons between Togo's Combined Fleet and the Second Squadron were circulated among the seamen. These helped to generate an epidemic of minor mutinies that were further stimulated by the arrival of detailed newspaper reports of St. Petersburg's "Bloody Sunday" massacre on January 22nd, when soldiers had shot down scores of hungry peasants outside the Czar's Palace. Rozhdestvensky dealt sharply with the mutineers, sending the worst offenders back to Russia, along with chronic invalids and mental patients, in one of his more unreliable transports.

Burly in stature, extravagant in speech, and given to fits of despondency, rage, and sudden euphoria, Rozhdestvensky was the mirror opposite of his tiny, taciturn, and phlegmatic adversary in almost every way except two: both were specialists in gunnery and both had a streak of incorrigible stubbornness, which in Rozhdestvensky's case may have been the element in his character that determined his eventual fate. Given his own conviction of the futility of his mission, the Hamburg-Amerika Line's objection to fulfilling its contract, and the slothful response of his superiors at St. Petersburg, Rozhdestvensky, without this trait, might have used the impasse as a legitimate pretext for justifying Semenoff's hopes and giving up the venture entirely. Instead, the Russian commander in chief took the problem into his own hands and summarily solved it by buying ten colliers outright on behalf of his government. Thus assured of enough fuel to get him across the Indian Ocean, he arranged for four others, crossing on a separate course, to meet him in Saigon.

During the last weeks of his enforced detention, after the ships' boilers had been cleaned and urgent repairs to their machinery completed, Rozhdestvensky turned his attention to ameliorating so far as possible the incompetence demonstrated by his gunners in the Dogger Bank Incident which was the last time the guns had been fired. The effort met with scant success. The order to practice a few simple fleet maneuvers revealed that some of the ships were carrying new signal-code books, in which the flags that meant "single line ahead" in the old books meant instead "search the coast," thus causing the recipients of the order to scatter in all directions. Reassembled with some difficulty, the destroyers subsequently undertook to fire torpedoes whose erratic performance Commander Semenoff described succinctly: "One never ran at all. Two went off to the right, one to the left. . . . Another began describing a circle, occasionally coming to the surface and threatening the boats which sought safety in flight."

Replenishment of the squadron's depleted supply of ammunition had long been expected but, when the ship supposedly bringing it arrived, her cargo proved instead to be twelve thousand pairs of boots and an ample stock of fur coats for use in Vladivostok. When the Admiral did finally undertake to expend some of his ammunition in a drill intended to simulate a night attack by torpedo boats, the results failed to arouse his enthusiasm: "As regards the firing . . . one really feels ashamed to speak of it. By daylight, the entire squadron did not succeed in scoring a single hit . . . although the targets differed from Japanese torpedo boats to our advantage inasmuch as they were stationary." The next day, in response to this rebuke, the *Suvorov* did manage to score one hit—a shot that landed on the bridge of the unlucky cruiser *Dmitri Donskoi* while it was towing the target.

Early in March Rozhdestvensky had divers scrape off as much as they could of the tropical moss and seaweed that had accumulated on the bottoms of his vessels, cutting their speed by two knots and raising their coal consumption thirty percent. Then, on March 16, after cabling St. Petersburg that he was leaving but without stating either his route or his destination, the Admiral ordered his ships to get up steam, and abruptly departed. As the fleet steamed out to sea, the *Kamchatka,* true to her peculiar tradition, signaled "I'm sinking," but soon found that she had only burst a pipe in the boiler room. The next reports the world heard of the Second Pacific Squadron came three weeks later, when it appeared in the strait of Malacca, forming a long, straggling, but nonetheless formidable line which, under a thick cloud of black smoke, stretched out for five miles and took almost an hour to pass by the Singapore waterfront. A correspondent for Reuters observed that the ships had a foot or so of seaweed along the waterline and that their decks were covered by coal.

As the Second Pacific Squadron steamed past Singapore on the afternoon of April 7th, a launch flying the Russian flag came out of the harbor and signaled the *Suvorov* that the Russian consul was on board and had important messages to deliver to the Admiral. The flagship signaled back that it would be too dangerous to stop and that the message should be handed to the destroyer *Bedovyi*. Having delivered his dispatches to the destroyer, the Consul came alongside again and shouted the latest war news through a megaphone: "Mukden has fallen . . . General Kuropatkin has been dismissed and replaced by General Linevich . . . Admiral Nebogatov with the Third Squadron has just sailed from Djibouti to join forces with you . . ."

That evening, as he studied the papers from St. Petersburg in his cabin, the Admiral became acquainted with further details. He was to proceed to Camranh Bay, on the coast of Cochin China, and there await his unwanted reinforcements—which, if Nebogatov had already left Djibouti, might arrive three weeks or so later. As an insulting postscript to these unwelcome instructions, his further orders, after he had defeated Togo and reached Vladivostok were to hand over command of his squadron to Admiral Birilev, who would come out by rail to receive it.

As the Squadron steamed northward during the ensuing days, along the coast of Malaya and then that of French Indo-China, Rozhdestvensky reached a bold decision. This was that, instead of waiting for the Third Squadron at Camranh Bay and thus impairing his chances in the coming battle on at least two counts, he would simply by-pass this port and head for Vladivostok without stopping at all. Since Togo would certainly be aware of the impending reinforcements and expect him to await them, this plan might offer some possibility of surprise; and if not slowed down by Nebogatov's old ships, he might even be lucky enough to slip past without a major fleet engagement. Once establish at Vladivostok, the squadron could at least harass the Japanese communications with Manchuria. Short of using the fleet as a lever for immediate peace negotiations, of which there was no apparent prospect, this was about all that could now be expected of it.

What prevented Rozhdestvensky from carrying out this insubordinate but perhaps practical scheme was one of those trifling details that so often decide the major events of history. It occurred on the afternoon of April 12th when, just sixty miles south of Camranh Bay, Rozhdestvensky, in line with his new plan, paused to take on the coal that he hoped would see him through to his final destination. Early that morning, in accord with regular routine, each ship had signaled the amount of fuel she had in her bunkers, as estimated by subtracting the previous day's consumption from the amount on hand. After lunch, to make sure that these figures were accurate, Rozhdestvensky sent out an unusual request, to the effect that each ship now make a fresh count of the exact amount actually on board. As was to be expected, each ship showed about a hundred tons more than it had when the coaling had started that morning, with one note-worthy exception. This was the *Alexander III*, which at first made no reply whatever and then, after a reminder, ran up a signal showing that she had four hundred tons *less* than the quantity shown in her report earlier in the day.

Despite the forebodings of her Captain Bukhvostov, the *Alexander III*, named for the Czar's father, had thus far shown herself to be the most efficient ship in the entire squadron. She had experienced the fewest mechanical breakdowns and, when taking on coal, had regularly won the prizes awarded for the fastest loading. What now developed was that the *Alexander III*, presumably in an effort to maintain her fine reputation by hook or by crook, had been falsifying her loading figures by a few tons at each stop, with the result that the compounded error had now reached an amount that would require two more days of loading to rectify. Meanwhile, the fuel she now had on board was insufficient to enable her to reach Vladivostok; and there would be none available to make up the deficiency until additional colliers could be summoned from Saigon.

Admiral Rozhdestvensky was an uncommunicative commander who confided in his own staff almost as little as he did in his superiors in St. Petersburg. Whether he now concluded that this new delay would be enough to destroy the element of surprise, or whether he simply regarded the *Alexander III's* misdemeanor as an augury that deserved to be heeded, he revealed to no one. When she hoisted her message that the four-hundred-ton shortage she had reported was not an arithmetical error, the Commander in Chief stood for several minutes, staring at the signal flags, his hands gripping the rail and his jaws working in his characteristic nervous grimace. Then he turned to Captain de Colongue and instructed him to issue new orders: the Fleet would go to Camranh after all and there await the arrival of Nebogatov.

The Eastertide detention at Camranh Bay was a nightmare that, though briefer than the one at Nossi Bé, had special horrors of its own. At Nossi Bé, through some quirk of French indulgence, the squadron had at least been allowed to stay on for almost three months, unmolested by a strict interpretation of the rules of neutrality. Now, perhaps as a reflection of more recent events on the battlefront, this leniency was sharply curtailed. A few days after the ships anchored in the spacious bay on April 14th, the Commander in Chief received a call from Rear Admiral de Jonquières, second in command of the

French Far East Squadron, a charmingly courteous officer who merely voiced a gracious welcome and then politely departed on his cruiser, the *Descartes*. On the 22nd of April de Jonquières reappeared, this time with new instructions: very reluctantly, in accord with neutrality regulations, he would have to ask the squadron to depart within twenty-four hours. Rozhdestvensky complied, but went only as far as Van Phong, the next harbor, a few miles farther north. This time it was the local administrator who turned up presently with the same request. Thereafter, caught between the shortage of coal that made it imprudent to steam up and down offshore and the neutrality rules that prevented him from lying quietly at anchor, the squadron spent its time cruising at low speed by day and ducking into the harbor at night, like a burglar dodging in and out of a doorway to hide from the policeman on the beat.

The feast of Easter, even dearer to the Russians than Christmas, was celebrated at Van Phong in a style appropriate to the sorry conditions. On board the battleship *Orel,* whose crew had proved troublesome throughout the voyage, the livestock taken on at Camranh Bay included a thin and presumably diseased cow that presently became so far gone that she could no longer stand. Informed of her approaching demise by the ship's butcher on Saturday the 16th, the eve of the feast, the executive officer made a hasty decision. "Slaughter her at once," he ordered, "She'll do for the men's dinner tomorrow."

Well aware that, as related by Novikoff-Priboy, "the head cook was preparing roast fowls, cakes, and dainties for the officers' mess," the seamen, when they got word of the character of the holiday repast they had to look forward to, reacted as might have been expected. Surly mutterings and clandestine gatherings below decks led to a protest meeting of the whole crew, which presently came roaring onto the afterdeck to demand better beef for their dinner and also the release of a seaman who had already been put in the brig for insolence. Informed of these demands by his deputy, the ship's captain, Nikolai Yung, gave way to the extent of ordering that the prisoner be released and two choice bullocks slaughtered for the men's supper. The next day, on hearing of the near mutiny, Admiral Rozhdesvensky appeared on board and mounted to the upperdeck to castigate both officers and men. "As for you," he shouted at the entire complement gathered below him, "only in the sea battle and in your own blood can you wash out your sins . . . If you don't, I'll skin you alive!" Eight culprits, picked at random from the ranks, were sent off to the transport *Yaroslavl,* which served as a prison ship.

A further embellishment of the holiday was the condition of Admiral Folkersham, whose health, never robust, had deteriorated rapidly ever since his arrival at Nossi Bé. Now, during the stay at Camranh Bay, he had suffered a stroke that left him unable to leave his cabin, where he lay at the point of death. At Camranh also, the Commander in Chief had dutifully wired St. Petersburg: "Have arrived Camranh Bay. Await orders." The reply came promptly: "Remain until the arrival of the Third Pacific Squadron and please keep informed of movements."

After several days of skulking along the coast by day and hiding in Van Phong Bay by night, it finally became evident that Nebogatov was drawing near. The ships of the Second Pacific Squadron were equipped with wireless instruments of a new and untried type, manufactured by the Slaby-Arco company of Germany and installed at a special low price. They had proved practically useless during the voyage but now, on May 9th, the cruiser *Ural,* which had the most powerful receiving set, began to intercept ship-to-ship messages that indicated that Nebogatov, whose Third Squadron had passed through the strait of Malacca on May 5th, was at last near at hand. Early that afternoon, dark smoke trails became visible in the southern sky and toward three o'clock, having completed their ten thousand-mile passage via Suez in less than three months, Nebogatov's ships came slowly over the horizon.

The two squadrons approached each other on opposite, parallel courses, the ships in long line-ahead formations, while the guns boomed out a salute and the seamen stood at the rails, waving their caps. Presently, the Third Squadron swung into a wide turn and lined up on Rozhdestvensky's starboard beam. A steam launch brought Nebogatov to the *Suvorov,* where, a small, paunchy figure with a round face mottled by eczema, he mounted the ladder at the head of which Rozhdestvensky stood waiting to receive him. The two admirals embraced and then, with Rozhdestvensky's staff, vanished into the Commander in Chief's cabin for a conference that Nebogatov later had occasion to describe:

My first impression was that the Admiral had no mind to disclose his plans in the presence of his staff and that soon he would give me a private interview. But after half an hour's general conversation he intimated that I could return to my own flagship . . . That was the only time I saw Rozhdestvensky in the whole course of the cruise . . . He did not again invite a visit, nor did he come on board the *Nikolai I.* We never discussed a plan of campaign. He gave me neither instructions nor advice.

The arrival of the reinforcements caused a new delay of four days. While his ships coaled, took on supplies, and made a few urgent repairs at Van Phong, Nebogatov read through a fat portfolio of his Commander in Chief's fleet orders and battle directives. Finally, on May 14th, the combined squadrons, now more than fifty strong, set off on the last lap of their amazing journey.

It was a voyage without precedent in naval history. Rozhdestvensky's accomplishment in getting from Madagascar to Camranh—over forty-five hundred miles, without touching at any port en route—had aroused admiration even in England, where talk of "the mad-dog fleet" gave way to candid applause for a nautical feat of the first order. In the U.S. *The Scientific American* for April 22nd, 1905, struck a note of sober reappraisal in a long article pointing out that Russia was, after all, the world's third greatest naval power and that Rozhdestvensky's battleships outnumbered Togo's by a substantial margin. The summing up was respectful: "Should Rozhdestvensky, by crushing the enemy, obtain command of the seas, and cut off Oyama and his armies from Japan, he will have wrested victory from defeat and saved to Russia an empire that has all but fallen from her grasp."

Within the fleet, as the day of decision approached, a new loyalty to the Commander in Chief and a new confidence in itself began to be widely felt. On the way across the Indian Ocean frequent target practice in conjunction with fleet exercises had substantially improved the squadron's competence. Danger, always threatening but never appearing, had created an illusion that perhaps the Japanese would in fact never show themselves at all; and sheer force of habit, if nothing else, helped to convince the crews that having come so far, they would surely be able to keep on. Just as Makarov had been affectionately known to the First Pacific Squadron as "Old Beardy," Rozhdestvensky, for all his tantrums and sarcasm, had somehow endeared himself to the Second. Officers and men, both of whom understood intuitively some part of the agony he had experienced, the trials he had had to put up with, and the hazards he had overcome, referred to him proudly as "Our Man." They felt that Our Man, having brought them thus far, somehow would take them the rest of the way as well.

For seven days after departing from Van Phong, the fleet plodded northward through the passage between the Philippines and Formosa and into the Yellow Sea, with Nebogatov's flagship, the *Emperor Nikolai I*, and his three coast-guard "flat-irons," as the Second Squadron had nicknamed them, lined up behind Folkersham's as the Third Battleship Division while the *Monomakh* joined the other cruisers under Enquist. Amazingly, the huge armada was to get past the Ryukyu Islands without being sighted by Japanese scouts or experiencing other untoward incidents such as had marred the earlier reaches of the outward passage.

On the 19th a British merchantman, the *Oldhamia*, was encountered and found to be carrying contraband cargo. Rozhdestvensky ordered her seized and sent to Vladivostok, meanwhile dispatching her captain and four British crewmen to the hospital ship *Orel* for safekeeping. When the *Orel* plaintively enquired, "What shall we do with five healthy Englishmen you sent over?" Rozhdestvensky signaled a good-natured reply: "Keep them healthy until you reach port!" On the 21st, two armed transports, the *Kuban* and the *Terek*, were detached to cruise off the east coast of Japan and if possible to create there an impression that the rest of the fleet was close at hand. On the 23rd, the ships coaled for the last time. On the 25th, ninety miles southeast of Shanghai, Rozhdestvensky dispatched to that port six of his auxiliaries, including two colliers for which he had no further immediate use.

Up to the morning of the 25th, no one in the fleet—including Admiral Nebogatov, who was also left ignorant of Folkersham's mortal illness, although it might at any moment make him second in command—had known which of three possible entrances to the Japan Sea Rozhdestvensky meant to take. After the dispatch of the auxiliaries to Shanghai, he altered course to North, 70° East, making it clear that he meant to take the eastern passage of Tsushima Strait, which, divided in two by the island from which it takes its name, separates Japan from Korea. On the night of the 25th, the weather turned cold and the men, their spirits rising as the thermometer fell, turned in to sleep under blankets for the first time in six months. With the change came rain and the welcome mists that might enable them to get through the strait unseen.

On the morning of the 26th, the sun broke through from time to time and toward noon the *Suvorov* amazed the fleet by signaling all ships to slow down to 5 knots and then ordering practice maneuvers. To minimize the danger of a torpedo attack that night, Rozhdestvensky had calculated that by bringing the ships to the narrowest part of the strait toward midday of the 27th, he had four hours or so to spare, and this was the first and only chance he would have for the Second and Third Squadrons to execute formations together. That afternoon, furniture and loose wooden fittings were hurled overboard, decks hosed down and sprinkled with holy water, and wet paddings of hammocks, coal sacks, and tarpaulin bound around rails and fittings as protection against shell splinters. Late in the day, the *Suvorov* signaled "Prepare for action. Tomorrow at the hoisting of colors battle flags are to be sent up."

That evening, the mist thickened to a fog through which a moon in the last quarter shone dimly and visibility was reduced to a few hundred yards. Wakeful after midnight, Commander Semenoff made a tour of the ship and, after looking in at the deserted wardroom, went up to the bridge, where he found the ship's captain, an irrepressibly good-humored officer named Vassaly Ignatius, wide awake and in especially high spirits.

元帥伯爵東鄕平八郎

Fleet Admiral Heihachiro Togo

"What are you doing, wandering about?" he asked his visitor.

"Just having a look around. Gone to sleep?" And Semen-off nodded toward the admiral, dozing in his wicker chair.

"Only just. I persuaded him to. Why shouldn't he? We can take it that the night has passed all right. Up to the present we haven't been discovered . . . It will be day-break in a couple of hours. Even if their torpedo boats are near us, they won't be able to collect. Besides, they won't be able to find us in weather like this. Look, you can't see the rear of the fleet. It's two hundred thousand to one against anyone running into us accidentally . . . If it is the same tomorrow, we'll give them the slip . . . My! what a stew they must be in! What fun!" At this Ignatius began to laugh so hard he had to stuff his handkerchief into his mouth to avoid waking the Admiral.

Ignatius was wrong on several points, including his esti-mate of the chances of discovery. That evening the fleet had been ordered to proceed with only running lights turned on but the hospital ship *Orel*, far behind the rest and completely out of their sight, had felt sufficiently safe from the flagship to ignore this order with impunity. On the other hand, he was completely right about one thing. The Japanese, who had spent several months preparing for the Second Squadron's arrival, were indeed in a stew and had been for several days. Despite all their prepara-tions they had not been able to locate their enemy and, according to all their calculations, he was long overdue.

VI

During most of the seven months it took Russia's Second and Third Far East Squadrons to complete their voyage from Reval to Van Phong, the whole world received week-to-week or even day-to-day reports on their progress. No comparable reports appeared concerning the activities of the Japanese Combined Fleet, of which even the whereabouts remained a mystery. Speculations on this subject by the world's press were extensive but the results varied widely and few came close to the mark. The usually prescient Captain Alfred Thayer Mahan, so often accurate as a geopolitical commentator and prophet, erred woefully when confronted by the specific problem of figuring out where Togo was lying in wait for his adversary. Writing for a popular magazine, he deduced that Togo's lair might be Keelung, the port on the northern coast of Formosa whose advantages had, in fact, been called to his attention some years before by young Captain Joffre. Admiral Sir E. R. Freemantle, commanding the Far East Squadron of the British Navy, offered—perhaps with questionable sincerity—the surmise that Togo might be concealed somewhere in the Pescadores.

In fact, the hiding place of the Combined Fleet was a good deal closer to home than either one: the deep-water harbor of Masampo, near the tip of the Korean peninsula. Masampo, where the Russians had planned eventually to establish a base of their own, was well situated to ensure just the kind of privacy which Togo had succeeded in achieving. Remote both from land population centers and —unlike Japan's fleet base of Sasebo, on the south coast of Kyushu,—from normal sea-traffic lanes, the bay was big enough to contain the twelve ships of his First and Second Battle Divisions. On the adjacent waters, gunnery practice could be carried on with a minimum of attention or hindrance.

Togo's views on gunnery, as implied in his earlier comment on the *Ting-Yuen,* were well summed up in one of his favorite maxims: "A gun that can score a hundred hits in a hundred shots is worth a hundred guns that each score one hit in a hundred." For offsetting Rozhdestvensky's advantage in long-range armament by his own three-to-two superiority in guns of 6 inches or less, the appropriate procedure was expressed in another familiar Japanese saying; *"Nanji no katana mijikakeraba, ippo susunde,"* meaning "If your sword is too short, take one step forward."

Even before the fall of Port Arthur, on the premise that Rozhdestvensky might reach the sea of Japan by January, Togo had been sending some of his smaller vessels back to Sasebo or Kure for repairs in groups of two or three. By the time General Nogi's troops finally took Hill 203 it had also become clear that Rozhdestvensky's arrival would be delayed at least until mid-February. Released from blockade duty by the destruction of Russia's First Pacific

Squadron, the whole Combined Fleet had returned to Kure and Sasebo, where repairs and refitting were rushed through as fast as possible. When the additional Russian delay at Madagascar had allowed him several extra weeks, Togo used them for target practice of the most intensive sort.

While by no means as severely handicapped as Rozhdestvensky had been at Nossi Bé by the shortage of shells, Togo had to consider both the expenditure of ammunition and also the wear and tear on barrels, which, in the urgent case of the 12-inch guns, needed re-boring after every hundred shots. To overcome this difficulty the Japanese used an ingenious system of inserting small-caliber rifles in the barrels of their big guns so that the gunners could at least get practice in range-finding, in laying the guns on the target, and in using the firing mechanisms, without wearing out the barrels. While there was nothing unique or even unusual about this procedure, it was not one favored by Togo's opponents. In his book *Rasplata,* Commander Semenoff relates the reply of a Russian admiral to a subordinate who had recommended the use of a similar method: "Then you are a believer in the saying: 'Better a louse in the soup than no meat at all.' I am not."

Unimpeded by such fastidious pride, the Combined Fleet at Masampo engaged in every kind of target practice, at all times of day and night, and with every kind of ammunition. A fair clue to the intensity of this drill was the quantity of subcaliber ammunition used by the flagship itself. Normally, the *Mikasa* fired 29,000 rounds of such ammunition in a whole year, but within ten days of the time that Togo rejoined her at Masampo she had used up 30,000 rounds and sent back for more. Years later the *Mikasa's* Gunnery Officer, Lt. Commander Kiyotane Abo, recalled that the constant rattle of gunfire at Masampo

made the harbor sound like the scene of a marathon pop-
corn roast.

In addition to the superior marksmanship that he hoped
to develop through this practice, Togo already had another
advantage where gunnery was concerned. This was the type
of powder used in the Japanese shells. Known in Japan as
"Shimose," after the naval engineer credited with devising
the formula for its composition, its acquisition actually
dated back to the summer of 1888, when a clever young
Japanese naval officer named Sadayasu Tomioka had been
sent to France to witness a demonstration of a new kind of
powder developed there by a professional inventor who
had indicated willingness to sell his formula to the Japanese. Unfortunately for the success of this plan he, like
the San Francisco hosts of Student Fukuzawa, had made
the mistake of underestimating the sophistication of his
visitor. While examining the novel powder, Tomioka contrived to get a few grains of it under one of his fingernails.
Placed under a microscope a little later, these sufficed to
show that the secret ingredient in it was nothing more
than picric acid, a chemical well-known in Japan and
readily procurable from local sources.

The advantages of Shimose powder, as subsequently developed in Japan, were that it not only exploded faster
than ordinary powder but also generated more heat, setting fire to anything inflammable near a shell burst. Its disadvantage was that its extra sensitivity also made Shimose
shells liable to premature explosion, with the result that
during the Port Arthur blockade a good many Japanese
gun barrels had been opened up like lily pods, often with
attendant casualties to the gun crews. Subsequent alterations in the formula to correct this fault were tested in the
weeks of gunnery practice at Masampo, where the morale
of the crews was raised by the discovery that the changes
had had the desired effect.

In the early 1900s, there were two schools of naval gunnery, of which one, adhered to by the French and the Russians, was that the primary purpose of any projectile was to sink an enemy ship if possible. The war heads of their shells were accordingly made of hard steel intended to penetrate whatever they encountered and equipped with delayed fuses so that the explosion would take place well after the penetration. The other school of gunnery, followed by the British and the Japanese, was that the prime purpose of projectiles was to render an enemy vessel ineffective as a fighting mechanism, after which sinking it would amount to a mere formality. Hence, while the Japanese had armor-piercing shells for use when a *coup de grâce* was in order, they relied chiefly on shells fused to explode on contact, for which their Shimose powder was ideally suited.

Another useful device, which had been acquired by the Japanese navy more recently than Shimose powder but by somewhat similar methods, was wireless. Invented by Guglielmo Marconi, who patented his apparatus in Britain in 1906, Marconi's equipment was available thereafter to all nations on a royalty basis. However, while Japan was a member of the International Industrial Patent Protective Association, her strict regulations provided that, in order to be valid in Japan, a patent had to be applied for there within sixty days of its becoming effective in its country of origin. Since Marconi's application for a Japanese patent had arrived in Tokyo sixty-two days after the patent became effective in England, it was automatically disqualified. Japan's electronic scientists thus felt legally entitled to go ahead with experiments of their own along the same lines.

There was also another, deeper reason why the Japanese, though by no means insensitive to ethical scruples, felt that these hardly applied to such devices as wireless or

the formulae for explosives. Japan's industrial race to catch
up with the Western world was predicated on the belief that, if she failed to do so the West would try to subju-
gate her, just as it had already subjugated most of the
other nations of Asia. Industry in general was therefore
considered not, as it was then and is still in the West, as a
means to personal prosperity, but rather as the means of
national survival. From the Japanese viewpoint, such
products as gunpowder or wireless indisputably belonged
much less to the category of peacetime conveniences than
to that of military equipment. As such, they were fair game
for anyone.

One of the minor confusions of the battle of Tsushima,
from the point of view of Westerners, may be the similarity of the names of some of the principals involved. Thus,
in addition to Fleet Admiral Heihachiro Togo, there was
Rear Admiral Masamichi Togo, commanding the Sixth
Battle Division, who was not related to his Commander in
Chief, and Captain Kichitaro Togo, the Commander in
Chief's nephew and skipper of the First Division battle-
ship *Asahi,* who later wrote a revealing little book of memoirs entitled *The Naval Battles of the Russo-Japanese
War.* Even more ubiquitous than the Togos involved at
Tsushima were the Yamamotos, headed by the Com-
mander in Chief's old wardroom companion and fellow
Satsuman, Gombei, the Minister of the Navy. Another
Yamamoto who, like Gombei, played a key role at Tsushima was the Navy Minister's nephew, Eisuke. Son of
Gombei's older brother, Eisuke Yamamoto had foreseen
the forthcoming importance of wireless as a means of communication between warships and had made himself one
of the top Navy specialists on the subject.

In 1902, just after the conclusion of the Anglo-Japanese
treaty whereby Britain had promised to aid Japan if any
other power aided Russia in a war between the two, Japan

sent appropriate representatives to the coronation of Edward VII. The wireless officer on one of the two warships assigned to carry them was Eisuke Yamamoto, who as such got a chance both to experiment with the primitive sets then available there and to visit British ships at Malta, where more advanced instruments were in use and accessible to inspection. In England, hospitable cooperation by Japan's new ally opened up opportunities for further progress that were not overlooked.

By the outbreak of the Russo-Japanese War, Japan had succeeded in equipping her fleet with instruments of her own manufacture which were reliable for distances up to sixty miles and sometimes worked for considerably greater ones. Eisuke Yamamoto had also ascertained that wireless transmission was more effective at night than in daytime, and under high rather than low atmospheric pressures, conclusions that he reported to Navy headquarters in Tokyo well in advance of similar revelations by the Marconi company. While these independent researches might well have entitled Japan to a reasonably clear conscience in regard to its use of naval wireless in wartime, a nice sense of deference to Western notions in such matters gave rise to a suggestion after the hostilities had ended that some token of appreciation be awarded to Signor Marconi. Action on this proposal was deferred until 1933, when, invited to visit Japan as a guest of the government, the Italian inventor was awarded the Order of the Rising Sun, first degree.

Possibly even more important than the contributions to Tsushima of Lt. Eisuke Yamamoto—who in the battle itself served on the staff of Admiral Hikonojo Kamimura and is not to be confused with Ensign Isoruku Yamamoto who served on the *Nisshin* and lost two fingers of his left hand during the action—was a fourth Yamamoto, whose given name was Jyotaro. Not related to any of the others and not even connected with the Navy, Jyotaro Yamamoto was the Shanghai representative of the two-hundred-year-old Mitsui Company, whose famous example set the pattern for the Japanese family-owned trading firms later to be known as *zaibatsu*. Even in this civilian capacity, Jyotaro Yamamoto found opportunities for furthering the national interest of which he made full use, as part of an extensive espionage and propaganda network, which also had noteworthy representation in Europe and the U.S.

While no evidence was ever developed to support the suspicion that Japan's destroyers were concealed among the fishing boats of the Gamecock Fleet at Dogger Bank, there were ample grounds for the Russian belief that her intelligence agents were hard at work in the vicinity. In Europe the Japanese forerunner of Ian Fleming's James Bond and of his own namesake, John Marquand's Mr. Moto, was a singularly well-traveled and erudite thirty-eight-year-old ex-diplomat named Colonel Motojiro Akashi, who made his headquarters in Stockholm. Having learned Russian and developed a wide set of contacts during a term as an attaché in the Japanese Embassy in St. Petersburg, Colonel Akashi used these advantages to keep the Navy Ministry well supplied with data on the composition and progress of Russia's Second Pacific Squadron. An even more significant and far-reaching phase of Akashi's activities was that of furnishing guidance and financial support to Russia's political malcontents generally and to an energetic young exile known as Lenin in particular.

According to Professor Stefan Thomas Possony, in his authoritative *Lenin, the Compulsive Revolutionary*, the official Japanese decision to support Russia's hard-core subversives was reached only reluctantly and after a long period of indecision caused partly by conflicting advice from outsiders. As might have been expected, England, whose amiable Edward VII was the Czar's "Uncle Bertie," showed small inclination to encourage her Japanese ally in what might turn out to be a serious threat to the institution of monarchy itself. In the U.S., however, more progressive views were understandably supposed by Tokyo to prevail in the White House itself. On January 15th, 1905, a conversation took place between President Theodore Roosevelt's frequent companion and confidant, Henry Adams, and his equally close friend and Harvard classmate, Baron Kentaro Kaneko, whose role in the U.S. was that of a publicist and informal aide to the official Japanese Minister in Washington. When Kaneko later reported that Adams was strongly in favor of all-out support for the revolutionaries, it served to confirm the policy of giving Akashi's machinations in Europe the monetary scope for which he had been pleading.

Akashi's skill in using his increasingly generous backing showed a brilliantly precocious grasp of what is currently known as psychological warfare, and without his timely aid it seems quite possible that Lenin might never have survived to lead the revolution of 1917. Akashi and Lenin met through the good offices of the latter's young crony, Konni Zilliacus, a well-known and widely traveled writer of Finnish origin and revolutionary sentiments, who, apropos of Akashi's activities, once remarked to his son: "Half the people to whom Japanese money is distributed don't know where it comes from—and the other half don't care." After their initial encounter it did not take Akashi long to reach an accurate and far-sighted estimate of Lenin's capabilities: "Lenin is considered by other socialists to be a rascal. . . . On the contrary, he is a sincere man and lacks egoism. He gives everything to his doctrine. Lenin is the man who can accomplish the revolution."

In August of 1904, soon after contact had been established, a conference of revolutionary exiles financed by Akashi took place at Lac de Bré in Switzerland which "revived Lenin's organization." A few weeks later, in October, Akashi helped to organize as well as to pay for another gathering of thirteen subversive splinter groups which "contributed greatly to the unification of the revolutionary movement." In January of 1905 he provided sufficient funds to guarantee publication for the next five months of the revolutionary journal *Vperyed*. Distribution of *Vperyed* inside Russia was under the able supervision of Maxim Litvinoff, and one of its editors was the V. V. Orlovsky who, in 1917, was to help set up the scheme whereby Lenin was to be smuggled back to Russia through Germany.

Orlovsky, Litvinoff, and Lenin were by no means the only noteworthy beneficiaries of Akashi's largesse. Another was the enigmatic priest Father George Gapon, organizer of the "Bloody Sunday" march on the winter palace in St. Petersburg. At the time of that calamity, Gapon was in more or less open collaboration with the police to lead a lawful, rather than subversive, movement toward social reform. Disillusioned by the massacre that resulted, he broke his police ties and joined the illegal revolutionists outside of Russia. Of Gapon, Lenin's wife, Krupskaya, was later to write: "Gapon undertook to supply arms to the St. Petersburg workers. All kinds of donations had been put at his disposal and he used the money to buy weapons in England."

In view of Akashi's ubiquitous activities in Europe, later reports by fleet engineer Politovsky that Japanese spies had boarded the Russian ships at Nossi Bé and Camranh Bay, although never verified, are certainly far from implausible. The closer the Russian ships got to Japan the more essential it became to have prompt and reliable information about their whereabouts and movements. It was in this connection that Jyotaro Yamamoto's services—quite in line with the Japanese concept by which devotion to the national interest had precedence over everything else, including mere commerce—became of paramount importance.

About the same age as Colonel Akashi, Jyotaro Yamamoto had joined the Yokohama branch of Mitsui as a boy of fifteen and worked his way up through the ranks in a varied career that included service on board the Mitsui steamship *Yoritomo Maru,* staffed by British officers. As manager of the Mitsui branch at Shanghai, he had found office space for numerous Army and Navy officers charged with intelligence assignments and he used his own wide contacts to set up a private information network that extended down the coast as far as Hong Kong. Evidence of the extent to which patriotic zeal embellished his business activities included over one hundred cables to his head office containing items for transmission to Army or Navy headquarters.

Soon after the Russian Fleet cleared the harbor of Van Phong Jyotaro Yamamoto sent one of his ablest assistants, a young man named Kaku Mori, to scout its further progress in a company launch. On May 25 Yamamoto himself ventured out to sea beyond the river's mouth in a similar vessel. The result of these excursions was promptly conveyed by cable to naval headquarters in Tokyo, which recabled them to Masampo where the *Mikasa* was berthed close to shore in a cove off the main harbor. They had a substantial bearing on the events that followed.

Intelligence agents in Shanghai and elsewhere, experiments in wireless telegraphy, and chemical improvements in gun powder were essential ingredients in Japan's long-range preparations for making war on the world's biggest nation. Now, as the Russian Fleet approached the shores of the Japanese Islands, Togo was concerned with much more immediate questions. Most urgent of these, after the departure of Rozhdestvensky from Van Phong, were precisely where the Russian Fleet was, and where it was heading.

In sizing up the intentions of his adversary, Togo had certain basic assumptions on which to base his conjectures. To operate in Far Eastern waters at all, the Baltic Fleet, as the Japanese preferred to call it, would first of all need a base. The only base available was Vladivostok, and evidence from all sources indicated that this was in fact Rozhdestvensky's destination. The next question was, by what route would he try to get there? There were three available alternatives.

The northernmost entrance to the sea of Japan from the Pacific, and the closest to Vladivostok, was the Soya, or La Perouse, Strait between Hokkaido and Sakhalin. Twenty miles wide at its narrowest point, this passage was guarded on the East by the Kurile Islands, where Japanese outposts could readily observe the entrance of the Russian fleet in ample time to enable Togo, if he were anywhere in the northern part of the Japan Sea, to be waiting at the western end of the strait by the time the Russians got there. The passage was rendered perilous by a steep shelf of submerged rock that was hard to avoid even in clear weather, let alone during the heavy fogs customary in May, and the narrow channel that was deep enough for his ships would, of course, be heavily mined. In addition, to reach La Perouse from the south, Rozhdestvensky would have to go around all the Japanese islands, thus adding some thousand miles to his journey. Giving his adversary credit for a reasonable quota of common sense, Togo felt sure that he would discard this possibility.

Much the same objections held in the case of the Strait of Tsugaru, three hundred miles further south, between Hokkaido and Honshu, except that here they applied more forcibly. Tsugaru was only nine miles across at its narrowest point, and never more than eleven. Its navigable channel, made treacherous by a strong current, was never wider than seven. After running the gauntlet of strongly fortified Japanese ports on both sides and a continuous mine field in the channel, Rozhdestvensky would be lucky to get half his ships through intact—only to meet Togo's fleet, which, again, would surely be awaiting him at the other end.

That left only the Strait of Tsushima, between the western tip of Honshu and the eastern tip of Korea, which, at the southern extremity of the Japanese Sea, was both the shortest and the most navigable approach to his objective. The two separate channels into which this strait was divided by the central island of Tsushima were each about twenty-five miles wide at the neck. On every count except the somewhat faint chance of gaining some element of surprise by taking one of the two northern passages, it offered Rozhdestvensky by far the best of the three possibilities. However, while basing his plan on the supposition that Rozhdestvensky would choose it, Togo was careful to dispose his ships so as to be at no disadvantage in case his guess was wrong.

Togo's main force, comprising his own First Battle Division of four battleships and two armored cruisers and Kamimura's Second Battle Division, composed of six armored cruisers, was concentrated together at Masampo. The Third Battle Division under Vice Admiral Shigeto Dewa, composed of four 20-knot cruisers, along with most of Vice Admiral Shichiro Kataoka's Third Fleet comprising three more light cruiser divisions and five destroyer flotillas, were at the fine harbor of Miura Bay, which, except at low tide, divides Tsushima itself into two separate islands. This disposition enabled Togo to have his entire fleet waiting to meet Rozhdestvensky, if he chose to

come via Tsushima, at the northern end of either its eastern or western passage. On the other hand, if Rozhdestvensky, through some aberration, were to choose one of the
northern straits, Togo expected to learn of it in ample time
to move north to meet him there. In case of the latter contingency, he had prepared a secondary base on the small
island of Okinokuni, three hundred miles north of Masampo and about equidistant from the western portal of
either La Perouse or Tsugaru.

While Togo felt that he had done everything possible in
order to be ready for any contingency, he still needed to
find out as soon as possible which one he would actually
have to deal with. In the unlikely event that Rozhdestvensky did go around Japan to one of the northern passages it
was essential to move to Okinokuni in time to meet him
there. On the other hand, it would be fatal to let Rozhdestvensky trick him into going north too soon, thus leaving
Tsushima unguarded and letting the enemy get loose in
the Japan Sea, where it might be difficult or even impossible to find him.

From the time that Rozhdestvensky departed from Van
Phong at dawn on May 14, Togo had remained without
reliable information on his progress. Calculating his speed
at around 11 knots, it seemed reasonable to suppose that
he might reach Tsushima on or about the 22nd. When that
date approached and passed without any sign of the Baltic
Fleet, tension began to build up on board the *Mikasa* and
the other ships at Masampo. Togo, as usual, had little to
say, but his officers and those on the staffs of the subordinate admirals became increasingly articulate.

For ease of communication, the waters south of Tsushima Strait had been divided into squares each one of
which represented ten minutes of latitude and longitude.
As in Togo's favorite game of *go*, in which the pieces are
played not from within squares, as in chess or checkers,

but from the intersections of the lines that form them, each of the corners of these squares was given a number representing the area around it. Thus, any ship in the picket line of scouts patrolling the entrance to the strait could indicate the location of the enemy by giving a single number, which would be meaningless without the key to the grid. By evening of the 22nd it seemed likely that if the enemy were really coming by Tsushima, he must be somewhere on the grid, but none of the ships had yet so reported. Did this mean that Rozhdestvensky had in fact decided to circumnavigate Japan? And, if so, was he already well on his way up the east coast?

On the evening of the 23rd a young midshipman named Toyokazu Wanami, on duty as officer of the deck on the old battleship *Fuso*, flagship of the Seventh Battle Division, leaned over the rail as the destroyer *Ikazuchi* came alongside. A seaman on her bow held up a long bamboo pole in whose tip, split to serve as a holder, was inserted a manila envelope. Midshipman Wanami slid the envelope out of the split pole, saw that it was marked "TOP SECRET—OPEN 5 P.M. ON MAY 25," and took it to a staff officer who carried it in to the Admiral's cabin. Not until several days later did Wanami learn what the envelope contained: orders for the fleet to move north immediately to the alternate base at Okinokuni.

The sealed orders not to be opened until the 25th were a precautionary measure, taken by Togo so that, in the event that he did eventually decide to move, no time would need to be wasted in drafting the instructions and circulating them to the fleet. Meanwhile, however, he retained the option to cancel the sealed orders and stay on. On the afternoon of the 24th, a conference was held on board the *Mikasa* to consider this decision.

Present in the admiral's big staff room that ran the width of the ship just forward of Togo's private office, which opened off it, and just aft of his Spartan cabin on the starboard side, were the chiefs and deputy chiefs of staff attached to Admirals Kamimura, Kataoka, Misu, Dewa, and Taketomi, along with Akiyama and Kato himself. Since the object of the meeting was to get a working-level consensus as to the best course of action and at the same time to let the staff officers exchange ideas and blow off steam, Togo and his immediate flag-rank subordinate commanders were not present.

The conference started around three o'clock on a cold, rainy afternoon and went on through the long spring twilight. Most of the facts were already well known to all present. On the one hand, headquarters reported that neutral ships had seen two Russian warships heading east off the coast of Kyushu. On the other, one of the officers on a Japanese scout ship disguised as a merchantman and briefly detained by the Russians had heard one of the latter say that the Baltic Fleet was headed for Tsushima. Would a Russian really give away his fleet's real destination so casually? Had not the merchantman been recognized for what she was, and this remark planted so as to mislead the Japanese officer who heard it? And as to the neutral ships, were they really neutrals? Or were they feeding false information to mislead headquarters?

How widely opinion was divided and how high feeling ran was shown by a good-natured but nonetheless spirited exchange between the First Battle Division Chief of Staff, Commander Kenkichi Matsui, and Commander Keisaburo Moriyama, his opposite number for the Fourth Battle Division. Moriyama felt that the Combined Fleet had already waited too long and was for going north at once. Matsui, feeling sure Rozhdestvensky would come via Tsushima, was dead set against it. The two bet each other a dinner on the outcome, which the winner did not live to collect.

Among the most famous rules laid down by Mahan was his axiom that "Communications dominate war." Mahan might well have gone on to show that, in a more limited sense of the term, communications also dominate most other human pursuits, and that what often dominates communications is the important detail of who signs them. The cable that was sent to naval headquarters in Tokyo after the staff meeting on the *Mikasa*—though never made public and later destroyed—was a good case in point.

The cable indicated that a meeting of staff officers had been held and that the consensus of those present was that the time had come to move north. It was unsigned, and addressed, not to Navy Minister Gombei Yamamoto, but to the strategy section of headquarters, representing roughly the same echelon as that of the officers who had been at the meeting. Its purpose was not to suggest that any definite decision had been reached but rather to let headquarters know that the question of moving was very much under discussion and to invite a further exchange of ideas with the Strategy Section in Tokyo.

By the time the message reached Tokyo, Gombei Yamamoto had left his office for the day. Still on duty at headquarters was his son-in-law, Takeshi Takarabe, along with the Strategy Section Chief, Captain Gentaro Yamashita. As both men were well aware, the consensus of the section was that a move north would still be dangerously premature and the message accordingly alarmed them both so much that they decided that it called for an immediate answer signed by the Minister himself. Takarabe jumped on his bicycle—in that era, the fastest form of urban transportation available—and pedaled at top speed through the darkening, dusty streets the three miles to his father-in-law's residence. Did his father-in-law not agree, Takarabe anxiously inquired, that a strong message should go back, signed by the Minister himself, to the effect that the fleet should on no account move?

For Yamamoto the moment was perhaps as testing as any he would encounter until September 1st, 1923, when, as a newly elected Prime Minister, he was to have the responsibility for forming a cabinet on the day of the great Tokyo earthquake. After considering the *Mikasa* cable carefully, he appraised it for what it was—an expression of opinion calling for a collaborative opinion rather than for a direct order of any sort. He sent no message that night but the next morning instructed Takarabe to draft a deliberately noncommittal reply to the fleet staff giving no explicit directions but worded so as to indicate that, while headquarters had full confidence in the man on the spot, the feeling still was that the decision to move north should not be taken without very careful, and perhaps additional, thought. He added—to make doubly sure that his intentionally ambiguous reply would not usurp a decision that properly belonged to the field commander—that the cable should be sent not in his name but merely in that of the Strategy Section.

Even before the *Mikasa*'s cable to Tokyo had been sent off, another development had occurred at Masampo. Just as the meeting on the *Mikasa* was breaking up, Rear Admiral Hayao Shimamura, Togo's former chief of staff, who was now in immediate command of the Second Fleet's fast cruisers, came on board the *Mikasa*, too late for the meeting but not too late to join his successor, Tomosaburo Kato, and Togo himself in their subsequent discussion of the views that had been expressed at it. On his flagship, the 20.8-knot *Iwate*, Shimamura, hurrying back from a scouting assignment far to the south, had been delayed by a heavy rain squall. Asked for his opinion of the move before he had had time to remove his dripping oilskins, Shimamura bluntly said: "If Rozhdestvensky knows anything at all, there is no question about what he will do—he must come by Tsushima."

Togo himself, stubborn as usual, still had confidence in his own hunch that Rozhdestvensky would choose the Tsushima passage. This diagnosis by his most trusted subordinate commander confirmed his own judgment. He cancelled the sealed orders and decided to wait at least through the next day. It was on the next day, the 25th, that Jyotaro Yamamoto, who had seen the Russian auxiliaries coming into Shanghai, sent his cable off to headquarters in Tokyo.

Jyotaro Yamamoto's message, relayed to Masampo late that evening, reported the arrival at Shanghai of the six Russian auxiliaries, including the colliers, and thus served once more to substantiate Togo's previous judgment. Almost as familiar with the composition of Rozhdestvensky's fleet as with that of his own, he knew that these must be the last colliers the Russians had and that if Rozhdestvensky were planning to take the longer course around the Japanese islands, he would have kept them with him, since he would need to coal at least once more en route. Had he not received this message Togo might well have moved to Okinokuni on the 26th. As it was, he decided to stay on at Masampo through one more night.

About seventy miles south of Tsushima Island—like gateposts on either side of the Eastern Passage of the strait —lie two small island groups: Quelpart on the west, Goto on the east. These two gateposts marked the limits of Togo's first line of patrols, comprising the fast cruisers *Akitsushima* and *Izumi* at the two extremities, with a picket line of four "subsidized," or auxiliary, cruisers between them. The latter were actually Japan's fastest passenger-liners, taken off the European and American runs and converted to war duty by the addition of 6-inch guns. On the early morning of the 23rd, one of these auxiliaries, mistaking Admiral Shimamura's *Iwate* for an enemy ship, had sent in an ambiguous alarm not corrected until two hours later. By then the First and Second Battle Divisions had gotten up steam and, to make use of it, Togo had taken the ships to sea and put in the day on maneuvers. No harm had been done; but still, none of the auxiliaries wanted to repeat the error. Now, at 2:45 in the misty predawn darkness of May 27th, when Captain Ki Narukawa, of the auxiliary cruiser *Shinano Maru*, sighted an unknown ship on his port bow, he was determined to make absolutely certain of her identity before sending off a report.

Narukawa turned south, passed the stranger on an opposite course, and then made a U-turn around her stern, so as to come up on her port side, where her silhouette would be between him and first light in the eastern sky. Though her shape did not, so far as he could make it out through the mist by the dim glow of the waning crescent moon, resemble a warship, the lights she was carrying—red and white lanterns at her masthead—were unusual and hence suspicious. Though the Russian Fleet was presumably blacked out, she might be some sort of an auxiliary. Herself completely unlighted, the *Shinano Maru* shadowed the stranger for an hour and three quarters until the first streaks of dawn appeared, at about 4:30. It was only then that Narukawa at last recognized her for what she was: the Russian hospital ship, *Orel*, whose characteristically lighthearted failure to conform with the fleet's blackout had now brought its predictable result.

The *Shinano Maru* sheared away from the stranger, but by this time she, too, had been seen, and another ship flashed a recognition signal, which went unanswered. A few minutes later, the mist parted abruptly and Narukawa suddenly became aware that he had not only discovered the Baltic Fleet but got himself right into the middle of it. No fewer than ten warships were visible, strung out ahead of him in a long line—with those closest starting to train their guns on him.

As they did so, the mist closed in again, and the *Shinano Maru* once more became invisible as her wireless operator sent the long-awaited signal: "dot-dash-dot, dot-dash-dot," repeated again and again, meaning "enemy fleet sighted." At intervals *Shinano Maru* included the location—Square 203. A better omen could hardly have been imagined since the number of the square was the same as that of the hill whose capture by General Nogi had brought about the fall of Port Arthur and with it the final destruction of the first Far East Squadron.

Shinano Maru's message was received first by Admiral Kataoka's flagship, *Itsukishima,* at Miura Bay. Relayed to the wireless room of the *Mikasa,* forward of and adjacent to Togo's bare cabin on the starboard side, it was brought to the Commander in Chief just after 5 A.M. Sleeping in uniform, as was his custom, Togo sat up to read the message and—for the first time since the war started, it was later said—his impassive face was softened by a broad smile.

When the *Shinano*'s wireless message reached the other ships in the squadron, though most of their officers were still asleep, a few were already up and about, motivated either by nervousness or by a perhaps compensatory impulse to display nonchalance. Admiral Hikonojo Kamimura—the Second Fleet's imperturbable Commander in Chief, whose Tokyo house had been stoned after his apparent blunder in a battle during the period of the blockade—was among the latter. He had, as was his recent habit, taken a dinghy to go off fishing, and it had been all his chief of staff, Captain Koichi Fujii, could do to persuade him not to take several other officers with him. Now Fujii had to set off in one of *Izumi*'s launches to bring the Admiral back, while the flagship was getting up steam.

On returning from maneuvers after the false alarm of the 23rd, Kamimura's Second Division and five of the six ships of Togo's First Division, which together formed the main body of the Combined Fleet, were moored in the outer reaches of the bay. The *Mikasa* had returned to her berth in the cove, so as to be near the cable head of the direct line to Tokyo. Now, since the *Mikasa* was out of sight of the others, *Izumi* took over her function of signaling to the fleet—first the news that the enemy had been sighted, and then successive orders to shorten anchor cables, weigh-anchors, and move out to sea in line-ahead, with the *Shikishima*, normally second in line, leading the First Division. Meanwhile, *Mikasa* sent off a final message to Tokyo: HAVING RECEIVED WARNING THAT THE ENEMY FLEET HAS BEEN SIGHTED, THE COMBINED FLEET IS SETTING FORTH TO DESTROY IT. THE WEATHER IS FINE BUT THE SEA IS ROUGH. The wording of the second sentence was an afterthought, added by Akiyama, with his customary verbal felicity, making the weather conditions seems symbolic of prospects for the events that were to follow.

During the preceding days, while the move north had been under consideration, all ships had taken on extra coal so as to be prepared for this possibility. Now—since the coal, stored on the decks in wicker baskets, would no longer be needed—all hands were ordered to throw it overboard, baskets and all, as the fleet moved out to sea. On the *Shikishima* a question arose as to whether the gunnery crews should take part in this operation. Ordinarily, to avoid any possible impairment of their sight by coal dust—and in line with the Japanese propensity for specialization which also exempted deck sailors from work in the stokeholds—gun crews were at all times exempt from coaling duty. Now the *Shikishima*'s Captain Izo Teregaki ruled otherwise; since the coal weighed the ship down two feet below her waterline and diminished her speed, getting rid of the coal took precedence over everything else and even the gunners were instructed to help.

Disposing of the coal took some two hours, varying with the amount carried by each ship. When the job was finished the decks were sprinkled with sand, to reduce fire hazard and to make them less slippery in case of copious bloodshed later. On the *Shikishima*, with conspicuous nonchalance perhaps modeled on Drake's game of bowls while waiting for the Armada, officers passed the time playing deck quoits. On another ship they practiced archery. Between ten and eleven, lunch was served in the mess halls and at duty stations. On the bridge of the *Mikasa* it consisted of rice balls, canned meat, and *nigiri meshi,* or pickled plums. On several of the other ships it was the traditional pre-battle delicacy of salted sea bream.

Bandage packages were distributed—some recipients used the boxes they came in for cigarette cases—and with the extra coal out of the way men and officers put on fresh uniforms, partly in honor of the coming fight and partly to minimize the chances of infection in case of wounds. There was a feeling on all the ships of impatience for the long awaited action but, in place of the hostility between officers and men so often discernible on board the Russian ships, an atmosphere of friendliness prevailed. Gunnery lieutenants shared their cigarettes with their crewmen, who, in chatting with their superiors, showed easy good humor instead of surly subservience. On the *Shikishima* an ensign named Takeo Yamagata saw a seaman immersed in a novel and asked why he was so intent on his book. "Well, sir," the seaman answered, "This may be my last chance to finish it."

It was while the coal was still being tossed overboard—
four hundred tons from *Shikishima* alone, enough to warm
a dozen villages through a whole winter—that the *Mikasa*
came out and swept past the rest of the line to take her
place at its head. As she sliced through the choppy seas at
18 knots, with spray flying back from her underslung ram
bow as far as her bridge, the ship's band, seventy strong on
the fantail, played the Navy March. Ensign Yamagata
never forgot the sound of the music, blowing louder and
louder across the water on the crisp southwest wind as the
flagship overtook the *Shikishima*, and then diminishing as
she drew ahead and cut in to take her place two hundred
yards ahead.

On the assumption that Rozhdestvensky would come
through Tsushima, as he was now doing, Masayuki Akiyama's plan for the battle comprised seven distinct
steps. The first two of these, based on the reasonable assumption that the invader would be discovered the afternoon before he entered the strait, called for a late-
afternoon torpedo attack by the destroyers, followed by a
night action of the same sort carried out by torpedo boats.
By getting through the entrance of the strait undetected,
Rozhdestvensky had contrived to dodge both of these.
Now it was time for the next step, third on Akiyama's time-
table, consisting of a general fleet action. This would have
to be undertaken without helpful preliminaries—as though
a bullfighter were called upon to kill without the preliminary services of his picadors. In Togo's subsequent report
on the battle, also composed by Akiyama, a famous passage makes the opening of this action sound extremely
simple: "The ocean was quite foggy and visibility was limited to five miles and yet the wireless reports presented so
complete a picture of the enemy situation that it was as if
they were passing directly before our eyes."
Tsushima was the first major sea battle in which wire-

less played any role whatsoever, and this wholehearted tribute to its effectiveness was quite understandable. Nonetheless, on the morning of May 27th, to Lt. Junichi Kiyokawa, who was receiving these reports in the wireless room of the *Mikasa,* they conveyed a distinctly different impression.

⌐ After the *Shinano Maru* had sighted the Baltic Fleet, sent her message of discovery, and made her escape, the Baltic Fleet was once more lost in the mist. Now, however, Togo's scouts knew where to look, and before 8 A.M. *Izumi,* the former *Esmerelda,* picked up the Russian ships on their starboard flank and accompanied them just outside of maximum range of their biggest guns, giving a detailed report of their course and formation. Presently, Admiral Shigeto Dewa's four light cruisers also passed the Russians on their port flank and took a position ahead of them and just out of range.

During this period, in the wireless room of the *Mikasa* Kiyokawa was receiving constant and simultaneous messages from Dewa, the *Izumi,* and later the *Itsukushima,* flagship of Admiral Kataoka's Third Fleet. With his rudimentary equipment, which could handle only one message at a time, it was hard enough to keep these reports separate fron one another. What made things even more confusing was that the messages gave different positions for the Russian fleet and conflicting reports on its formation and maneuvers. From what Kiyokawa could make out, the enemy fleet was approaching along three parallel lines at a distance of five miles from each other. As he said later:

> We wondered which line we should trust—and in accordance with which we should therefore adjust our speed and course. Kato and Akiyama kept pressing me to answer the question: "In short, where is the enemy now?" *Izumi*'s report was the neatest and I wanted to trust it—

actually, it was the most accurate one—but *Itsukushima* of the Third Fleet had more rank so at the start I followed its information. In the midst of this confusion, we sighted Dewa's flagship, *Kasagi*. An hour before this, we had received information from *Kasagi* but were not clear about the direction in which she had sighted the enemy. Now, watching *Kasagi* right in front of me, I should have been able to locate the enemy on the map. But due to the fact that we were moving at full speed and changing direction continuously, plus the fact that I was already confused by the conflicting reports and that it was such an important assignment—the fate of the Empire actually depended on my decision—I was really having a very difficult time.

At any rate, one report that proved to be reasonably dependable was Akiyama's original estimate of the weather. The stiff breeze from the southwest raised whitecaps in the Sea of Japan and four-foot waves made the going too rough for the torpedo boats—tiny vessels comparable to World War II PT boats. At ten o'clock Togo ordered them back into Miura Bay, where they were to stay until the wind died down enough to allow them to rejoin. Meanwhile, the *Mikasa* led the First Battle Division southeast across the strait until 12:45, when, almost in sight of the Honshu coast, the ships turned in succession and started back across the strait to the southwest. At 1:30 smoke was seen off the *Mikasa*'s port bow and thought to be the Russians' until it proved instead to be that of Admiral Dewa's light cruisers, which reported the enemy to be about five miles astern. Thinking therefore that he had by now crossed the Russians' bows, so that they were to the east of him, Togo turned sharply south to meet them. It was while on this course that, ten minutes later, he saw on the southern horizon first the long smudge of heavy black smoke that he was looking for and then, a few moments afterward, the tall yellow-and-black funnels of the long-awaited Baltic Fleet.

When first sighted, the ships themselves were, as they had been most recently reported, in two columns that now appeared to be converging, with the one to the east taking station ahead of the other. What troubled Togo, however, was that the Russians, now about six miles to the south, were coming up not, as he had been led to expect, on his port but on his starboard bow, and hence to windward of him. Togo's plan, under the existing conditions, had been to start the battle to windward of his adversary and for this there were two compelling reasons. One was that the heavy seas now being driven against the west, or weather, side of his ships were throwing so much spray across the lenses of the telescopic sights as to make these valuable devices practically useless. The other was that Japanese shells fired from the west of the Russians would hole the enemy ships on the windward side and thus make hits that were anywhere near the water line far more damaging than Russian hits on the leeward side of his own ships. The problem for Togo was whether his superiority in speed of some 4 knots would now allow him enough time to get his fleet across the Russians' bows and so start the battle from the obviously more advantageous position.

Faced, as so often before, with a difficult question requiring an instantaneous decision, Togo reacted characteristically and perhaps the best description of this dramatic moment was a typically understated one provided by a neutral observer on the *Asahi,* fourth ship in the Japanese line. Though technically only an observer, Captain, and later Vice-Admiral, William C. Pakenham was an extremely knowledgeable one. One of the two British naval attachés accompanying the fleet, he had arrived in Sasebo early in March of the previous year, having given as his reason for leaving Tokyo a desire to see the cherry blossoms in Kyushu, where the spring arrived much earlier. Thereafter he had gone aboard the *Asahi* and remained afloat, without once setting foot on shore until after the battle just now starting. After it, when asked by the Emperor to name the bravest man in his fleet at Tsushima, Togo had at once avoided invidious comparisons and paid gracious tribute to an ally by singling out Pakenham for this distinction.

What made the latter's behavior so noteworthy was that, urged to take shelter in the conning tower or some other post of relative safety, he had instead watched the entire battle from a wicker chair on the forward deck, taking notes "like an official judging a yacht race." When a nearby gun crew was blown to bits a few feet away and Pakenham rose to his feet to disappear below decks, some observers thought that he had at last decided to accept discretion as the better part of valor. On the contrary, he returned a few minutes later, having changed to a fresh white uniform because the mishap to the gun crew had spattered some gore on the one he had been wearing. Now, after inspecting the hostile fleet through the monocle that he habitually wore in his right eye, Pakenham set down his impression.

> The moment was one calling for prompt and decided action. In the then state of the atmosphere, distance could not be accurately estimated. The enemy looked so close that the Japanese must have . . . been tempted . . . to accept the simplest and most obvious way of opening the action, namely by a broadside rush past the foe on parallel, but opposite, courses. [Instead, they] turned in succession to northwest, altering again to port (2:0) when directly ahead of the Russian fleet.
>
> It was then possible to see down the length of the Russian line. In the right column the four biggest battleships loomed enormous, dwarfing all others into insignificance. It was not easy to realize that the battleships of Japan

were probably producing at least equal effect on the minds of the Russians."

By this time the order had gone down to Signalman Takizawa to hoist the Zed flag. A few moments later Togo was to make the boldest decision of his career and one of the most daring recorded in the long annals of sea warfare.

The *Mikasa* in action

VII·

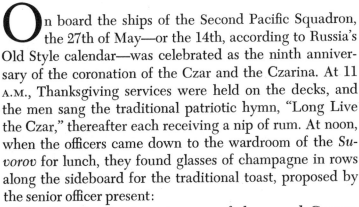

On board the ships of the Second Pacific Squadron, the 27th of May—or the 14th, according to Russia's Old Style calendar—was celebrated as the ninth anniversary of the coronation of the Czar and the Czarina. At 11 A.M., Thanksgiving services were held on the decks, and the men sang the traditional patriotic hymn, "Long Live the Czar," thereafter each receiving a nip of rum. At noon, when the officers came down to the wardroom of the *Suvorov* for lunch, they found glasses of champagne in rows along the sideboard for the traditional toast, proposed by the senior officer present:

"On this, the great anniversary of the sacred Coronation of their Majesties, may God help us to serve with them our beloved country. To the health of the Emperor! The Empress! To Russia!"

As the cheering subsided and they drained their glasses, the call to action-stations sounded, timed as neatly as though in a scene on the stage, and the officers hurried out of the big paneled room, through the passages and up the ladders.

It had been an anxious morning. Shortly after the sighting of the *Shinano Maru* at dawn, the wireless officer on the *Ural* began to pick up a sharply increased volume of code signals—presumably reports of their discovery and consequent orders for the disposition of the Japanese Combined Fleet. The *Ural* came alongside the flagship and signaled to ask whether her operator should attempt to jam the Japanese messages, adding that four cruisers had been sighted astern, following the squadron at a safe distance.

Rozhdestvensky ignored the news of the cruisers and ordered that no attempt be made to interfere with the Japanese messages—suspecting that, if one were, it might prove less of a hindrance than a help, by giving away the Russian position in case the mist had impaired visual contact. About seven o'clock a Japanese cruiser, presently identified as the *Izumi*, appeared on the starboard beam and steamed along on a parallel course until the *Suvorov* swung a 12-inch gun of her after-turret into position to fire, whereupon the *Izumi* hastily vanished into the haze. A few minutes later several cruisers put in an appearance on the port beam, just out of range, to be relieved an hour later by four light cruisers accompanied by several destroyers whose presence so tried the patience of Captain Yung of the *Orel* that, at a few minutes before noon, the *Orel* opened fire. Since she used smokeless powder, thus preventing the other ships from detecting the origin of the shot, several of them surmised that it must have come from the flagship and began firing also.

"Ammunition not to be wasted," signaled Rozhdestvensky, and the booming of the guns presently died down and ceased. The crews were ordered to have their dinner and at noon, abreast of the southern portion of Tsushima Island and in sight of its twin peaks known to mariners as "the Donkey's Ears," the flagship altered course at last onto the homestretch of her eighteen thousand-mile voyage—North, 23° East, direct for Vladivostok.

During the entire battle of Tsushima Admiral Rozhdestvensky issued only two fleet orders—both of them before the action was actually joined. The first, which he gave shortly after setting the new course to North, 23° East, has been something of a puzzle to naval historians ever since. It was for the four leading ships of his battle line to turn *in succession* eight points—that is, 90°—to starboard and then eight points *together* to port, thus putting the four again on the same course as the rest but in a line-abreast rather than a line-ahead formation.

One possible reason for this move was that indicated by Captain Semenoff in his account of the battle—i.e., to frighten off the Japanese cruisers and the accompanying destroyers, which Rozhdestvensky suspected of intending to cross his bows to lay a string of mines in his path. An alternative, or perhaps additional, purpose was the one nowadays attributed to him by authorities on the battle at the U.S. Naval Academy. This was to place his four newest and most powerful ships in the formation from which they could most readily establish a line-ahead in either direction on sighting the Japanese and thus, if Togo was himself approaching in a single column, start the battle by crossing his T.

In any event, like so many of Rozhdestvensky's practice exercises, the maneuver was incorrectly performed. Instead of making the turn to port together—simultaneously with the flagship—the *Alexander, Borodino,* and *Orel* made it in succession, due to a misreading of the signals by the *Alexander* which caused her to follow in the *Suvorov's* wake and thus caused the other two, thinking *they* had misread the signal, to follow in hers. This compound error placed Rozhdestvensky's ships in two parallel columns, one led by the *Suvorov* and the other, on her port side, led by the *Oslyabya.* Shortly after attaining this unwieldy and impractical formation—which did, however, serve the purpose of causing the Japanese cruisers to vanish into the mist—Rozhdestvensky gave his second fleet order of the day, which was for the four ships in his right-hand column to resume their previous position at the head of the left-hand column, while the *Oslyabya* and the seven others again fell in behind them, thus reforming a single line. In swinging back to do so, however, the four leaders inevitably lost distance, so that the eight ships in the left-hand column were forced either to reduce speed as best they could or else to swerve out of line to one side or the other. Of the formation thus established Admiral Nebogatov was later to provide a succinct description: "One vessel had to turn to starboard, another to port, so that there was absolute confusion . . . 'Mob' is the only word to describe our formation at this time."

It was while starting this unhappy rectification of the mismanaged maneuver that had preceded it that Rozhdestvensky saw at last the spectacle, awaited for so long that it had begun to seem almost mythical, of Togo's deadly First Battle Division, taking shape through the mist as it cut across his bows from starboard to port.

"There they are, sir—all six of them, just as on August 10th," said Semenoff, standing beside the Admiral on the upper forebridge. He was recalling the way in which Togo's ships had put in their appearance at the battle of the Yellow Sea, where Kamimura's cruisers had fought as a separate unit, and in which he had predicted that they would appear again.

"No," replied Rozhdestvensky, his binoculars still focused on the horizon, "there are more—they are all there." The Admiral turned and went down the ladder to the conning tower, followed by his chief of staff.

On the bridge of the *Mikasa,* even with the aid of his

Zeiss binoculars, Togo could not discern what lay behind his adversary's moves, but he could at least see that Rozhdestvensky was attempting to form a single line-ahead with his most powerful ships in the lead. When the *Mikasa* reached a position about four miles to the west of the Russians, Togo turned southwest again and for a few moments steamed on a course almost parallel but opposite to theirs. It was at this point that he took his tremendous gamble, in which the stakes were, just as the Zed flag stated, the rise or fall of his nation.

What the gamble consisted of, in practical terms, was an order for all twelve ships of his First and Second Battle Divisions to reverse direction in the flagship's wake while within range of the Russian guns. Such a U-turn meant that while the ships were making it, each following the path of the ship ahead of her, each would pass through a fixed turning point as though rounding an invisible buoy, thus presenting in effect a stationary target to the enemy's fire. Moreover each ship, until it had completed the turn, would be unable to return this fire, since its guns would be intermittently "masked", i.e. blocked, by the presence between it and the enemy of the ships that had already straightened out on the new course. Since it would take some fifteen minutes for all twelve ships to complete the U and get sufficiently steadied on the new course for the gunners to take aim, Togo was in effect giving Rozhdestvensky a priceless head start in opening fire, and at the same time presenting him with a target of maximum vulnerability.

The reward in view was commensurate with the risk. If he could make the U-turn successfully, Togo would put his main force on a parallel course in the same direction as, instead of the opposite direction from, Rozhdestvensky's, and on its windward flank. Thereafter, his superior speed should enable him either actually to cross the Russians' T or to force them to alter course away from their objective to prevent him from doing so. Meanwhile, by shortening the range, he could make both his superior marksmanship and his preponderance of smaller guns count to the fullest. And by executing the turn at once, while Rozhdestvensky's ships were still trying to sort themselves out of the jumble caused by their attempt to resume a single line-ahead, he could reduce to a minimum the interval in which Rozhdestvensky's gunners had a free shot at the Japanese First Division.

There were two ways in which Togo could, had he wished, have made a modified or more cautious version of the same maneuver. One would have been to have his ships make the U-turn "together"—simultaneously instead of in succession—thus reversing the order of the ships in the line. This, however, would have resulted in putting Admiral Shimamura's flagship, the *Iwate*, at the head of the reversed line, and Togo, despite his full confidence in Shimamura, felt that the responsibility for leading the main body of the combined fleet into its climactic battle must remain his own. The other way would have been to get completely out of range by going farther west before making the turn—but this, in addition to giving Rozhdestvensky precious moments in which to straighten his line, might have meant a further loss of time sufficient to have led to another indecisive encounter like that of the previous August 10th. Togo preferred to take the risk—with no bets hedged and no margin for error—that the advantage he would hold after making his turn would more than compensate for any damage that the Russian guns could do while he was making it.

That the gamble was for enormous stakes and that the decision to take it had to be made rapidly by no means indicated that it was either rash or unpremeditated. As Togo said to a friend years later: "The way to win a naval engagement is to strike hard at the right moment; and the ability to judge the opportunity cannot be acquired from books, but only from experience." In the high wind, vocal orders were hard to hear on the *Mikasa*'s exposed forward bridge, but there was no need for many words to be spoken. Kato and Akiyama both knew exactly what the Commander in Chief would want to do under the circumstances and were only awaiting his choice of "the right moment." At 1:55 Togo raised his right hand to draw in the air a half circle to the left. Instantly, Kato turned to pass the command to the ship's captain:

"Hard to port!"

"Hard to port!" Ijichi shouted to his helmsman. A moment later the *Mikasa* heeled over, listing sharply to starboard as she turned her bow toward the enemy fleet, and the turn began.

On board the *Mikasa* Second-class Seaman Seiichi Goto, a gunner's mate serving the forward 12-inch turret, occupied at this moment a position of peculiar distinction. Assigned to relay word-of-mouth orders from Chief Gunnery Officer Abo, on the bridge, to Second Lieutenant Otomei Suzuki, in charge of this turret, his station was nearer to the *Mikasa*'s bow than that of anyone else on board and thus, of the entire Japanese fleet, he was the man closest to the enemy as the battle started. Youngest of four brothers who had all joined the Navy as volunteers, Gunner Goto had barely squeaked in, a month before his seventeenth birthday, by persuading his parents to give their understandably somewhat reluctant approval, but he had little time now to gloat over the singular bit of good fortune that had resulted.

In the moments that had preceded the order to make the turn to port, while the *Mikasa* was still headed as though to pass the Russian fleet on an opposite course, Goto, even more directly than his Commander in Chief,

was worried by the heavy spray that, with the flagship
again headed diagonally into the fresh southwest wind,
still flew across the foredeck. The affect of the spray itself
and of the salty deposit it left on the lenses of the telescopic
sights, with which in the last few weeks they had spent so
much time practicing, made these devices entirely unusable. If the flagship stayed on a southwestward course and
fired at the Russians with her port batteries, the forward
12-inch guns would have to depend on the old-fash-
ioned hairline sight, with consequent loss of accuracy.
No one in the Japanese fleet was better pleased than Goto
when the *Mikasa* swung into her U-turn. As the ship came
around to head northeast, the starboard batteries would
be engaged—and with the wind astern, the spray coming
across the bows would no longer be a problem.

What remained a problem, not only for Goto but for
everyone else on the *Mikasa*, was just how well the flagship would weather the next few minutes—and indeed
whether she would survive them at all. As she started her
turn, the Russians were not slow in perceiving their opportunity, nor in trying to take full advantage of it. The first
Russian shell, a near miss, sent a sixty-foot column of water
into the air only twenty yards astern. A few moments later
the first hit crashed into the flagship's superstructure just
behind the bridge, carrying away her wireless aerial. Fifteen more shells hit the *Mikasa* within the next five minutes and it was not until 2:09 that, as the flagship at last
straightened away on her new course, Gunner Goto finally
received and passed on to Suzuki the order to open fire.
The first ranging shots, at six thousand and sixty-two hundred meters, were short and over, respectively. As the other
ships followed the *Mikasa* around the turn, each under
heavy fire through the bend of the U but none of them
seriously damaged, they, too, picked up the range and by

2:15 the battle began to be a more or less evenly contested two-sided exchange.

To each of the men in it—as Togo had painstakingly explained to his crews before the battle—a gun duel at sea necessarily offers convincing evidence that his own side is losing. Only too plainly visible and audible are the death and destruction on board his own ship, while the damage done to all of the enemy's—except in the relatively rare case of a hit on a mast or a smoke-stack—remains largely imperceptible. Every man can see the flash of each of the opposing guns and, by an optical illusion like that which makes the eyes of a portrait seem to follow a viewer across a room, each shot appears to be aimed directly at him. Meanwhile, most of the gun-flashes of his own ships remain wholly invisible.

For somewhat similar reasons, an observer who could have seen the start of the Battle of Tsushima from directly above might have found it extremely difficult to tell which side held the advantage. Since the encounter took place the year before the Wright brothers got off the ground at Kitty Hawk, and since neither fleet used observation balloons, no such observer existed. Even if there had been, he would not have been able to see much after the first half hour, for by then the smoke from the guns, combined with that from the stacks and with the mist already in the air, formed a dense cloud that at times prevented the fleets from even seeing each other.

While no planes or observation balloons were present, there was, nonetheless, one person who did get an unobstructed panoramic view of the battle of Tsushima for a few minutes just at the beginning—both the most decisive part and the only time when the whole action was completely visible. This was a thirteen-year-old boy named Ichisaburo Sato, the youngest son of one of several fishermen whose fleet sheltered at the tiny islet of Okinoshima, some twenty miles west of Tsushima, bounding the eastern channel of the strait on the east side, ten miles off the coast of Kyushu. In peacetime the only inhabitant of Okinoshima beside the fishermen and the Sato brothers was a Buddhist priest in a tiny temple near the shore, for whom Ichisaburo acted as errand-boy and acolyte. Since the start of the war the navy had established an observation point on the top of the four-thousand-foot hill of which the islet was mainly composed, manned by four sailors and a telegraph operator.

Early on the morning of May 27 Ichisaburo climbed the hill to tell the telegrapher that during the night a squid-fishing boat from Tsushima had taken refuge from the rough seas in the bay down below and that its skipper wanted word that he was safe sent to his family. The telegrapher replied that no civilian messages were allowed, because he had just got notice that the Russian Fleet was headed for Tsushima strait and he had to reserve his wire exclusively for naval traffic. Ichisaburo hurried down again to carry this news to his father, the other fishermen, and the Buddhist priest.

The priest and the boy had just finished their lunch, shortly before noon—after which devout Buddhists traditionally fast until the next day—when a message came from the observation post that the Russian Fleet was now entering the strait. Ichisaburo and the priest ran down to the shore, removed their clothes, and waded into the water, where the priest said prayers for victory. While they were there they heard the first shot of the battle— *Orel's* at the intrusive cruisers—followed by several more. All this was too exciting for Ichisaburo to ignore, and he rushed out of the water, hurried into his clothes, and climbed the high hill for the second time that day. At the top, the crew of the observation post said that he would be in their way if he stayed and that he should go straight down the hill again. Ichisaburo, after leaving the post, could not bring himself to obey. Instead, he found a tall pine tree on the seaward side of the hill, climbed up it as far as he could, and then crawled out on a limb. There, as he looked toward the west, "were two rows of scores of warships. They looked as neat as two rows of go-stones. I never thought that warships looked so beautiful in the midst of a battle."

Ichisaburo had missed Togo's turn, which must have occurred at about the time he was climbing the tree, but he was in his perch for what Captain Pakenham, much more precariously situated on the deck of the *Asahi*, described as "the scenic part of the battle," when "Two long lines of ships were attacking each other vigorously; formations were as yet unbroken; damages were still conjectural; and the fate of the day seemed to hang on every shot. . . . Range was observed to have become 6,562 yards. . . . Russian fire was still well-sustained. With the object, perhaps, of varying the range, the *Mikasa* was zigzagging in her course and the ships in her immediate neighborhood were attentively following her slightest turn."

As Ichisaburo watched from his tree branch, the two long lines of warships, like toy ships on the bright blue surface far below him, curved gradually toward the east, drawing closer together as they did so. "Countless shells were flying around. And as they fell into the sea they turned into hundreds of water-columns. The guns flashed like lightning and roared like a thousand thunderstorms. . . ."

For those less advantageously placed than Ichisaburo, and those whose viewpoint was less detached than that of Captain Pakenham, the battle presented a very different aspect. On board the *Suvorov,* Staff Officer Semenoff, whose roving assignment left him free to watch the battle from wherever he could see it best, had moved to the after 12-inch gun turret when his Commander in Chief went to the conning tower. The turret was a vantage point from which he could see not only the Japanese ships but also all those of his own squadron—the battleships in a still somewhat irregular line astern and the cruisers making off toward the east, where they had been instructed to protect the auxiliaries and stay out of the way. With him stood a talkative young officer named Lieutenant Reidkin, who, since he was in charge of the after starboard 6-inch turret and since the action was clearly going to start on the port side, was also temporarily at liberty to assume the role of a spectator.

"Hello, look, what are they up to?" said Reidkin peering through his glasses as Togo's ships started their U-turn. Then, as the nature of the maneuver became clear, he added, "*How* rash! Why, in a minute we'll be able to roll up the leading ships."

"Please God we may," thought Semenoff, who, remembering the Battle of the Yellow Sea, had good reason to feel less sanguine.

Glancing at his watch—the time kept on the Russian ships was fifteen minutes behind that of the Japanese— Semenoff noted that the first Russian shots were fired at 1:49, with the two leading Japanese ships already halfway through their turn. As the rest of the squadron's guns came into play astern of the *Suvorov,* he noted also that most of their "shorts" and "overs," marked by water spouts that rose more than sixty feet in the air, were near misses, indicating a satisfactory standard of marksmanship. He reminded himself also that the absence of noticeable hits could be explained, in part at least, by the fact that the slow-fused Russian shells were meant to explode only after penetrating the target and even then would cause little smoke. According to Semenoff's estimate—about two minutes short of the true interval—it was only two minutes from the time that the *Suvorov* opened fire until the first ships in the Japanese line began to reply.

The Russian nickname for the projectiles—a foot thick and four feet long—fired from the biggest Japanese guns was *"chemodani"* meaning "portmanteau" or "duffel bag." "Are these the *chemodani?*" asked the chatty Lieutenant Reidkin with a cheerful smile as the first big ones flew overhead, clearly visible and making a strange wailing noise as they passed.

"Yes, those are the ones," said Semenoff, noticing, however, that unlike the big shells used by the Japanese in the battle of August 10th these exploded as soon as they touched the water. Splinters from the near misses whistled as they flew past, or jingled as they hit the sides and superstructure, even before the first direct hits. These came soon afterward, and Semenoff later described them with commendable precision:

> Abreast the foremost funnel arose a gigantic pillar of smoke, water and flame. . . . the next shell struck the side by the center six-inch turret. . . . Smoke and fire lept out of the officers' gangway; a shell, having fallen into the captain's cabin, and having penetrated the deck, had burst in the officers' quarters, setting them on fire. . . .
>
> The men at the fire mains and hoses stood as if mesmerized, gazing at the smoke and flames, not understanding, apparently, what was happening. I went down to them . . . and with the most commonplace words, such as "Wake up! Turn the water on!" got them to pull themselves together and bravely to fight the fire.

A minute or two later, another explosion caused "something large, and soft though heavy" to hit Semenoff from behind, knocking him unconscious. When he came to, sitting on the deck some minutes later, he noticed that his watch, which he had taken out of his pocket just before the explosion, was still ticking, but that its crystal was missing. He spied the crystal on the deck, picked it up, and spent several more minutes laboriously fitting it back into place, before realizing that repairs to his timepiece were of distinctly secondary importance. Reidkin, by this time in his own gun-turret, looked out to give him a cheery greeting: "Hello! A scene that you are accustomed to? Like the tenth of August?"

"Just the same," replied Semenoff.

In fact, as the Commander later noted, it was completely different:

> On August 10th, in a fight lasting some hours, the *Czarevich* was struck by only 19 large shells, and I, in all seriousness, had intended in the present engagement, to note the times and places where we were hit, as well as the damage done. But how could I make detailed notes when it seemed impossible even to count the number of projectiles striking us? I had not only never witnessed such a fire before but I had never imagined anything like it. Shells seemed to be pouring on us incessantly. . . .

Semenoff attributed the devastating effect of the Japanese shelling in part to the volume and accuracy of the firing and in part to some new ingredient in the Japanese powder which caused instantaneous fires to break out in the vicinity of each explosion.

> I actually noticed a steel plate catch fire from a burst. Of course the steel did not burn, but the paint on it did. Such almost non-combustible materials as water-

drenched hammocks and boxes flared up in a moment. At times it was impossible to see anything with glasses, owing to everything being so distorted in the quivering, heated air. No! It was different to the 10th of August!

Wondering "Was it all imagination? Was it all a nightmare? Had I become jumpy?" Semenoff felt that he might gain some reassurance from a visit to the Admiral. When he reached the conning tower, after a near fall when his foot slipped in a pool of blood that until a moment or two earlier had been an ingredient of the *Suvorov*'s first signalman, Semenoff found little to encourage him. The Admiral and the flag captain were both bent over so as to peer out through the narrow aperture between the ceiling and the circular walls, protected by a belt of steel seven feet wide and ten inches thick.

"Sir," Captain de Colongue was saying, "We must shorten the distance. They are all being killed. They are on fire."

"Wait a bit. Aren't we all being killed also?" answered the Admiral.

As though in confirmation of this observation, Semenoff noticed two corpses in officers' tunics lying face-downward—those of the helmsman and the flag-gunnery officer. Nonetheless, the rangefinder was being efficiently worked by an officer shouting his orders in a clear voice to the electricians, who obediently turned the handle of the indicator, transmitting the range to the various turrets and gun batteries. This evidence that something at least was going forward properly cheered Semenoff for a moment. "We're all right," he thought to himself, but when he left the tower for the more exposed forebridge, where he could again get a panoramic view, his elation rapidly subsided.

The enemy ships were in perfect order, steaming parallel to us but gradually forging ahead. No disorder was noticeable. It seemed to me that with my Zeiss glasses (the distance was a little more than 4000 yards) I could even distinguish the mantlets of hammocks on the bridge and groups of men. But with us? I looked around. What havoc! Burning bridges, smouldering debris on the decks—piles of dead bodies. Signalling and judging-distance stations, gun-directing positions, all were destroyed. And astern of us the *Alexander* and *Borodino* were also enveloped in smoke. . . .

According to Commander Semenoff's reassembled watch, it was now only sixteen minutes after the start of the battle, and if the scene on the *Suvorov* seemed to him disheartening, it was perhaps as well that he was unaware of conditions on board the flagship of the second division. *Oslyabya* had entered the battle under a serious disadvantage, supposedly known only to her own captain, the ship's surgeon, two orderlies, and Admiral Rozhdestvensky. This was that Admiral Folkersham, whose flag still flew from her masthead, was actually no longer in command. Though Rozhdestvensky had ordered the news withheld, lest the crews consider it a bad omen, he had died on the night of the 25th and his body, now attired in full dress uniform for the formal funeral service that was to take place in Vladivotok, lay in a sealed coffin in the ship's chapel.

At the start of the battle, while the *Mikasa* and the five ships of the First Division that followed her were concentrating their fire on the *Suvorov*, the *Oslyabya* had been forced to slow-down her engines and turn to port to avoid ramming the *Orel* as she squeezed into the line. A few minutes later, as Admiral Kamimura's heavy cruisers followed the First Division into the new course and saw that the *Suvorov* was already being well taken care of, they chose for their prime target the conspicuous flagship of the Russian squadron's second division. With her tall sides and three lofty stacks, *Oslyabya*, as she lay almost motionless in the water, was ideally suited to this role. Each of the Second Division's cruisers carried four 8-inch and either twelve or fourteen 6-inch guns, and these soon reduced her whole superstructure to rubble.

According to then universally accepted theory, a properly armored battleship could almost never be sunk by gunfire alone—which was why little torpedo boats, admittedly able to sink such ships, were so thoroughly dreaded. Whether *Oslyabya* actually qualified as armored was perhaps a moot point, for one thing because her armor was not so thick as her design had specified, and for another because, like many of the other Russian ships, she was so overloaded with coal that much of her armor belt was submerged. In any case, before she got under way again, three hits in succession that penetrated the forward part of her port side at almost the same spot opened up what one of her officers later described as "not a hole but a regular gate." When the *Oslyabya* was finally able to resume speed in order to keep place in line, she shipped so much water that she developed a severe list to port, which one of her engineers tried to correct by flooding the forward magazine. Now with her bows even lower, the list to port increased rapidly and at ten minutes to three, with her guns silenced and fires raging on deck, the *Oslyabya* swung out of line to starboard to await her rapidly approaching end.

Captain Baer of the *Oslyabya*, a tall, bald-headed officer, whose hawk nose and full, double-pointed beard gave him a notably commanding presence, had been running his ship from the conning tower. At a few minutes after three o'clock, just an hour after the start of the battle, he came out on the forebridge to shout to the men on the deck below him: "Abandon ship! All hands to the boats, or jump overboard!"

Baer's servant, a boatswain's mate named Mikhailov,

tried to pull the captain off the bridge in obedience to his own command, but Baer pushed him aside. A compulsive smoker, with a spray-soaked cigarette even now stuck between his lips, and a severe cut from a shell splinter showing red across his bald head, he held himself up by the stanchion of what had been an awning and went on shouting his last orders to the men already in the water: "Goodbye, shipmates. Get further away from the ship, the devil take you! If you don't, you'll go down in the suck!"

With the decks at a sixty-degree angle and the bow under water, some brave souls thought to open the bulkheads, to give the stokers and mechanics in the engine rooms a slim chance to escape. In most cases it was too late and the engine-room crews stayed on below, trapped in an inferno of furnaces that spilled out red-hot coals and bursting boilers that spouted scalding steam. In the sick bay the ship's surgeon went on treating the wounded —of whom many, already bandaged, were unable to move and had no one to help them reach ladders and hatches. On the steep decks, the seamen scuffled and fought each other for cork vests, or struggled to launch the lifeboats, of which most were already too battered or burned to keep out the sea. The chaplain, a fat, middle-aged monk, his thin hair blown into tufts by the wind, uttered a pathetic plea: "Brothers, shipmates, I can't swim. Save me'!"

It was about 3:30 when the huge ship, the most impressive in appearance of the entire Baltic Fleet, finally turned over on her side and lay there for several seconds before rolling the rest of the way. Then, with her weed-grown bottom uppermost and one of her propellers still spinning crazily in the air, she plunged head-first under the sea. She was the first ship sunk in the battle of Tsushima and the only armored battleship ever sunk by gunfire alone— though the latter distinction was not one she was to hold for long.

Oslyabya

Although the *Oslyabya* was the first ship sunk at Tsushima, she was not the first to be forced to drop out of the line of battle. This dubious honor went to a Japanese cruiser, the *Asama*, whose Captain, Rokuro Yashiro, an enthusiastic amateur musician, had astonished the officers on his bridge by playing a flute solo while his ship was engaged in making the hazardous U-turn. When asked later on what had inspired this melodic outburst, he explained that the object was to provide simultaneously an example of serenity and a soothing influence. Thus encouraged, the *Asama* safely completed the turn, but shortly thereafter she came under intense fire from the ships at the tail end of the Russian column. A 12-inch shell from the *Nikolai I* smashed her steering gear, forcing her out of action for the rest of the afternoon while she had it repaired.

Just as the Japanese gunners had made the *Suvorov* their prime objective, the Russians chose the *Mikasa* and in the first half hour of the action she took a total of thirty direct hits. One of these smashed into the starboard side of the upper deck, just aft of the bridge, killing the entire crew of one of the forward 6-inch guns along with the ship's deputy commander, Tatsuo Matsumura. Another crashed into a washroom, inflicting wounds on several seamen, including signalman Jinzaemon Takizawa. A third struck the ladder leading to the bridge, where shell fragments wounded two young staff officers called Hisatsune Iida and Junichi Kiyokawa. Another fragment plowed into the hammock wrappings around the ship's compass, a few inches away from Admiral Togo's chest. His staff were later to extract it and present it to the Commander in Chief as an addition to his collection of lethal souvenirs.

From the point of view of the flagship's efficiency the most damaging hit of all was the very first, which had torn through the rigging of the foremast, smashing the wireless. For the rest of the afternoon the *Mikasa* was obliged to relay her signals to the rest of the fleet by semaphore to the *Shikishima,* which then broadcast them to the other ships. But while the *Mikasa* took the brunt of the punishment—almost a quarter of all the hits scored by the Russian guns, which did all their damage during the first half hour of fighting—she was not the only one to suffer serious losses. The imperturbable Captain Pakenham, before going below decks to change his theretofore immaculate whites, related the occasion for his departure in grisly detail:

> An explosion under the afterbridge of the *Asahi* filled the air with flying fragments. Of these, one fell underfoot. It was the right half of a man's lower jaw, with teeth missing. Everything and everybody for twenty yards round was bespattered with tiny drops of blood and minute particles of flesh that adhered to whatever they struck. A six-inch shell had exploded against a twelve-pounder gun, killing the officer and crew and some of the bystanders. In spite of the quantity scattered, the amount of blood left on the deck looked sufficient to fill a big cask. . . .

During the first few moments of the battle, Togo's U-turn had given Rozhdestvensky at least an even chance, and perhaps considerably more than that, to make up for all the miseries and trials his ships had experienced up to that time. The poor discipline of the crews; their incompetence in maneuver; the decks over-loaded with coal; the encumbrance of seaweed and barnacles acquired in seven months at sea; the handicap of the slow Third Squadron; even the faulty gunpowder in his shells and the defects in the construction of his ships might all have been annulled and forgotten had his gunners, in those few minutes, had the ability, or even the mere good luck, to score enough hits to impair the enemy's fighting efficiency.

In fact, though their fire had been more accurate than perhaps Togo and certainly Rozhdestvensky could have expected, they had failed to do this. All twelve of the Japanese First and Second Division had made the turn without being badly hurt in the process; and even the temporary loss of the *Asama* a few minutes later diminished their firepower by only a fraction more than eight percent. But even now, in the gun duel that followed the turn, despite Togo's advantages of speed, fighting-fitness, and marksmanship, the outcome of the encounter was by no means a foregone conclusion.

Rozhdestvensky had never entertained the absurdly sanguine though cynical illusions of the captain of the cruiser *Oleg*, who had offered to bet that Togo would allow the whole fleet to pass unharmed to Vladivostok—with the objective of making all of its ships eventual prizes by blockading them there. He was aware, however, that while all war is full of uncertainty, an engagement between two great fleets, even more than most battles, offers any number of unforeseeable chances. As he approached Tsushima there was the possibility that Togo might have divided his fleet to protect the different entrances to the Sea of Japan; or that a heavy fog might allow the Russians to pass by unseen; or that their gunners might score more than their share of effective hits in the first few minutes. Even with all these inviting eventualities totally cancelled, even when both fleets had opened fire on even terms, there was still at least an off chance of recouping, to greater or less degree, the golden opportunity lost in the first fifteen minutes.

That this chance was never to be realized was due to numerous causes, of which the most immediate was perhaps the sinking of the huge *Oslyabya*. In the seven months of their cruise halfway around the globe, the mere habit of continuous association had given the men in the Russian crews a spurious sense of invulnerability. To their occupants the ships of the fleet had come to seem permanent entities, as reliable as castles, as indestructible as hills. That one of these mighty fortresses could simply turn over on its side and then vanish under the supporting waves seemed at first unbelievable and then—since they had after all watched it happen with their own eyes—a dire confirmation of all the monstrous and paralyzing fears created by the hail of shells from the Japanese guns.

The ships ahead of the *Oslyabya* were close enough for the sailors to see her turn out of the line, her bow down, enveloped by smoke and clearly doomed. The seven ships that caught up and passed her got a clearer view of what happened thereafter. Said a sailor from the *Nikolai I* when the battle was over: "The impression caused by the capsizing of a vessel of such a gigantic size was awful. We saw how the men thrown off the deck clutched and clung to the sides, or crawled and fell, or were crushed by falling top-hamper, or swept away. . . ." The speed with which the disappearance of the *Oslyabya* took place was an added element in the horror. One moment, though a virtual wreck, she was still there like the rest, with smoke pouring out of her broken funnels and flags flying from her ruined masts. A few moments later there was nothing except the rough water, in which a few tiny figures could be discerned, clinging to each other or to bits of the wreckage. Could it be that the same dreadful catastrophe would soon, and just as quickly, overwhelm them too?

As a matter of fact, very few were to be so fortunate. Of the *Oslyabya's* total complement of some nine hundred, more than two hundred were to be saved by the destroyer *Buiny*, which hurried to the scene of the sinking to search for survivors. Almost as many again were picked up later by the Japanese. The three other battleships that were to go down that afternoon mustered fewer than a score of survivors among them.

The next ship to drop out of line was the *Suvorov* whose condition had deteriorated rapidly since Commander Semenoff had consulted his watch after leaving the forebridge. More fires had broken out on her deck, but now there was no way of even trying to control them, since the hoses were burned or broken and the lifeboats, filled with water for use in such emergencies, had been smashed or punctured by shell splinters and had thus themselves become fuel for the flames. Both masts were down, and a hit on the forward funnel had caused it to crash to the deck, covering it with thick smoke and smoldering debris. Movement from bow to stern became impractical except below decks, but in trying to make his way aft through the officers' quarters Semenoff found them still burning furiously. Turning back, he met a lieutenant coming down the ladder and asked where he was going.

"Into the steering compartment," was the reply. "The rudder is disabled."

Making his way back to the forebridge, Semenoff at first found it hard to get his bearings, because the ships that the *Suvorov* should have been leading could now be seen steaming past her on an opposite course. Suddenly it struck him that what the lieutenant had just said supplied the explanation for this: her disabled rudder had caused the flagship to swing around 180° to starboard, so that the *Navarin*, whose proper place was sixth in the line, was now on the *Suvorov*'s starboard beam, going past at full speed.

In the event of such a disaster to the flagship, two destroyers, the *Biedovy* and the *Buistry*, had been detailed to come to the *Suvorov*'s assistance in order to transfer the Admiral to some other ship. Neither destroyer was in sight and now, with both masts gone, and all the flag halyards with them, the *Suvorov* had no means of summoning aid. Toward four o'clock she found herself wallowing helplessly in the rough sea, ignored even by the enemy except for an occasional 6-inch shell from one of the cruisers, which after the 12-inch portmanteaus came almost as a relief.

It was during this lull that Commander Semenoff encountered a good-natured and high-spirited young midshipman named Werner von Kursel, who greeted him with a cheerful enquiry:

"Well! How are you passing the time?"

"Badly," growled Semenoff, and explained that, having smoked all his cigarettes, he was on his way to get a fresh supply from his cabin.

"To your cabin?" Kursel grinned. "I've just come from there. I'll go with you."

Semenoff accepted the offer and followed his guide through a maze of smoking wreckage and smashed passages. What ensued was a practical joke of the kind in which Kursel specialized and to which Semenoff was later to recall his adverse reaction: "Having got as far as the officers' quarters, I stopped in amazement. Where my cabin and two adjoining ones had been was an enormous hole! Kursel laughed heartily, thoroughly enjoying his joke, but growing angry I waved my hand and quickly retraced my steps. Kursel overtook me in the battery and offered me a cigar."

At about three o'clock, the *Suvorov* had taken a direct hit on the conning tower, of which the effect was to incapacitate those of its instruments and controls which had up to then been still workable. At the same time, the Admiral—who had already suffered several severe cuts from flying splinters—received a major head wound from another shell fragment, which drove a sliver of skull into the top of his brain. Experiencing intense pain but still conscious, Rozhdestvensky allowed himself to be led down from the tower—which meant wriggling through a narrow hatch and descending a thirty-foot ladder to the foredeck —in search of some more functional command post. Rozhdestvensky, assisted by Semenoff, Colongue, and several other refugees from the tower, made for the relative security of the center 6-inch turret on the port side, but before the group could reach it another shell exploded nearby. A splinter from this one cut through the main nerve in the Admiral's left ankle, paralyzing the foot. Dragged into the turret and propped up on a wooden ammunition crate, Rozhdestvensky lost consciousness, but only for a moment. When he opened his eyes again, it was to hurl a characteristic question and command at his flag captain: "Why isn't this turret firing? Fall in the crews immediately."

Before the *Suvorov*'s departure from the head of the line Togo's ships, by drawing ahead of the Russians and at the same time gradually closing the range to less than three thousand yards, had forced Rozhdestvensky to alter course gradually, veering first east and then southeast. When the *Alexander* replaced the *Suvorov* in the lead, her captain tried a bold move: a sharp turn to port, by which he hoped to escape to the northwest by cutting across the rear of the Japanese line. Togo countered this by turning his First Division together sixteen degrees to port, thus paralleling the new Russian course while allowing Kamimura's Second Division cruisers, which thereafter fought independently, to continue eastward. The *Alexander*, her escape thwarted, now resumed a northeastward course in a second effort to pass astern of the Japanese line, and Togo repeated his port turn-together, thus re-establishing the original order of his First Division and their position relative to the Russians.

During these fleet convolutions, while the *Alexander* and the *Borodino* now took the brunt of the Japanese fire, the helpless *Survorov* twice found herself within range of Togo's ships. Both times the Japanese tried to sink her, without pausing in their pursuit of more active prey, but both times without success. As the Japanese battleships moved away the second time, a Russian destroyer, the *Buiny*, came close enough to see the plight of the flagship and asked if she could be of assistance. Staff Captain de Colongue sent an officer to semaphore, with his hands in lieu of flags, the request that the *Buiny* stand by to take the Admiral off.

Since neither the flagship nor the destroyer had a launchable boat, the only way to effect the transfer was for the *Buiny* to come alongside. With so much smoke and flame pouring out of the *Suvorov*'s leeward side that it was impossible for the destroyer to get close to it, she was obliged to approach from windward. As the smaller ship rose and fell in the high seas close to the battleship's bow, she was in constant danger of being holed by a broken gun barrel or by one of the smashed torpedo-net booms projecting from the side. Nonetheless, she was made fast there while the semiconscious Admiral was carried by his staff from the turret toward the forward embrasure, from which it was planned somehow to hand him across to the waiting destroyer.

Under the direction of Werner von Kursel, shouting his orders through a megaphone, seamen on the battleship hung over the side, forming a sort of human buffer or slide, while others on the destroyer waited, lined up at the rail. As the destroyer rose on a wave, its plates grating against those of the flagship, the Admiral's inert body half

slid and half rolled into the hands of the men on the destroyer. Three members of Rozhdestvensky's staff—de
Colongue, Semenoff, and Flag Lieutenant Leontiev—
jumped across to the destroyer at the same time, as did a
dozen or so of the *Suvorov*'s seamen. "Aren't you coming
with us?" Colongue shouted up to von Kursel.

"No, sir," the midshipman shouted back, "I shall stay by
the ship."

As the *Buiny* backed swiftly away—both ships were
now under heavy fire from Kamimura's cruisers—Midshipman von Kursel was the only able-bodied officer left on
the flagship, whose jolly Captain Ignatius had been blown
to bits early in the afternoon. Her only workable gun was
a 75-millimeter rapid-fire weapon on the rear deck. By
the time that the Admiral was removed, most of the
Suvorov's below-deck hands were already unconscious
or dead, as a consequence of inhaling the poisonous fumes
and smoke drawn into the holds by the ventilators instead
of fresh air. A hundred so so surviving deck-hands now
gathered on her stern and under von Kursel kept the last
gun firing until, as darkness fell, Togo sent his destroyers
in to make the kill. The credit for this went to Lieutenant
Commander Umejiro Fujimoto, in command of the Elev-
enth torpedo-boat Flotilla, who was later to write the only
eyewitness report of the *Suvorov*'s last moments: "Although she had only one serviceable gun, she still opened
fire, showing her determination to defend herself to the
last moment. . . . At length, about 7 P.M., after our torpedo boats had twice attacked her, she went to the bottom." Fujimoto's report does not mention survivors.

Battle-smoke mist and the early spring twilight combined to make visiblity so poor that for a time in the late
afternoon Togo's First Division lost contact with the
enemy. At about six o'clock, however, the *Mikasa* sighted

several of the remaining ships "flying in a cluster to the northward." Togo's official report of the First Division's activities goes on to relate the consequences.

> Approaching at once, it steamed parallel to these and then renewed the fight, gradually emerging ahead of them and bearing down on their van. . . . This fight on parallel lines continued from 6 P.M. to nightfall. The enemy suffered so heavily that his fire was much reduced, while our deliberate practice told more and more.

During this period the *Alexander III* fell out of line and, enveloped in fire and smoke, drifted out of sight of the others. Admiral Kamimura's cruisers, functioning on their own initiative after parting from the First Division at the time of Togo's first turn-together to port, noted having seen her capsize and sink at a little after seven. No more detailed account of her end than his was ever to be provided, for out of her crew of nine hundred, not one, including her outspoken Captain Bukhvostov, survived.

The last major casualty of the day was the *Borodino*. At 7:28, just as the sun was touching the horizon, Togo signaled to his First Division to withdraw from the action so as to give the torpedo boats a clear field and eliminate any chance of a mistake in the identity of their targets. As the *Fuji* turned aside to comply, she let go a final shot from her stern 12-inch turret toward the *Borodino*. The shell struck the target with results that provided Pakenham with his final coolly objective notation of the day:

> Entering the upper part of the *Borodino* near the foremost broadside turret, it burst, and an immense column of smoke, ruddied on the under side by the glare from the explosion and from the fire abaft, spurted to the height of her funnel tops. From every opening in engine-rooms and stokeholds steam rushed, and in two or three

minutes the ship from foremast to stern was wrapped in fiercely whirling spirals of smoke and vapor, gaily illuminated by frequent tall shafts of flame. It was evident that the conflagration had reached a stage where it could defy control . . . though even so it was not realized how near was the end. . . . Though sudden, this was not dramatic. While all watched, the unfortunate ship disappeared (7:30), her departure only marked by a roar not greatly louder than that of one of her own bursting shell, and, until dispersed by the wind, by a great increase in volume of the dense cloud that brooded over the place she had occupied. . . .

Early the next morning, a Japanese destroyer picked up a huge, naked seaman named Semyon Yushchin, who had spent the night clinging to the floating mast of one of the *Borodino's* shattered lifeboats. He proved to be her only survivor.

PART THREE

Consequences

Katte kabuto no o wo shimeyo—
In victory, tighten the strings of your helmet.

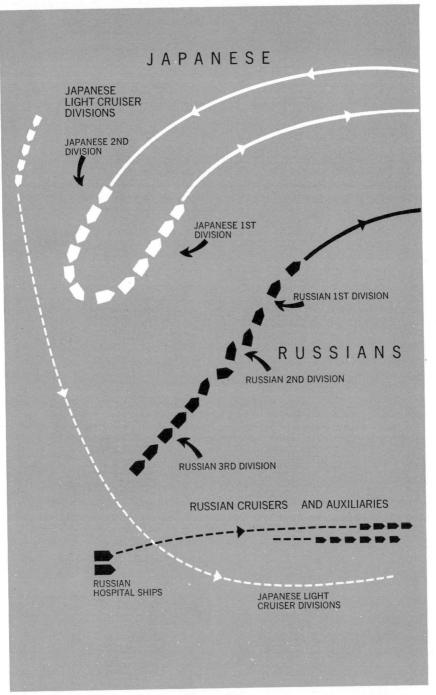

BATTLE MAP I, SHOWING POSITION OF JAPANESE
AND RUSSIAN FLEETS AT START OF BATTLE

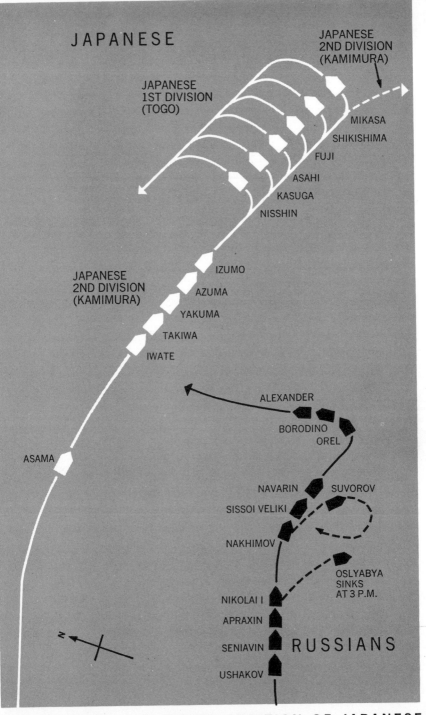

BATTLE MAP II, SHOWING POSITION OF JAPANESE
AND RUSSIAN MAIN FORCES AT 3:30 P.M.

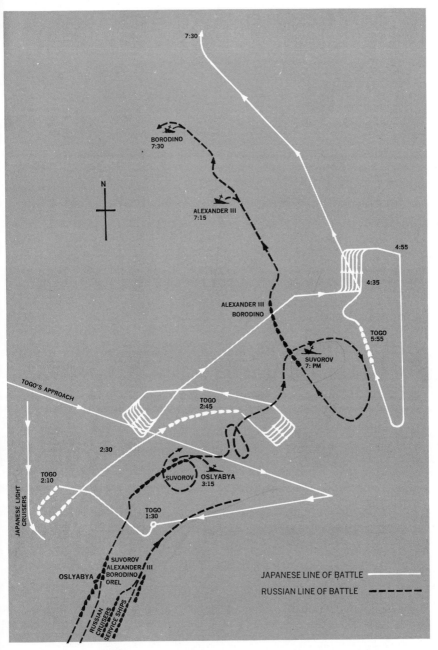

**BATTLE MAP III, SHOWING PROGRESS OF BATTLE
FROM APPROXIMATELY 1 TO 7:30 P.M.**

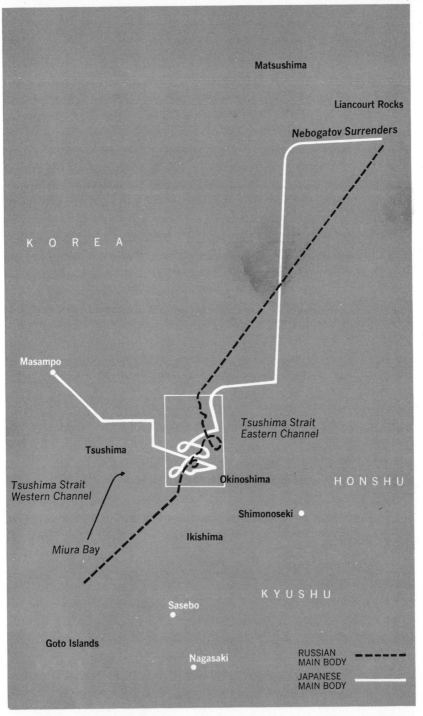

Matsushima

Liancourt Rocks

Nebogatov Surrenders

K O R E A

Masampo

Tsushima

Tsushima Strait Eastern Channel

Tsushima Strait Western Channel

Okinoshima

H O N S H U

Miura Bay

Shimonoseki

Ikishima

K Y U S H U

Sasebo

Goto Islands

Nagasaki

RUSSIAN MAIN BODY

JAPANESE MAIN BODY

BATTLE MAP IV, SHOWING TRACKS OF BOTH FLEETS
AND NEBOGATOV'S SURRENDER ON MAY 28TH

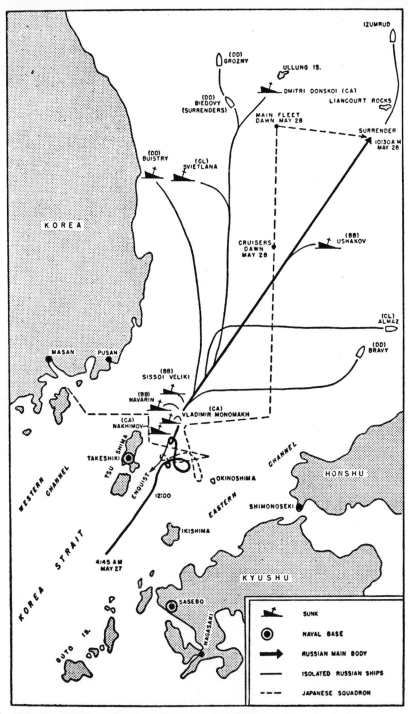

FLEET TRACKS, BATTLE OF TSUSHIMA

VIII

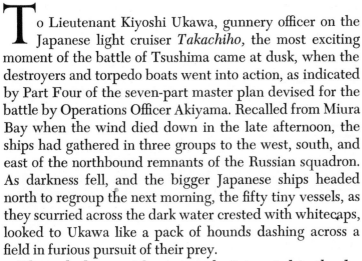

To Lieutenant Kiyoshi Ukawa, gunnery officer on the Japanese light cruiser *Takachiho*, the most exciting moment of the battle of Tsushima came at dusk, when the destroyers and torpedo boats went into action, as indicated by Part Four of the seven-part master plan devised for the battle by Operations Officer Akiyama. Recalled from Miura Bay when the wind died down in the late afternoon, the ships had gathered in three groups to the west, south, and east of the northbound remnants of the Russian squadron. As darkness fell, and the bigger Japanese ships headed north to regroup the next morning, the fifty tiny vessels, as they scurried across the dark water crested with whitecaps, looked to Ukawa like a pack of hounds dashing across a field in furious pursuit of their prey.

Ukawa had a special reason to be interested in the destroyers, because he had served in one, the *Shirakumo*, throughout the siege of Port Arthur, and he knew how the men in them felt. While the destroyers, most of them weighing around 300 tons, and the torpedo boats, mostly under a hundred, had performed heroically at Port Arthur, their desperate efforts to block the harbor passage had not succeeded. The destroyers had also failed to finish off the Port Arthur Squadron after the battle of the Yellow Sea on August 10th and now they were all the more eager to make up for these failures by a brilliant success. The spirit of self-sacrifice with which their crews were imbued was well expressed by one of their skippers in a letter to a friend describing their plan of action:

> We ought to be able to close within twenty yards of the target before she is sunk. If we hit, we shall go down with the Russians; if we are hit, the Russians shall come down with us, for the last man alive will steer the spare torpedo into the water. What is life but a summer night's dream?

For defense against night torpedo attacks there were two schools of thought in the Russian Squadron. One, adhered to by Admiral Rozhdestvensky, was to use searchlights to pinpoint the attackers and then—since neither main nor secondary batteries could be brought to bear on such close, fast-moving targets—to try to drive them off by machine-gun fire. The other, adhered to by Admiral Nebogatov, was to use no lights whatever and merely try to escape under cover of darkness.

The disadvantages of the former system were convincingly demonstrated by the sequel to the fleet action, as this developed during the evening of the 27th. It then became apparent that the attackers often got in close enough to discharge their deadly missiles before even the one-pounder Hotchkiss-Nordenfeldt machine guns devised for the purpose could be trained on them, and also that the targets were too small and too elusive for the gunners to deal with effectively even when they did start firing in time. The *Navarin*, already badly damaged during the afternoon battle, sank with most of her crew after taking two torpedo hits. The *Sissoi Veliky* and the *Admiral Na-khimov*, then the only two ships remaining of Folker-sham's division, also took hits but managed to struggle along as far as the coast of Tsushima, where both were scuttled to avoid capture.

Comparable misfortunes befell most of Rozhdestvensky's smaller vessels during the night of the 27th and the next day. Of the seven auxiliary ships that had accompanied the squadron into battle, three—the wireless-monitor *Ural,* the troublesome repair ship *Kamchatka,* and the transport *Russe*—had been sunk when they strayed into convenient range of Japanese battleships or cruisers during the afternoon. Meanwhile, Admiral Enquist's cruisers, whose assignment had been to protect these and the other auxiliaries from the Japanese light-cruiser divisions under Admirals Dewa, Uriu, Taketomi, and Masemichi Togo, gave up the attempt either to fulfil it or to break through towards Vladivostok on their own. Instead, when darkness fell, most of them made off for the neutral port of Manila, where they could be safely interned, in preference to being either sunk or made enemy prizes.

Three of them got there—the *Aurora,* the *Zhemchug,* and the *Oleg,* whose optimistic captain, pleading for permission to try to use his 23-knot speed to reach Vladivostok alone, Enquist felt obliged to overrule. The fate of two other cruisers that got separated from the rest before their departure tended to substantiate Enquist's judgment. One of these was the *Svetlana,* which on the 28th encountered three Japanese cruisers; these sank her after a hotly contested running battle. Another was the *Dmitri Donskoi,* which ran into twice that many, with somewhat similar consequences.

Meanwhile, the Nebogatov theory of torpedo-boat defense proved surprisingly workable in the case of the remnants of the Russian line that were to survive the night of the 27th. At about 6 P.M. that evening a Russian destroyer had come alongside the *Nikolai I* to signal Nebogatov that he was now in command of the fleet, and to convey Admiral Rozhdestvensky's last command, that he shape course for Vladivostok. Nebogatov received the order without surprise. A kind-hearted commander, well along in his fifties, whose consideration for his crewmen was to be even more dramatically shown the next day, he ordered supper served to them at action stations and steamed on at full speed, signaling the other ships to follow in his wake and show no lights. The four ships capable of following these directions were the coast-defense "flat-irons," *General Admiral Apraxin* and *Admiral Seniavin,* whose more severely damaged sister ship, the *Admiral Ushakov,* struggled along far behind them; the fast cruiser *Izumrud;* and the battleship *Orel.* While the latter's superstructure had been so thoroughly demolished that only two of her guns were still capable of firing, no more than a score of her crew of nine hundred had been killed, and fewer than one hundred wounded.

The survival of the obsolete "flat-irons," far from being a confirmation of Klado's argument in favor of sending them to the Far East, amounted to a convincing rebuttal of it. Instead of attracting fire away from the more powerful ships, and thus helping the latter reach their destination, Nebogatov's ships, whose gunners had done surprisingly well for the first few minutes, had thereafter fallen so far behind the eight Russian ships ahead of them that the enemy fleet was out of their range, and vice versa. At one point, happening on Enquist's cruisers when these were taking severe punishment from Kamimura's more powerful ones, they had helped to drive the latter off. Thereafter they had not only been unable to help offensively but had even remained too far away to serve as adequate targets for Togo's First Division, whose chief concern remained the eight leading ships in the Russian line. No such lack of attention, however, was to favor Nebogatov on the second day of the battle.

During the night of the 27th, his five ships had fought off two torpedo attacks without suffering serious damage before darkness enabled them to escape the hunting packs. As May 28th dawned, clear and bright with none of the mist of the day before, they found themselves between the island of Matsushima and a barren group of smaller islands to the east known as the Liancourt Rocks, some two hundred miles north of Tsushima and only three hundred miles short of their goal. Soon after sunrise, scanning the horizon from the bridge of his flagship at 6:25, Admiral Nebogatov saw smoke to the southwest.

Any glimmer of hope that this smoke might betoken the approach of additional Russian survivors vanished in short order when the hulls became identifiable as three of the enemy's light cruisers. Nebogatov had enough firepower to engage these but, before he could do so, they moved out of range. The speedy *Izumrud* was then sent to reconnoiter ahead and returned to report the approach of Togo's dreaded First Division, accompanied by the now reactivated *Asama*. These, soon joined by Kamimura and his five other heavy cruisers, presently formed a ring around the Russians, which was gradually augmented by other warships until the visible total reached twenty-seven, not counting destroyers. The ring closed slowly until, at a signal from the *Mikasa*, their big guns opened fire.

As the first shells sent up sixty-foot geysers close to his ship, Nebogatov turned to his gunnery officer and asked for the range.

"Twelve thousand yards," was the reply.

Since none of his ships carried workable guns that could possibly reach more than eleven thousand, Nebogatov realized at once that the Japanese could destroy what re-

mained of the Squadron at their leisure, with no risk whatsoever to themselves. The only question that arose was
therefore whether to scuttle the ships and try to get the
crews away in the boats or, more simply, to surrender.
Since most of the boats had been too severely damaged
the day before to be seaworthy, and it would be suicidal to
launch them under fire in any case, the former course
would presumably mean the loss of practically all of the
twenty-five hundred men under his command, in addition
to that of the ships. Russian naval regulations included a
paragraph which, Nebogatov felt, was meant to cover just
such contingencies:

> During an action the Commanding officer will set an
> example of valor, and continue fighting to the last. To
> avoid useless shedding of blood he is permitted, but only
> with the concurrence of all the other officers, to deliver
> up his ship, if all the ammunition is spent, the guns are
> disabled and means of defense generally are exhausted,
> and if it shall be found impossible to destroy his ship and
> at the same time for the crew to seek safety on shore or in
> the boats.

The Admiral sent for the ship's captain, Vladimir Vasil-
yevich Smirnov, who lay severely wounded in his cabin,
and for his staff officers. When they were gathered round
him in the conning tower, he put the question: "What are
we to do?"

It was Smirnov who gave the definitive reply: "Yester-
day, we did our duty, sir. Today we are no longer in a
condition to fight. There is nothing for it but surrender."

Looking around the circle of faces Nebogatov read
agreement in them all. A signal was made to the other
ships requesting their concurrence, which was promptly
forthcoming. Nebogatov then ordered his signal officer to

send up the international code flags XGE, meaning "We surrender."

Since they had the whole day in which to finish their job, the Japanese gunners were firing without haste. A considerable interval occurred between incoming shells and, because of the long range, hits were infrequent. Nonetheless, the first portmanteaus had come crashing into the flagship by the time the XGE flag went up. When the firing continued thereafter, Nebogatov, somewhat puzzled, sent for a white tablecloth and had this hoisted to the masthead. Still the shelling continued, and now Nebogatov, ordering the ships' engines to be stopped, accepted a final humiliation. This was to order the Rising Sun flag sent to the mast head of the *Nikolai I*—named for his Czar's grandfather, who in 1829, had sent the ships of his navy to destroy a Russian frigate in punishment for having surrendered to the Turks.

As the *Mikasa* headed north on the night of the 27th, Captain Hikojiro Ijichi had given orders for the crews to stay at action stations. During the evening, while the officers gathered in the wardroom to exchange reminiscences, he had gone below to pay respects to those who had died in the battle. The casualties on board the flagship—seven killed and eighty-three wounded—were, as was to have been expected, the heaviest in the fleet, whose total of killed in action was only one hundred seventeen. This number, however, included several of its ablest young officers, of whom one was Commander Kenkichi Matsui, who had won his bet against Keisaburo Moriyama when the message from the *Shinanu Maru* had revealed the appearance of the Baltic Fleet in Tsushima Strait that morning. When Moriyama tried to send his friend a message of congratulations he learned that Matsui—a student of strategy, who took his duties so seriously that he had had a map of the world painted on the ceiling of his cabin so that he could study it in off hours—had been one of the first casualties on board the *Nisshin*.

On board the *Mikasa* the seven dead bodies—among which the only officer's was that of Ijichi's second in command, Tatsuo Matsumura—had been carefully laid out in the immaculate seamen's bathroom. There, in the presence of crew members not on duty, the captain went to each of the dead and, kneeling beside him, said farewell as though to a living person. The names of the seven were then inscribed on a white handkerchief, with a drop of blood from each beside his name. The handkerchief was enclosed in a wooden box that already contained another one like it, inscribed with the names of whose who had fallen in the battle of the Yellow Sea. Ijichi kept the box in a place of honor in his cabin.

At dawn the next morning the *Mikasa*, followed by the other ships of the First Division, was some sixty miles northwest of the slower Russians, and thus, as planned, between them and Vladivostok. Informed by wireless at 5:35 that what appeared to be the remainder of the Russians' main body had been sighted between Matsushima and Liancourt Rocks, the First and Second Divisions moved eastward to start closing the circle around them.

To Togo, Kato, and Akiyama, standing together on the forebridge of the *Mikasa*, the behavior of the enemy ships now seemed puzzling in the extreme. Instead of returning the Japanese fire, which Togo ordered his 12-inch guns to open when the ring was completed at 10:30, the Russians continued to steam along on their course, as though they considered themselves in some way immunized to further injury. At the same time, the *Nikolai I* hoisted three signal flags which even with the aid of binoculars were difficult to read at a distance of more than five miles. Eventually, the letters XGE were deciphered, but that hardly helped much. There were several thousand three-letter combinations in the international code, and no commander could be expected to know by heart more than the few hundred that he might find occasion to use. When it developed that neither Akiyama, Kato, nor the Commander in Chief had the slightest notion of what XGE stood for, Kato proposed the obvious solution: send down for the code book and look it up.

Staff errands of this kind were normally handled by Lieutenant Junichi Kiyokawa—no favorite of Kato, who had nicknamed him "the hairy caterpillar" in disparagement both of his appearance and of his celerity. Perhaps fortunately, Kiyokawa, whose flesh wound of the day before had not proved serious, was in the conning tower at the moment and the assignment went to an even more junior officer, Ensign Shinjiro Imamura. Instructed to hurry to the chartroom two decks below, where the international code was kept, Imamura scrambled down the ladders and after a brief search located the object of his quest— a large volume, bound in red, on the top shelf of the bookcase to the left of the door.

Hurrying back to the bridge, Imamura handed the code book to Akiyama, who thumbed through its pages, with the top officers in the Japanese Navy peering anxiously over his shoulders. Finally, they found the signal whose meaning, as stated in English, made it clear at once why no one of the three was familiar with it. "We surrender" was not a message for which any Japanese naval officer would ever be likely to have the slightest need—and Togo could not believe that the Russians really meant it now. He suspected that Nebogatov was trying to play some sort of trick and continued to hold that opinion despite a wireless message from Admiral Shimamura—who had correctly guessed that Togo would not understand the *Nikolai*'s flags—giving him the code-book translation.

Even when the white tablecloth was hoisted to the *Nikolai*'s masthead Togo—remembering the Chinese warship that had escaped under a similar banner on July 2nd 1894—could not bring himself to believe that the surrender was genuine. His doubts received temporary confirmation when the *Izumrud*, which, like the other Russian ships, had hoisted the XGE signal, suddenly pulled it down and made off at full speed toward the east. Togo despatched two cruisers and several destroyers in pursuit of the fugitive and continued to fire on the *Nikolai*, to the growing distress of Commander Masayuki Akiyama, who stood at his left elbow.

Tokyo's distinguished specialist in plans and operations officer was an eccentric whose numerous idiosyncrasies were, as a rule, indulged by the rest of the staff on account of his unquestioned brilliance in his field. Akiyama quite often came to mess in his bedroom slippers, gobbled down his rice without a word, and then, rising unceremoniously, shuffled back to his cabin before the rest of the staff was half finished. He often worked till all hours of the night and in the late afternoons liked to jump over the side for a swim, sometimes not even bothering to remove his trousers. On the bridge he made a habit of wearing his sword belt over, instead of under, his tunic, in accord with some theory that the extra abdominal support thus provided was helpful in reinforcing resolution and the ability to concentrate.

A profound student of history and philosophy as well as of warfare, Akiyama experienced all the self-doubts to which intellectuals are so often subject and had many qualms about his own capabilities and fitness for his job. In one of his letters to his wife, he spoke of planning to become a Buddhist priest when the war was over. In another, somewhat contradictory one, written after the victory for which his seven-part plan had provided the foundation, he remarked with characteristic diffidence that perhaps now Togo would have enough confidence in him to want to keep him on as a member of the staff. Akiyama, essentially a creative rather than a destructive personality, was basically much more interested in designing battles than in fighting them. To him, his Commander in Chief's persistence in firing on ships that were obviously making no effort to defend themselves seemed not only inexplicable but also ethically wrong. His disapproval and surprise, overcoming the awe in which he held Togo, forced him to protest:

"Sir, the enemy has surrendered. Shouldn't you give the order to cease fire?"

For decades after the battle of Tsushima, Admiral Togo was to devote much of his spare time to boar-hunting, often in company with the Emperor. In this bloodthirsty pastime his specialty was administering the *coup de grace* to the wounded quarry, and his companions of the chase recalled that he would quite frequently offer to despatch their kills as well as his own. While he was quite prepared to indulge the oddities of an Akiyama—whose mind was said to be a filing cabinet containing the answer to every conceivable problem in naval strategy—Togo found the eccentricities of his Planning Officer entirely foreign to his own nature. To him, the present situation presented itself quite differently from the way in which it appeared to his highly sensitive subordinate.

One of Togo's basic maxims was: "Never fear a strong enemy—and never despise a weak one." So far in this battle all had gone well—though just how well he had as yet no sure means of knowing—and this was no time to jeopardize through some weak sentiment a victory already almost won. With his left hand still grasping the hilt of the

Emperor's sword and his cheeks puffed out in the angry expression habitual to him in time of battle, he did not trouble himself to make any reply whatever.

By now the Rising Sun had been hoisted to the *Nikolai*'s masthead, and the other Russian ships were following her example. Akiyama was almost choking as he put his question again, this time even more pointedly:

"Sir, doesn't the spirit of bushido compel us to stop firing?"

This time Togo, out of his knowledge of naval law, gave him a cold reply: "Their ships are still in formation and still moving. If they mean to surrender, they should first stop their engines."

Akiyama had nothing further to say but by now, at last, Nebogatov had said it for him, by ordering his ships to stop their engines. When they lay unmistakably dead in the water, Togo finally brought himself to give the order to cease fire. Many years later he explained his feelings, during this second instance when his instinct for the kill went well past conventional limits:

"It was utterly beyond our expectations. We had opened fire with the strongest determination to annihilate them at once, but all in vain. It really was the strangest occurrence, and we were astonished and somewhat disappointed."

To initiate the surrender arrangements Togo sent Akiyama, accompanied by a French-speaking lieutenant, to the *Nikolai* on the torpedo boat *Kiji*. On board the Russian flagship, the lieutenant translated the message with which Togo had entrusted them: the Russian ships were to be maintained intact and Admiral Nebogatov was to come to the *Mikasa* to discuss the terms of surrender. Nebogatov agreed and requested permission, which was granted, to change into a dress uniform.

Admiral Nebogatov had taken command of the Third

Pacific Squadron under no illusion about its capabilities. He had brought it from the Baltic to Camranh in less than half the time utilized by Rozhdestvensky in reaching the same objective, and with fewer confusions en route. He had then been allowed to lead his ships into battle ignorant of the death of his immediate superior and even, for three hours after Rozhdestvensky's transfer to the *Buiny*, of the fact that he was in command of the entire fleet. Now, at the end of a long and reasonably distinguished career, he went to his cabin to put on his dress uniform with medals for the last time. So attired, he reappeared a few minutes later and stepped to the rail of his forebridge to address the crew assembled on the deck below him.

"Comrades, this is a sad day for Russia, for the Imperial Navy and for all of us who have survived this terrible battle. But I have decided to capitulate to the enemy because otherwise we should have been annihilated to no purpose. I do so with a heavy heart but in the knowledge that no more human suffering can alter our fate or the fate of our fatherland. I am getting on in years, and my life is of trifling importance. Let the shame of this action rest on me alone. I am ready to be tried by court-martial and am prepared for the extreme sentence. I accept the entire responsibility for this surrender . . ."

On the *Mikasa*, with punctilious regard for protocol, stairs had been rigged on the starboard side for the visiting admiral. Nebogatov mounted them slowly and the two admirals, followed by their staff officers, retired to Togo's staff cabin to agree on final details: the ships to be boarded by prize crews, officers allowed to keep their swords, crews treated as prisoners of war. When the two Admirals had toasted each other formally in champagne, Nebogatov—who, had he failed to make contact with Rozhdestvensky, had been planning to take his ships through the strait of La Perouse—had only one question to ask: "How did you know that we would come through Tsushima Strait?"

Togo permitted himself a small, enigmatic smile. "I didn't know," he replied, "I merely thought so."

Now there remained only the laborious business of getting the surrendered ships back to Sasebo, a task for which arrangements were speedily outlined. The *Orel*, whose engines were in the worst shape of the four, would proceed under tow. Seamen from the Japanese ships would board the others to help their own crews and to familiarize themselves with the ships. In charge of the hundred sailors assigned from the *Shikishima* to the *Nikolai I*, because he spoke fluent French, was Takeo Yamagata, the young midshipman who had questioned the sailor whom he had seen hurrying to finish reading his novel the day before. Young Yamagata's interest in reading matter was by no means accidental. He was himself by way of being an amateur poet, and often sent samples of his compositions home to his parents. His father, who was also a *littérateur* had, Takeo later learned, made a habit of telling his friends that his son was the bravest young man in the Japanese fleet and, when asked why, would reply: "Because he dares to send me such terrible *haiku*."

Before the war, young Yamagata had been for some years an indignant critic of the Far East policy followed by Russia and often submitted letters to the papers denouncing it. Now, on board the *Nikolai I*, when he saw Russians close up and face to face for the first time, he found all nationalistic resentment vanishing. Yamagata perceived at once that, despite differences in size and appearance, Russians were really human beings much like himself, and he felt sorry for them in their present hard predicament. He started his tricky assignment on the *Nikolai* by making a speech in French, in which he expressed these feelings and found that it went over very well. Then he obtained the permission of the Russian officers to let their seamen listen to Japanese gramophone records to help pass the time on the cruise back to Sasebo. Finally, he distributed a pack of picture postcards of the *Shikishima* which he had thoughtfully brought along with this idea in mind. One of the Russian officers tried to reciprocate by giving him a pair of German binoculars, but this was a gift that Yamagata under the circumstances felt obliged to decline.

Owing largely to Yamagata's *savoir faire*, better order prevailed on board the *Nikolai I* on the way back to the Japanese base than on some of the other prizes. On board the *Orel*, a group of unruly seamen got drunk and broke into the officers' cabins. The paymaster was persuaded to share out the contents of the ship's treasury with officers and men, of whom some got much less than they considered a fair share. The ship's captain, Nikolai Yung, died of his wounds and was ceremoniously buried at sea, with the Rising Sun flag at half-mast.

If the behavior of the Russian seamen on some of the prizes gave their new owners some clue to the causes of their victory, the converse was equally true. Another ancient Japanese maxim dear to Togo was *"Katte kabuto no o wo shimeyo,"* meaning "After a victory, tighten the strings of your helmet." One of the exchange officers on Admiral Kamimura's flagship, *Iwate*, was the captain of the captured coast defense ship *Apraxin* who witnessed an impressive demonstration of how strictly this principle was observed in the Japanese fleet. Invited to the bridge on the morning of May 29, the Russian was amazed to hear the captain turn to his Chief of Staff, Commander Tetsutaro Sato, and say: "Let us have target practice," whereupon the orders were given and the gunners on the ships of the Second Battle Division blazed away at a towed target for more than an hour. The Russian captain said to Sato, "Now I know why we lost. You defeat the whole Russian fleet and the next day you practice gunnery!"

Recalling the incident years later, Sato inadvertently drove the point home. "The captain noticed such a little thing, a mere trifle that we might have overlooked. I think he was a brilliant man."

After his transfer to the *Buiny* on the afternoon of the 27th, Admiral Rozhdestvensky had been put to bed in a hammock slung in the skipper's cabin, where the ship's surgeon examined his wounds. The Commander in Chief, he found, had a dangerously fractured skull, and he warned that the slightest jolt or shock might prove fatal. The Admiral spent the rest of the day in a coma broken by brief intervals of consciousness during one of which Commander Semenoff asked him whether he wished to retain his command. The reply was an incoherent mumble in which Semenoff made out the words: "No . . . where am I . . . You can see . . . command . . . Nebogatov . . . Keep on Vladivostok . . . course North, twenty-three degrees East."

While the two hundred survivors from the *Oslyabya* huddled shivering in her passages and on her deck, the *Buiny* ploughed along northward during the night, undetected or ignored by the hunting packs of Japanese torpedo boats and destroyers. Early the next morning, with her fuel running low and her engine starting to fail, the destroyer had the good luck to fall in with three other survivors: the cruiser *Dmitri Donskoi,* accompanied by two other destroyers, the *Groznyi* and the *Bedovyi.* Since both of the latter were in better shape than the *Buiny,* it seemed prudent to transfer the *Oslyabya*'s survivors to the *Donskoi* and move the Admiral—who had now regained fairly continuous consciousness and some capacity for making decisions—to one of the other destroyers. He chose the *Bedovyi,* whose Captain Baranov was one of the few officers in the fleet who apparently enjoyed his favor.

Asked what orders he had for this pitiful remnant of his huge armada, Rozhdestvensky muttered what was to be the last command of his long career: for the *Donskoi* to escort the faltering *Buiny* while the *Groznyi* and the *Bedovyi,* capable of more speed, steamed together on the familiar course, North, 23° East. He then relapsed once more into intermittent coma. What happened thereafter was reported not by Semenoff, whose graphic account of the battle ends with the destruction of the *Suvorov,* but by the skipper of the *Groznyi:*

> At a little after three o'clock . . . we saw two vessels coming from the straits of Korea, . . . which rapidly overtook us. At close quarters the vessels were seen to be Japanese destroyers, one with two funnels, the other with four. Approaching the *Bedovyi,* I asked her by semaphore what we should do, and received for reply: "How much speed can you make?" I replied: "Twenty-two knots." In reply to the order, "Go to Vladivostok," I asked, "Why go away and not join battle?" To that I received no reply but seeing that the *Bedovyi* did not increase speed, and not wishing to leave her by herself, I decreased speed and stayed near her until I saw her hoist the flags for parley and the Red Cross. Then I gave orders for full speed ahead. . . ."

What was happening on board the *Bedovyi,* as later reconstructed by Novikoff-Priboy, was a conference among Rozhdestvensky's staff officers. Though the *Bedovyi* was capable of as much speed as the *Groznyi,* the chances of either one reaching Vladivostok after giving battle seemed remote. The alternative of an attempt to escape at top speed would mean vibrations that would surely prove fatal to Rozhdestvensky before they could reach their objective. With the concurrence of his colleagues, Chief of Staff de Colongue ordered hoisting the signal "I have critically wounded men on board," which, accompanied by the Red Cross flag, might serve to give the *Bedovyi* the immunity to attack of a hospital ship.

Not surprisingly, the skipper of the leading Japanese destroyer, the *Sazanami,* a young lieutenant named Tsunezo Aiba, was as puzzled by the *Bedovyi's* signals as his superiors had been by those of the *Nikolai I.* Like the *Mikasa* a few hours before, the *Sazanami* opened fire, and it was only when the protesting wail of the *Bedovyi's* siren and the stopping of her engines made unmistakably clear her intention to surrender that Aiba gave his gunners the order to cease. He then had a boat lowered to row him across to the *Bedovyi.* At her rail he saw a collection of officers whose wealth of gold braid seemed as incongruous with their vessel as the admiral's pennant at her masthead.

Aiba was taking no chances. Springing on board with drawn sword—and thus giving the officers assembled for parley the impression that he had much more gory business in mind—he slashed at the wireless antennae with which, in his ignorance of its deficiencies, he had supposed the destroyer might try to summon assistance. With the antennae reduced to an unworkable tangle, he turned to the highest-ranking officer present and asked in English: "Are you the Captain? I am now in command of this ship."

De Colongue's attempt to explain the unusual circumstances did not altogether dispel Ayiba's doubts. The surrender of a ship still capable of combat seemed implausible enough but now he was being asked to believe also that the Commander in Chief of the whole Russian fleet was his prisoner as well as the destroyer itself. Told that Rozhdestvensky must on no account be disturbed, Aiba answered: "I won't disturb your admiral but at least I must see him with my own eyes."

Having peeked in at the bloody and bandaged figure of the Commander in Chief, Aiba was sufficiently convinced to return to his own ship, taking the staff officers with him and leaving a guard at the cabin door. Two days later, under tow and flying the Rising Sun, the *Bedovyi* reached the end of her voyage—not Vladivostok but Sasebo Naval Base, where Nebogatov's battleships were already on view, tied up along the sea-wall.

By the afternoon of May 28th the surrenders of Rozhdestvensky and Nebogatov, the departure of Enquist, and the prebattle death of Folkersham had deprived the Second Pacific Squadron of its entire high command, while the sinking or surrender of all twelve of its most powerful ships had effectively ended its existence as a fighting fleet. Nonetheless, no one person in either fleet was yet in a position to be sure of the magnitude of the victory. Meanwhile, the day was to include a series of individual encounters and actions involving widely separated units of which the results—some heroic and some the reverse— were also to have a bearing on the outcome.

While the *Groznyi* was making good her escape from the scene of the *Bedovyi's* capitulation, the *Dmitri Donskoi* vanished northward, followed by the *Buiny*. They had not gone far before the latter's engine troubles made it clear that she could never reach Vladivostok. After a consultation with his engineer, her Captain Kolomeitsev decided to transfer his crew to the *Donskoi* and then blow up his ship to prevent her capture. The transfer was effected in due course but the explosive charge set to demolish the *Buiny* for some reason failed to go off. The procedure then decided on was for the *Donskoi* to demolish the destroyer by gunfire, but this also turned out to present difficulties.

At point-blank range of three hundred yards, the first

shell from one of the cruiser's 6-inch guns went wide of the stationary target, as did a second and third. After two more somewhat closer misses, the sixth and seventh shells grazed the destroyer without doing serious damage. Finally, the eighth shot made a hole in her bow through which she gradually shipped enough water to cause her to sink.

The destruction of the *Buiny* took place early in the afternoon. Thereafter, the *Dmitri Donskoi* steamed northward unimpeded until almost 5:30, when smoke appeared on the horizon to port—caused, it developed, by the two cruisers that had just sunk the *Svetlana*. These were joined presently by all four cruisers of Admiral Dewa's Fourth Division. During the one-sided engagement that followed, the two hundred survivors from the *Oslyabya*, terrified by this second exposure to Japanese gunnery, screamed, wept, and threatened mutiny unless the ship surrendered. When they were herded below decks and hoses were turned on them to keep them there, some managed to jump overboard, to die by drowning or the percussive effects of near misses. By six o'clock the *Donskoi* was within sight of Matsushima Island, where the skipper planned to run her aground unless darkness enabled him to escape his attackers. When darkness fell, he successfully repelled two Japanese torpedo attacks, and brought his ship to temporary haven in a small bay. There he landed the *Oslyabya* survivors and his own crew, of which every member was wounded. In the morning, a few of them took the ship into deep water and sank her.

Comparable in its gallantry to the end of the *Donskoi* was that of the *Admiral Ushakov*, which, unable to keep up with the other "flat-irons", had maintained the same course through the night. The next afternoon, long after they had surendered, the *Ushakov* encountered Admiral Shimamura in the *Iwate*, accompanied by the *Yakumo*.

Both Japanese ships opened fire while at the same time signaling. "Your admiral has surrendered. We advise you to do likewise." Confronted by an even more discouraging situation than that which had faced Nebogatov earlier, the *Ushakov*'s acting captain Miklukh-Maklai responded quite differently, and, having deciphered only the first half of the signal, gave the order to return the fire. The subsequent duel lasted for barely half an hour, by which time, with the *Ushakov* too battered to offer further resistance, Miklukh-Maklai ordered her seacocks to be opened and her men to take to the water. Moved by this courageous resistance, the Japanese cruisers managed to rescue all but eighty-three members of her crew of four hundred and fifty—not including her indomitable captain, who went down with his ship.

The defiant departure of the fast cruiser *Izumrud*—her 23 knots gave her more speed than any Japanese ship of comparable power—was likewise rewarded by success of a sort. Pursued by two slower cruisers as she withdrew from the scene of the surrender, she outdistanced them with ease and the next morning found herself off the Siberian coast. Then, having heard that the islands near Vladivostok were in Japanese hands, her captain imprudently headed for Vladimir Bay, almost two hundred miles farther north, where he ran aground in a fog the next night. He and his crew then scuttled their ship and made the last lap of their journey on foot.

Of the Russian fleet of thirty-eight ships that went into battle, only three actually reached their final objective. The first was the small auxiliary cruiser *Almas*, orginally designed as a yacht for Viceroy Alexeyev, which carried nothing more deadly than six 4.7-in guns. Detached from Enquist's division during the night of the 27th, she shrewdly chose to run along the Japanese coast, where she encountered no enemy ships at all. Nearing Vladivostok on the morning of the 28th, the *Almas* ran out of coal and wirelessed for assistance. A collier was sent out to meet her and guide her in through the mine field that Shima-mura had laid down as Part Seven in the Akiyama plan. Thus escorted, she entered the harbor in the late after-noon of May 29th.

Eagerly awaiting the arrival of Rozhdestvensky and his mighty armada, the citizens of Vladivostok had prepared a tumultuous welcome. The hospitals were equipped to solace the heroic wounded and a crowd of several hundred lined the waterfront as the *Almas* tied up at a ready moor-ing. Fishermen had already brought back word of hearing gunfire and seeing the flash of cannon far to the south two nights before. Now the port would hear the whole epic story of the great battle.

There was little that the captain of the *Almas* could give them except a sketchy account of being driven off by an immensely superior force of Japanese cruisers and of sev-eral Russian battleships burning, of which he had seen one capsize and sink. Later arrivals were the *Groznyi*, which had made good her escape after Rozhdestvensky's surren-der, and another lucky little destroyer, the *Bravyi*. Their fragmentary reports, and the even more eloquent failure of any other ships to arrive, were the only first-hand news they were to receive until the pedestrian crew of the *Izumrud* straggled in from the north a few days later.

The exploits of the two destroyers and the *Almas*, not to mention the stubborn defiance shown by the *Izumrud*, the *Ushakov*, and the *Dmitri Donskoi*, contrasted sharply with the behavior of some of the other Russian ships that had survived the first day's battle. Hardest to classify was pos-sibly that of the hospital ship *Orel*, which, on the after-noon of the 28th, was discovered by the *Sado Maru* steaming calmly along a few miles north of Tsushima. Like the *Shinano Maru*, which had earned a *Kanjo*, or special citation, by discovering the Russian fleet, the *Sado Maru*, owned by the Nippon Yusen K. K. Shipping Company, had been one of the crack liners on the European run before the war, but thus far she had distinguished herself much less favorably than her sister ship. It was the *Sado Maru* which, on the 23rd, had sent in the false alarm causing the Japanese combined fleet to get up steam and put out to sea.

Actually, there were several extenuating circumstances to be considered in connection with this error. In the first place, the *Sado Maru* had no way of knowing that the smoke trails that she had sighted belonged not to the Russians but to Admiral Shimamura's division of cruisers, which like herself were searching for the Russians. In the second place, her message, indicating merely that the smoke trails *might* be those of enemy ships, represented an entirely proper precaution. In the third place, insofar as the day of maneuvers resulting from her message had caused the ships of the Japanese First Division to anchor in the outer part of Masampo Bay on their return, thus enabling them to get to sea all the faster on the 27th, the consequences of the false alarm had been more advantageous than otherwise. Nonetheless, the *Sado Maru* had no intention of committing a second *faux pas*, which might not have such fortunate results.

If there was anyone on board the *Sado Maru* with an especially good reason for wanting to restore the ship's prestige, it was a thirty-year-old midshipman named Ichiro Fukuda. A graduate not only of Japan's Naval Academy but also of Annapolis, where he had stood twenty-sixth in the class of 1902, Fukuda's rate of promotion had been slowed down by his absence and he was eager both to rectify this and to do something special to justify his foreign training. His big chance arrived when, having spotted the hospital ship, the *Sado Maru* sent a shot across her bow, causing her to stop. In view of his knowledge of English, Fukuda was chosen to command the boarding party.

Although searching a ship flying the Red Cross flag was a somewhat unusual procedure, there were again on this occasion certain special circumstances to consider. Submarines, despite their use as long ago as the U.S. Civil War, were still a naval novelty and each side had reason to suspect the other of having some. Both had, in fact, ordered five such vessels—each about thirty feet long, armed with four torpedo tubes—to be built in the U.S. shortly before hostilities broke out, but both sides apparently were saving them for an emergency, since neither had so far used them.

For Japan's failure to use her submarines there was in fact a peculiarly compelling reason. In 1905 a submarine depended for its ability to submerge or to surface entirely on a pair of Kingston valves, one on each side, through which it could take on or eject water ballast. By some deplorable error, the ten Kingston valves sent to Japan for installation on her five submarines were all for the starboard side. This made the appliances unusable and confined the boats to dry dock.

The cause of the mis-shipment in the equipment for Japan's submarines was absurdly simple: the five port-side Kingston valves that should have been included, had instead been delivered to Russia with the submarines shipped there. The reason that Russia had not used her Philadelphia-made submarines thus corresponded exactly with that of Japan for not using hers, namely that she had received ten valves for the port side and none for the starboard.

Since no one in either Japan or Russia, including even the ubiquitous Colonel Akashi, was as yet aware of this frustrating coincidence, the Japanese theory was that the Russians were saving their submarines for use by the Second Pacific Squadron. Since they could hardly have been towed all the way from the Baltic, they were perhaps concealed inside another ship. For this purpose nothing could have been more suitable than the hospital ship *Orel,* and Fukuda's principal mission in searching her was to make sure that she did not have the component parts of one or more submarines stowed below decks, presumably to be assembled after her arrival at Vladivostok.

If the *Orel* was carrying submarine sections they would, of course, be crated to look like something else. The bulkiest kinds of crates on a hospital ship would probably be those containing food supplies and, in view of this, Fukuda had already given thought as to how he could best ascertain the contents of any suspicious crates her hold might contain. Concluding that the person best qualified to distinguish between a genuine food crate and a fake one would be a ship's cook, he had taken the precaution of adding the *Sado Maru's* head chef to his boarding party, in the uniform of an ordinary seaman. When the *Orel* shut off her engines in response to the shot across her bow, his party rowed to her side in a whaleboat.

Quite prepared to discover a submarine, or even a small fleet of them, secreted within the *Orel,* Fukuda was in no way prepared for what in fact he did find there. This was a sort of tropical garden installed on her afterdeck, in which luxuriant Madagascan plants of every imaginable variety were growing in a simulated forest glade. Through this glade were laid out scenic paths and trails leading to cozy bowers equipped with picturesque benches. Strolling along the paths or sitting on the benches were several of the ship's complement of nurses, wearing crisp uniforms and accompanied by what looked like completely convalescent officers.

In this peaceful sylvan scene there was only one discordant note. This was the head nurse, who was waiting for Fukuda at the top of the ladder and to whom he was prepared to show the special courtesy appropriate to the trying circumstances. Instead of allowing him to do so with the good manners and docility that could have been expected of a Japanese lady under comparable conditions, the head nurse seemed to think he had come on board to receive a lecture on naval etiquette. Before he could even utter his carefully rehearsed regrets for the necessity of intruding, she launched into a shrill rebuke, first for his impudence in stopping the ship at all and then for his effrontery in coming on board. What made this particularly disconcerting to Fukuda was that the head nurse could speak better, or at least much more voluble, English than he could.

Sending his cook and the other members of the party to conduct a thorough search of the hold, Fukuda tried hard to explain the situation to his unwilling hostess but found it difficult to interrupt her tirade. As this continued, he gradually realized that the *Orel* was not only quite unaware that she had betrayed the presence of the Russian squadron by showing lights on the night of the 26th but unaware even that the result had been a considerable battle—let alone of how that encounter had ended. The ship had stayed so far behind the fleet that, while the head nurse had heard gunfire in the afternoon and seen flashes of light during the following evening, she had taken these for some sort of unusually realistic fleet exercise.

In due course Fukuda also divined that the officers strolling through the tropical garden were not Russians at all but the "half dozen healthy Englishmen" from the *Old-*

hamia, sent to the *Orel* five days before. Their presence gave Fukuda ample reason for taking possession of the *Orel,* in order to examine her cargo more carefully later on. When his search-party, including the head chef, reported no signs of submarines or other illegal cargo in her hold, Fukuda, having ordered the *Orel's* captain to follow the *Sado Maru* to Sasebo, reembarked to return to his own ship in the whaleboat.

At Sasebo, when Fukuda learned that one of the *Orel's* nurses was Admiral Rozhdestvensky's niece, he felt sure this must have been the one he encountered—and that she had patterned her air of command on that of her uncle. Nonetheless, even after he had won his own admiral's stripes some twenty years later, his recollection of his inability to halt or even interrupt her tirade gave the Battle of Tsushima, for him, the mixed character of a national triumph but a personal defeat.

Only when most of the Japanese ships had re-assembled at the great naval base did it become altogether clear just how much of a national triumph for Japan the battle had been, and how complete a defeat for Russia. With consideration appropriate to the victor in such an engagement Togo saw to it that his wounded adversary had the best care that the base hospital afforded and provided him with facilities for reporting to his government. Rozhdestvensky promptly dispatched a telegram:

TO HIS MAJESTY THE CZAR, AT CZARSKOESELO:

ON THE 14TH MAY [27th May N.S.] AT 1:30 P.M., BETWEEN THE SOUTHERN EXTREMITY OF TSUSHIMA AND THE MAINLAND OF JAPAN, WE CAME INTO ACTION WITH THE MAIN FORCE OF THE JAPANESE SQUADRON, CONSISTING OF TWELVE VESSELS, AND THEIR CRUISER SQUADRON, CONSISTING OF NOT LESS THAN TWELVE VESSELS.

AT 2:30 P.M., THE SUVOROV HAD TO LEAVE HER POSITION IN THE FIRING LINE. AT 3:30 P.M. SOME OF THE MEMBERS

OF MY STAFF AND MYSELF WERE TRANSFERRED IN A SENSE-
LESS CONDITION TO THE *Buiny,* ON BOARD OF WHICH WE
FOUND A PORTION OF THE CREW OF THE *Oslyabya,* WHICH
HAD ALREADY BEEN SUNK. I THEN HANDED OVER COMMAND
OF OUR FLEET TO NEBOGATOV. DURING THE NIGHT. . . . I
WAS TAKEN TO THE *Bedovyi.* . . . I THEN LEARNED THAT
ON THE EVENING OF THE 28TH, THE *Bedovyi* SURRENDERED
TO TWO JAPANESE DESTROYERS. ON THE 31ST, I HEARD THAT
NEBOGATOV WAS AT SASEBO.

ROZHDESTVENSKY, AIDE-DE-CAMP TO THE CZAR.

According to legend, Czar Nicholas II, when told of the
outcome of the battle of Tsushima while playing tennis at
his country palace, remarked: "What a terrible disaster!"
and then went on to finish his set. In view of the Czar's
later unhappy fate, this makes a comforting story, but it
happens not to be true. In fact, according to A. A. Moso-
lov, chief of his court secretariat, Nicholas II received the
news while traveling on his Imperial train, absorbed its
true significance at once, sent for War Minister General
Sakharov and had a long discussion with him in which,
according to Sakharov, he "showed that he fully recognized
the problems ahead of us." In any case, by the time he received Rozhdestvensky's cable, the Czar was well aware
both of the magnitude of the defeat and of its meaning. He
sent a generous and sympathetic reply:

I HEARTILY THANK YOU AND ALL THE MEMBERS OF YOUR
SQUADRON WHO HAVE LOYALLY FULFILLED YOUR DUTY IN
BATTLE FOR YOUR SERVICE TO RUSSIA AND MYSELF. IT WAS
GOD'S WILL NOT TO GIVE YOU SUCCESS BUT THE COUNTRY IS
PROUD OF YOUR COURAGE. I WISH YOU A SPEEDY RECOVERY.
MAY GOD CONSOLE ALL OF US.

Telegrams from Admirals Nebogatov and Enquist, however, received no reply.

Togo's official report to his Emperor took somewhat longer to compose, comprising as it did, the entire tale of engagement and destruction. The gist, however, was contained, in the fashion approved by sensible editors the world over, in the very first sentence:

BY THE GRACE OF HEAVEN, OUR COMBINED FLEET HAS SUCCEEDED IN ALMOST COMPLETELY ANNIHILATING THE ENEMY'S SECOND AND THIRD SQUADRONS, WITH WHICH IT FOUGHT IN THE SEA OF JAPAN ON MAY 27TH AND 28TH.

In fact, this was an extremely modest summation. What Togo and his ships had done was to sink six of the enemy's eight battleships and capture the remaining two; sink, capture, or drive into internment twenty-five of his other warships, of which only three of the smallest reached their objective; and accomplish all this at a cost to the Japanese fleet of three torpedo boats.

Enemy ships sunk totalled 146,900 tons, with 58,000 tons more either captured or interned, as against 300 tons sunk for Japan. In terms of human life Japan lost 117 men to Russia's 4830, and took almost 6000 prisoners. In terms of tonnage lost Tsushima was then, and remains now, the biggest battle ever fought by ships on the sea. Even more important than the statistics of men and ships lost were its effects upon history. Among great sea battles, Tsushima may well eventually be judged the most decisive in history, not only in its immediate effects but in its ultimate consequences for the world as a whole.

IX

In the naval hospital at Sasebo, to which he was removed from the *Bedovyi*, Admiral Rozhdestvensky received scrupulous care from Japanese doctors. They extracted the splinter from his skull and, with the help of his niece, who was allowed to be one of his nurses, soon restored him to a condition in which he was well enough to receive callers. One of his first, on June 3, was Admiral Togo.

The meeting between the two Commanders in Chief, in the sparsely furnished room where Rozhdestvensky lay in bed with his head still bandaged, began with an apology from Togo for the austerities of the hospital itself. He explained that this had not been designed for the accomodation of such distinguished patients and went on to pay professional tribute to his recent adversary's prowess in battle which his official biographer has translated as follows:

"There is nothing for a warrior to be ashamed of in an honorable defeat. We fighting men suffer either way, win or lose, and the great point is whether or not we have done our duty. During the battle your men fought most gallantly for two days. I admire them all and you in particular. You performed your great task heroically until you were seriously wounded. You have my sincere respect and I hope you will recover as soon as possible."

"I am not ashamed to have been defeated by you," Rozhdestvensky is reported to have said as the two Commanders in Chief shook hands.

Since Sasebo lacked facilities for quartering six thousand prisoners of war, most of these were sent to an army prison camp near the town of Kumamoto, in Kyushu. A vivid account of their life there, including the bitter altercations between officers and men occasioned by the revolutionary fervor of the latter, was later to be provided by Novikoff-Priboy. Meanwhile, he himself apparently found ample consolation for the rigors of confinement in a fragmentary romance with the sister of a prison-camp interpreter, having struck up a friendship with the latter through their common interest in Russian literature. Early in January, many of the prisoners were repatriated by ship to Vladivostok and the former paymaster's steward of the *Orel* recorded their passage through Tsushima Strait, beneath which lay almost five thousand of their former comrades:

. . . In a violent northerly gale, with a falling barometer, we passed close to the isle of Tsushima. Most of the men mounted to the upper deck. With anguished eyes those who had lost friends and comrades scrutinized the turbulent waters, but there was no trace now of the terrible battle. . . . Someone took off his cap and, as if at the word of command, the others followed his example. For a minute or two we stood in silence, pale and gloomy, listening to the roar of the wind, which seemed to be sobbing over an enormous tomb. . . .

Stoker Baklanov strode to the middle of the deck and, stepping onto a closed hatch, planted himself there firmly. His square-chinned face, moistened by droplets of sea-water, had an expression of self-confidence. He spoke now in a booming bass:

"Dear shipmates of Tsushima, you witnessed here the sad fate of our comrades. Why did they go down to death? Who was to blame? We know well enough. I can't tell how you feel about the matter, but for my part I should like to wring the necks of the guilty and go on with the job so long as my heart continued to beat. Next time we go to war it won't be for the forest of Korea but to win a better sort of life for ourselves. We'll go for the enemies at home. Just as the Japanese sunk our ships here, so will we drown in blood the whole czarist system.

"Bravo!" came the hearty response.

The year 1905 had started for Russia with the "Bloody Sunday" massacre in St. Petersburg. As the progress of the war in the Far East deteriorated, internal dissension increased, and the catastrophe at Tsushima provided further fuel for the flames, which in the meantime were being skilfully fanned by Colonel Akashi. By autumn general strikes, violence, and open insurrection had spread into every corner of Russia and in mid-October an eloquent spokesman named Leon Trotsky led a nationwide strike in which a new organizational unit called the "soviet," or council, was formed, consisting of delegates elected by the proletariat, with one delegate for each thousand workers. The result was the Imperial Manifesto, which, on October 30th, created the first duma, or parliament, and transformed the nation from an absolute monarchy into a constitutional one.

In November, the return of several thousand embittered Tsushima veterans touched off naval mutinies at Kronstadt, the base from which the battleships of the doomed fleet had been launched, and in the Black Sea Squadron. These armed uprisings climaxed the year of revolt and, as a revealing preview of the events that were to follow a decade later, became a proud prelude to the bloody saga of the 1917 revolution. During the nineteen-thirties, movie audiences all over the world were to writhe with horror at the most gruesome scene in Eisenstein's *Potemkin*, in which sadistic officers had a tarpaulin placed over a group of rebellious sailors, who were then subjected to gradual massacre by gunfire. In fact, this scene was a perhaps superfluous embellishment by the celebrated director of what had actually occurred: execution of the rebel sailors on *top* of the tarpaulin, of which the purpose was to prevent their blood from staining the wooden planks of the deck.

During the winter of 1906, there took place in St. Petersburg the court-martial of the officers charged with handing over their ships to the Japanese, including Admiral Rozhdestvensky. The latter, though exonerated for his part in the surrender of the *Bedovyi*, on the ground that he was unconscious when it occurred, insisted on being tried with his former staff officers, also accepting as his the blame for the surrender of Nebogatov's four ships.

True to his promise on May 28th, Nebogatov did his own best to shoulder the onus for the surrender: "I alone lowered the flag, and I myself had raised the signal to surrender. And whatever may have been said with regard to the protests made by officers against the surrender, I can only say that I would not have allowed any such protests."

Seemingly anxious to avoid incriminating the government ministers in St. Petersburg, who were in fact mainly to blame, while at the same time satisfying the public demand for some sort of scapegoats, the court handed down severe verdicts. Both Nebogatov and Clapier de Colongue were sentenced to death and, though these sentences were later commuted by the Czar, both served long terms in prison, as did several other members of Rozhdestvensky's staff. Rozhdestvensky himself—possibly because he was better informed than the rest of the defendants as to the maladministration and corruption within the Ministry of Marine—was let off lightly with dismissal from the service for "failure to perform his duty". He lived on in obscure retirement for three years more, and died in January of 1909.

Meanwhile, in Japan, events took a different but in some ways perhaps more surprising turn. While the victory at Tsushima would theoretically have made possible further incursions on the continent of Asia, all that the Japanese army attempted during the early summer of 1905 was an invasion of the Russian island of Sakhalin, to which Russia could offer no substantial resistance. In fact, the situation was one wherein economics rather than communications dominated war: since neither belligerent had the cash for further military outlays or immediate means of raising additional foreign loans, an end to the hostilities became more or less inevitable. All that was needed was an appropriate mediator.

Since Britain had been an open ally of Japan and both France and Germany had assisted her enemy, no major nation in Europe was equipped to fulfill this role. In the U.S., however, Theodore Roosevelt, after serving three and a half years of the term of his late predecessor, had just been inaugurated as President in his own right, and the prestige thus acquired put him in an ideal position to act as peacemaker. At the instigation of both the Kaiser, who intimated that he was speaking for the Czar, and of the Japanese Ambassador in Washington, who was undoubtedly speaking for his Emperor, Roosevelt proposed a conference in the U.S., to which both sides agreed. Since Washington in August was too hot, the site chosen was the quiet little New England resort of Portsmouth, N.H., named after the British harbor where Togo had gone to naval training school aboard the *Worcester*.

Actually, the U.S. interest in mediation as interpreted by T.R. was by no means wholly altruistic. While he had been hoping for a Japanese victory that would curb Russian expansion in Manchuria, he was far from eager to have Japan replace Russia as a threat in the Far East; and he also suspected that, if Russia were to be completely removed from the situation, the power vacuum represented by the Manchu regime in Peking might encourage such intense European competition to carve up the remains of China as to result in a world war, along the lines of the one that was to develop from different causes a decade later. Keeping such considerations to himself, the President got the conference off to a good start with a luncheon—at a round table designed to obviate questions of social precedence—on board the presidential yacht in Oyster Bay, attended by the representatives of both sides. These were the two chief Plenipotentiaries, Former Finance Minister Sergius Witte for Russia and Foreign Minister Marquis Jutaro Komura for Japan, each assisted by his nation's envoy in Washington.

The issue upon which the conference nearly broke up was Russia's refusal (a) to cede the island of Sakhalin and (b) to pay a substantial indemnity, on the ground that to do either would be "beneath the dignity of a great power." T. R. proposed that this dilemma be solved by Russia's ceding Sakhalin but buying from Japan the right to retain the northern half, thus avoiding an "indemnity" and giving up only half the territory demanded by the victor. In the treaty eventually signed on September 5th Japan acquired the southern portion of Sakhalin but got no monetary compensation for relinquishing her claim to the remainder. Witte, who understandably regarded the treaty as a substantial diplomatic victory and was rewarded with a title for his part in achieving it, attributed Marquis Komura's acceptance of the final terms to an attack of indigestion, caused by his over-indulgence in the unassimilable food served by the local hotel.

By the terms of the Portsmouth Treaty, what Japan thus finally got, in addition to half of an island then considered of little economic or strategic value, was the Liaotung Peninsula, including Port Arthur, which it had already won once before in 1894, and Russia's promise to honor at last her previous promise to evacuate Manchuria, while recognizing Japan's special interests in Korea. These seemed a scanty reward indeed for her smashing victory in a war that had cost her a quarter of a million men and half a billion borrowed dollars. In Japan—where Russia's capacity to resume hostilities on land was under-estimated—publication of the treaty aroused widespread resentment, in large part shared by the navy, including its Commander in Chief.

On September 10, some days before Rozhdestvensky had even departed for home and only a month before a gala naval review that had been scheduled in honor of the victory, a sudden fire broke out on board the *Mikasa*. Reaching the after magazine before the flames could be brought under control, it caused an explosion that killed 590 members of the flagship's crew and ripped a 90-foot gap in the ship's side, sending her to the bottom of the harbor. That Togo was not among the dead—five times more numerous than the fleet's entire losses at Tsushima—was due to the chance that he had gone ashore for a visit to Tokyo earlier the same day. Whether the explosion on board the *Mikasa* was an accident caused by the spontaneous combustion of the highly volatile and over-heated Shimose ammunition, as decided by the Navy Minister's official investigation, or the result of a misguided act of protest on the part of some unbalanced seaman has never—like the cause of the explosion on the U.S. battleship *Maine* a few years earlier—been incontrovertibly determined. In any case, the tragedy was widely regarded in Japan as an appropriately symbolic expression of the nation's reaction to a peace treaty that failed lamentably to justify the sacrifices made during the war.

Despite the absence of the *Mikasa*, a gigantic naval review in honor of the fleet's contribution in general and the final victory in particular was held as scheduled a few weeks later, starting on October 21, the exact centenary of Trafalgar. Received at court by the Emperor, Admiral Togo read aloud his report of the entire war, from Port Arthur through the climax at Tsushima. The next day the Emperor reviewed the fleet in Tokyo Bay, where 160 warships were drawn up in orderly array, with Togo at his elbow on the deck of the now fully restored *Asama*, to explain what each ship, division or flotilla had done during the various engagements. The victory celebration ended with rites held at the Aoyama Cemetery, to honor the sailors who had failed to return with their ships.

Two months later, following the precedent whereby Admiral Ito had become Chief of the Naval Staff after his victory in the Sino-Japanese War, Togo replaced his former commander in that administrative post. Before taking his permanent departure from sea duty, he delivered a formal address to his officers on board the *Asahi*, now flying his flag. In effect a condensed version of his lifetime philosophy, generously seasoned with his favorite military maxims, this address so deeply impressed President Roosevelt, among others, that he had it distributed in full to both the U.S. Army and Navy in the form of a General Order, with an introduction in which he stated: "In the recent war in the East, Admiral Togo took his place among the greatest sea-fighters of all time." Said Togo, in part:

The war of twenty months' duration is now a thing of the past, and our United Squadron, having completed its functions, is to be herewith dispersed. But our duties as naval men are not at all lightened for that reason. To preserve in perpetuity the fruits of this war, to promote, to an ever greater height of prosperity, the fortunes of the country, the Navy, which, irrespective of peace or war, has to stand between the Empire and shocks from abroad, must always maintain its strength at sea and must be prepared to meet any emergency. This strength does not consist solely in ships and armament; it consists also in immaterial ability to utilize such agents. When we understand that one gun which scores a hundred percent of hits is a match for a hundred of the enemy's guns each of which scores only one percent, it becomes evident that we sailors must have recourse before everything to the strength which is over and above externals. . . .

If, keeping the instructions of our Sovereign ever graven on our hearts, we serve earnestly and diligently, and putting forth our full strength await what the hour may bring forth, we shall then have discharged our great duty of perpetually guarding our country. Heaven gives the crown of victory to those only who by habitual preparation win without fighting, and at the same time forthwith deprives of that crown those who, content with one success, give themselves up to the ease of peace. The ancients well said: "Tighten your helmet strings in the hour of victory."

In Japan, increasing faith in sea power, accompanied by an undertow of disappointment in diplomacy, and in Russia, increasing social unrest, accompanied by an undertow of bureaucratic alarm, were the first far-reaching ripples set in motion by the battle of Tsushima. Others were soon discernible elsewhere, including the United States, where President Roosevelt, all the more because of his admiration for the martial virtues of Japan as exemplified by Admiral Togo, was quick to see the implications for the Western hemisphere in Japan's new role as a major world power. In his own estimation the most significant single accomplishment of his presidency was the construction of a Panama Canal to confer, among other benefits, that of enabling the U.S. fleet to get from one ocean to the other without circumnavigating Cape Horn. Meanwhile, it seemed to T.R. prudent to demonstrate to all concerned that for the U.S. Navy, unlike Russia's, a voyage not merely halfway around the world but all the way around it presented so few problems that it could be regarded merely as a sort of extended fleet exercise. The last dramatic act of his second term, accordingly, was to send the Great White Fleet on a global goodwill tour, on which the first important stopover was Yokohama.

In Russia, restored to a shaky equilibrium by the convening of the first duma in 1906, the consequences of Tsushima continued to be felt in many ways, including their influence upon a complex crisis that arose the next summer involving the Serbian province of Bosnia. Russia's Foreign Minister by that time was Alexander Izvolsky, who, convinced of the futility of Russia's efforts to expand in the Far East, thought he saw a way to make progress in another direction and closer to home. This was to arrange a secret deal with Austria-Hungary whereby, in return for support of a move to make Turkey open the Dardanelles to Russian warships, Russia would refrain from opposing a simultaneous Austro-Hungarian annexation of Bosnia, despite the fact that Serbia was theoretically a Russian ally.

Where this interesting scheme went wrong was that Austria-Hungary coolly accomplished the annexation of Bosnia long before Russia was ready to execute its part in the plot. Far too depleted by her defeat in 1905 to attempt more than a face-saving gesture, Russia nonetheless felt obliged to assemble some troops on the Serbian border. This resulted in a direct confrontation with Germany, which, as the ally of Austria-Hungary, threatened immediate intervention on her behalf unless Russia backed down promptly and completely. At this point the real feelings of Kaiser Wilhelm II, the self-styled "Admiral of the Atlantic," who had so blithely encouraged his cousin, the "Admiral of the Pacific," in his Far Eastern foray, became painfully apparent in the tone of a note transmitted by the latter's ambassador in St. Petersburg: "We expect a precise answer, yes or no. Any vague, complicated or ambiguous reply will be regarded as a refusal."

This blunt ultimatum left its recipient—who was patently incapable of making war of any sort, let alone of taking on the strongest military power in Europe—no alternative but shamefaced compliance. According to the British Ambassador to St. Petersburg, "In the recent history of Russia there has never previously been a moment when the country has undergone such humiliation and, though Russia has had her troubles and trials both external and internal and has suffered defeats in the field, she has never . . . had to submit to the dictation of a foreign power." Czar Nicholas II, in a letter to his mother, referred to his chastisement more succinctly: "German action toward us has simply been brutal and we shall not forget it."

Any chance that the Czar might have been allowed to forget it was permanently dispelled seven years later by a second Serbian crisis, this one caused by the assassination of Austria's Grand Duke Ferdinand at Sarajevo. Now, when Austria-Hungary, backed by Germany, presented her ultimatum to Serbia, and when the latter again turned to the Czar for help, he had England and France on his side and reacted accordingly. As perhaps implied by Robert K. Massie in his fine biography *Nicholas and Alexandra,* it may be permissible to speculate that, without Tsushima and Russia's consequent humiliation in 1907, there might have been some chance for a compromise between Russia and Germany in 1914, whereby World War I might have been avoided or at least postponed. As things stood, the second Serbian crisis provided the Czar's pitifully shortsighted ministers with what looked like a priceless chance to even old scores. Alexander Izvolsky, architect of the first crisis, was by 1914 Russia's ambassador to France. "This is my war! My war!" he exulted that August.

Better established than the degree to which Tsushima may have been a contributing cause of World War I—and its concurrent upheavals in Russia—was Tshushima's obvious influence upon the strategy and tactics adopted by the navies involved therein. By 1914 the lesson inferred from Togo's superior gunnery and superior speed had helped to accelerate the development, first by the British navy under Lord John Fisher and later by others, of battleships of the *Dreadnaught* type, armed with no guns smaller than 8-inch and capable of speeds of over 20 knots. By the same token, Togo's destruction of a great fleet in the course of one afternoon had impressed upon both Germany and Britain, whose very existence depended on the Royal Navy, the importance of tactical caution.

No major encounter between the British and German fleets occurred until May 31st, 1916, just eleven years after Tsushima, when they met at Jutland. A victory for either side comparable to Togo's at Tsushima might conceivably have ended World War I that afternoon just as decisively as Togo had ended Japan's war with Russia a decade before, but nothing of the sort occured. Britain's fleet enjoyed a three-to-two advantage in ships and gunpower, and the 171,000 tons of warship sunk at Jutland were divided between the two fleets in roughly that ratio, with no ships either captured or interned. While counted as a tactical victory for England, since the German fleet withdrew from the action, the result was in effect a draw, since, per-haps due to Jellico's reluctance to try to pursue and de-stroy it, the latter remained a threat till the end of the war.

Through the renewal of her alliance with Britain, signed only a few days after the Portsmouth Treaty, Japan fought on the side of the Allies in World War I. With the enemy's battle fleet confined to Europe, this gave her an opportunity to even her own old scores with Germany for the latter's conduct at Shimonoseki in 1895 and, unlike Russia, she was able to take full advantage of the chance. German interests in China centered on the splendid port of Kiaochow, considered by some naval experts the most valuable on the entire coast of China. By November of 1914 Japan had taken possession of it, along with the city of Tsingtao, later to serve as a springboard for post-war inroads on the mainland, after an ultimatum couched in the same terms as those used by Germany in 1895. By the war's end she was also in possession of the several hundred German islands in the Pacific, later entrusted to her ease under a League of Nations Mandate.

After the war, Japan's status as one of the world's three greatest naval powers was officially recognized in the 5–5–3 ratio agreed upon by the Washington Disarmament Conference of 1922, giving Britain and the U.S. parity in first place. What made Japan's smaller share ample for her purposes was both her position of lonely eminence on the far side of the Pacific and the fact that, in the era of pacifi-cism and isolationism that followed, the U.S. neglected to build up to her assigned limit. Thus, between 1922 and 1930, Japan built 334 warships of all sorts, totalling 334,091 tons, while the U.S.—with incomparably greater financial resources—was building 21 ships of 115,120 tons, which included only 8 of the 15 battleships allowed her. Ten years later, Japan's naval strength was roughly equal to that of the U.S., a circumstance that had a significant bearing on events that ensued.

Even more noteworthy than the repercussions of Tsushima on naval developments during and after the First World War were their effect on Japan's foreign policy during the decades that followed it. During the 1920s, two conflicting theories contended for acceptance by Japan's politicians and public. One was the traditional line that the nation's prosperity, if not its actual survival, depended on the aquisition by conquest of a colonial empire like Britain's to provide both the raw materials that the home island lacked and a preferential market for the finished products that these materials would enable her to make. This theory had by that time been confirmed and encouraged not only by Tsushima but also, and even more convincingly, by the subsequent annexation of Korea, which had been successfully completed in 1910. The opposite theory was that Japan, now universally recognized as one of the world's great maritime powers, had by this time gone about as far as she needed to go by force of arms and that she should henceforth make progress primarily by building up foreign export markets through the application of diplomatic and industrial skills. This theory, supported by the influential zaibatsu, held its own until the onset of the world-wide Depression, when the imposition of protective tariffs in the U.S. and elsewhere made its continued application seem impractical.

During the early 1930s Japan's militaristic expansionists acquired zaibatsu support in the "Manchurian Incident" of 1931, whereby Japan took over Manchuria at no greater cost than a scolding from the League of Nations. Somewhat paradoxically, it was the army that, thus encouraged, took the lead in expansionism thereafter, while the more internationally sophisticated navy tried to act as a restraining influence. The restraint proved ineffective and by the end of the decade the army's aim of insuring national security by means of foreign conquest had become so thoroughly accepted that any other policy was regarded as not merely unsound but treasonable. In conformity with this, Japan launched her drive to create a "Far East Co-Prosperity Sphere" by means of the expanded China campaign, which was still in progress when World War II started in 1939.

The outbreak of World War II seemed, under the circumstances, to provide Japan with a unique chance to carry her then current aggression to a successful conclusion. In the first place, the European powers that might have tried to impede her efforts were fully engaged in fighting Nazi Germany. In the second place, the U.S., which was soon lending these powers naval support, seemed much too concerned with Europe to attempt to police the other side of the world as well. What abruptly changed the picture and confronted Japan with a decision even more fateful than that of going to war with Russia in 1904 was the sudden and unexpected U.S. refusal in July of 1941 to go on selling her the oil and scrap iron upon which the Japanese economy was largely dependent.

The tactical similarity between Japan's surprise attack on Pearl Harbor and her previous opening gambit at Port Arthur was so dramatically conspicuous that it has perhaps helped to distract attention from the even more significant resemblance between the policy decisions that lay behind both events. Like Imperial Russia in 1904, the U.S. considered Japan so far inferior in size and power that any possibility of her taking the initiative in starting a war seemed out of the question. When, just as Prince Ito had gone to St. Petersburg in 1903, Saburo Kurusu came to Washington in 1941 to try to get the embargo lifted, this seemed to corroborate the impression that for Japan to attempt any other sort of solution was wildly improbable.

Just as Prince Ito had done in 1903, Japan's emissaries in the U.S. in 1941 soon reached the conclusion that, far from really intending to reach some sort of workable compromise, their adversary meant to use the negotiations as a means of effecting delay that would be to Japan's military detriment. In the Japanese view of international ethics, employing diplomacy to gain military advantage amounts in itself to an act of war and invites an openly warlike reprisal. The question that arose in Tokyo was, therefore, whether to accept the embargo or to start a war that, even more clearly than that of 1904, would be an all-or-nothing gamble.

In 1904 Japan was gambling that by going to war at once instead of waiting until Russia was also ready to do so a year later, her Army and Navy would be able to bring off a carefully timed strategical sequence. First, the Navy would seize command of the sea; then the Army could occupy the requisite terrain; and with this accomplished, the Navy would be free to defeat any reinforcements that the enemy might bring to bear later on. In 1941 the intended sequence was almost identical. By knocking out the U.S. fleet at Pearl Harbor Japan would be able to control the Pacific; this control would enable her armies to take possession of the oil and other resources she needed; and with these in hand, she could hold her gains against any reinforcements that the U.S. might send out later. The major difference between the two gambles was that the stakes in the second were immeasurably bigger. This time victory would mean permanent aquisition of China and all Southeast Asia—that is to say, the greatest empire in world history, measured by either area or population—while defeat would presumably mean national annihilation. Japan, promptly and characteristically, took the gamble.

There were, of course, two additional differences, which

were much less perceptible. The first of these was that Japan's naval Commander in Chief in World War II, though his forces flew Togo's Zed flag as they approached Pearl Harbor, was not Togo but the former Ensign Isoroku Yamamoto, who had lost the first and second fingers of his left hand at Tsushima. Unrelated to either Gombei, Eisuke, or Jyotaro Yamamoto, Isoroku was, like Togo, a gambler prepared to take tremendous risks when the occasion demanded. Experience as a naval attaché in Washington during the twenties had convinced Yamamoto that, to win a war against the U.S., Japan would have to be prepared to go on fighting until she could, as he put it, "dictate the peace treaty in the White House"—a statement later twisted for propaganda purposes into a statement of Japan's intentions—and he had accordingly devised an opening gambit patterned directly on Port Arthur. Unlike Togo, however, Yamamoto was inclined to be careless about tying his helmet strings after a victory. A long succession of victories had in fact preceded the Battle of Midway in May of 1942, and it was there that he allowed overconfidence to mislead him. Instead of finishing off the U.S. Pacific Fleet, as he had planned and expected to do, thus giving the army a year or more in which to consolidate its holdings in Southeast Asia and the Pacific Islands, he lost the battle and with it, the war.

There was, of course, one other reason why, even if Yamamoto had won at Midway, Japan might still have lost the war in the long run. Because the facial differences between any two Chinese inevitably seem to any Occidental less conspicuous than the facial differences between any Chinese and any Caucasian, Occidentals often draw the false conclusion that all Chinese look alike—and Orientals often make the same mistake in regard to Occidentals. By a similar illusion on a much larger scale, the Japanese perhaps drew from Tsushima the thoroughly false conclusion that, because one huge Western power rent by internal dissension had proved hopelessly ineffective in war, another western power, superficially similar in several respects, would be similarly feckless and impractical. In effect, the Japanese may have mistaken the U.S. in 1941 for Russia in 1905—a confusion in identity which, while it had grievous results for them while the hostilities lasted, was perhaps what later on helped to make defeat even more advantageous than the grandiose victory for which they had hoped.

What Tsushima eventually led to in short was, for Japan, the first complete military disaster in her long history, followed by six years of occupation by a nation in many ways more antithetical to her than any other on the face of the globe. The result of all this, however, was not the national annihilation that might have been expected but a process of education and adjustment complementary to that started by Perry almost a century earlier. Forcibly prevented from conquering one corner of the world and squeezing a marginal prosperity therefrom, the U.S. Occupation helped Japan to achieve an immeasurably greater prosperity by using her remarkable talents to make all sorts of peaceful economic conquests all over the face of the globe.

To say that Tsushima was perhaps the most decisive sea battle ever fought in its ultimate as well as in its immediate consequences is not then to suggest that the former were in any way those envisaged by the victors. On the contrary, the encounter illustrates, perhaps better than any comparable engagement, the truism that Time is the wild card in the historical pack; and that only the most primary and short-range results of even the most seemingly conclusive events can be predicted with any assurance whatever.

When Togo ran up his Zed flag he was certainly correct in asserting that the fate of the nation depended on the outcome of the engagement to which it referred. Even more surely, however, he can have had no conception of just how that fate would be worked out, through a much greater defeat in a much greater war. And certainly neither Togo nor Colonel Akashi could have foreseen that one indirect result of Japan's victory would be that the Communist revolution so precociously encouraged by the latter, would eventually transform Russia into one of the world's two super-powers, and as such much more of a threat to Japan's new-found prosperity in 1969 than she was in 1905.

While the eventual effects of Tsushima in the political history of the participants are by definition largely conjectural and wholly insusceptible to any sort of proof, its effects on the history of the world as a whole have perhaps been at once less questionable and more profound. As the twentieth century moves into its final quarter, it seems increasingly possible that its most noteworthy achievement, and the global change by which it will be identified in the history books of a thousand years hence—if such books are then still being composed—may be simply the emergence of Asia from European domination and the consequent integration of Eastern and Western civilizations on a basis of political parity.

The revolutions in China; the emergence of India from colonial status as a unified subcontinent rather than a collection of squabbling principalities; the revolt of the vast Indonesian archipelago from rule by the Netherlands; the emergence as independent states of Burma, Ceylon, Malaysia, and the Philippines; and finally the upheavals in what was formerly French Indo-China, which are still going on in what are now Cambodia, Laos, and Vietnam, can all to some extent be ascribed—though of course to varying degrees and for varying reasons—to what occurred on that May afternoon early in the century at the entrance to the

Japan Sea. The victory there of one small Asian nation over a European empire that was the biggest on earth in less than an hour demolished forever the long-standing fallacy that there was some qualitative disparity between Asians and Europeans; or rather, it suggested that, if there were such a disparity, it favored the former.

Of the scores of warships that fought at Tsushima and survived the battle, most have long since been scrapped, sunk, or otherwise demolished. The *Shinano Maru,* whose discovery of the Russian fleet started the battle, eventually became a crab-fishing ship in the Bering Sea and, after outlasting World War II, was scrapped in the mid-fifties. A ten-year struggle, costing upward of $100,000, to extract a stock of gold bullion reportedly sunk with the cruiser *Nakhimov* resulted finally in the recovery of the ship's safe, which contained nothing of value. While three of the Russian prizes were restored to her during World War I, most of the rest of these wound up as targets for Japanese gunners and pilots in the twenties and thirties. The only survivor of the battle still extant and on view is the most famous of all—and the one that sank first. Raised from the mud of Sasebo harbor nine months after the 1905 explosion, Togo's flagship *Mikasa* was later moored at Yokosuka, like Nelson's *Victory* at Portsmouth, as a national monument.

During the post-World War II Occupation, most remnants and relics of Japan's expansionist era were laboriously destroyed by the idealistic U.S. visitors, apparently under some euphoric delusion that this would discourage the aggressive instinct among the Japanese and thus, by mystic osmosis, engender World Peace. Owing largely to more polite and more practical efforts on the part of U.S. naval authorities including former Commander in Chief for the Pacific Chester W. Nimitz and Former Chief of

Naval Operations Arleigh Burke, the *Mikasa* was made an exception to this process. Now moored in concrete, she remains at what is currently the U.S. naval base at Yokosuka as an appropriate object of veneration for Japanese school-children and historically-minded foreign visitors. On view between her decks, on which paint marks show the incidence of shell hits during the Russo-Japanese war, are such mementos as Togo's Zeiss binoculars, the original Zed flag, and the white linen handkerchief on which Captain Ijichi inscribed the names of his ship's dead. In what used to be the area of the crew's mess hall, a waist-high glass-covered exhibition case some twelve feet square encloses a miniaturization of the opening phases of the Tsushima Battle, including the famous U-turn. Now, at the flick of a switch, two dozen tiny vessels manuever across a green fiber-board sea where simulated gunfire and shell splashes make the reenacted encounter look rather the way the real one must have looked to Ichisaburo Sato from the branch of his tree on Okinoshima, where, as of this writing, he still resides.

While the *Mikasa* is the only ship that still survives Tsushima, many of the human participants in the engagement proved considerably more durable than their vessels. Most notable of these was Togo himself, who, born in the age of sail, outlived that of steam and then that of surface vessels as the major embodiment of sea power. Togo survived Tsushima by more than twenty-nine years, or almost as long again as the entire period of his service in the Japanese Navy after his return from schooling in England. When, at the age of eighty-seven, he was asked by a reporter whether he still felt capable of commanding a fleet in an action at sea, he calmly replied, "I might have some trouble getting up on the bridge but, once there, I believe I could do so."

Far from being spent in well-earned leisure, most of the

years that immediately followed his great victory were extremely active ones for Togo. They did, however, inevitably include an extensive round of ceremonials and an unparalleled harvest of international honors, starting with the award of the Order of the Garter in 1906. Later that year Togo, General Nogi, and War Minister Oyama also received the British Order of Merit, a group limited to two dozen members, of whom not even one had ever before been a foreigner.

Togo's subsequent array of medals soon came to exceed the severely limited expanse provided by his dress tunic, and at the time of his death the collection was such that twelve officers were needed to carry them at his state funeral. Among his more noteworthy Japanese distinctions were titles in the peerage, first of Count and later of Marquis; the Order of the Golden Kite, First Class; and the Grand Order of the Chrysanthemum, with Collar, of which one of the royal princes was the only other possessor. Even more significant than such public distinctions were Togo's promotions in court rank, climaxed in 1933 by the honor of being permitted to carry a cane while in the presence of the Mikado. Long before this, Togo's prestige at Court had become such that at formal receptions he had to sit all alone, since there was no one of sufficiently exalted rank, including even the remaining *genro*, or elder statesmen, to share his table.

In 1911 Togo and General Nogi were chosen to represent Japan at the coronation of King George V, an occasion that coincided appropriately with the date fixed for renewal of the 1905 Anglo-Japanese Alliance. This time the Admiral reached England traveling in State aboard a Japanese liner on whose deck he and his old comrade in arms passed much of their time playing go. The high point of Togo's sojourn in England was a dinner given for him by the Worcester Association, composed of the alumni of his old training ship, to whom he gave a brief, nostalgic address. Not present was Captain Thomas Ryder Galsworthy, formerly the commander of the *Kowshing* and himself a graduate of the *Worcester* two years after Togo, who had tactfully declined to serve on the reception committee on the grounds that his presence might embarrass the guest of honor.

On his way home from the coronation, Togo displayed his own sense of tact by not journeying through Russia, as did General Nogi, but instead through the U.S. and Canada. The high points of his brief stop in the U.S. were a banquet at the White House, whose occupant by then was William Howard Taft; a visit to the alma mater of Admiral Uriu, Commander Akiyama, and other Tsushima comrades at Annapolis; and a lunch with former President Theodore Roosevelt at Oyster Bay on August 13th. The meeting between the hero of Tsushima and the architect of the Portsmouth Peace Conference, which had convened almost exactly six years before, went off splendidly until after lunch, when they sat down on the porch for a postprandial chat. To T.R. this seemed an ideal moment to show his guest a sword presented to him by the Emperor Meiji, but when Togo drew the blade from its scabbard he was shocked to find it marred by numerous rust spots.

Realizing that these blemishes were the result of Occidental ignorance rather than intentional disrespect, Togo nonetheless felt obliged to instruct his host as to the character of any samurai sword, let alone one conferred by the Mikado himself. In his somewhat halting English he explained that such a weapon is a symbol of the owner's honor and must at all times be completely immaculate. Properly speaking, such a sword should be cleaned only with a certain kind of oil applied with a certain kind of cloth but, using the closest equivalents available at Sagamore Hill, Togo proceeded to polish up what to him was his host's most precious possession. Only when the sword had been restored to pristine brightness did the Admiral feel it permissible to take leave of the suitably chastened T.R., who later conveyed the gist of his guest's admonitions to the members of his family.

Not long after the reunion of Togo and Nogi in Japan there occurred the event that caused their final separation: the death of the Emperor on July 30th, 1912, which, for Nogi, had a special significance. He felt, that since he owed to the Emperor his reprieve from the obligation to end his life in 1875, the debt had now come due, and that it required prompt payment. Nogi and his wife discharged it together by quietly committing ceremonial seppuku in their home a few days later.

Togo's obligation to his late ruler, while equally profound, was of a totally different order. By continuing to live he was enabled to take over what had been General Nogi's prime duty during his last years, that of supervising the education of the Mikado's grandson and eventual heir, who now, at the age of eleven, had become the Crown Prince. As President of the Office for the Crown Prince's Studies, Togo was less a full-time personal mentor, as Nogi had been, than a kind of headmaster, traveling companion, and surrogate uncle. He indoctrinated the heir to the throne with his theories of duty, honor, and national preparedness, meanwhile also encouraging a love of the sea. In his royal protégé this took the form, not of any special concern with the Navy, but of an enduring devotion to the study of marine biology, in which by 1968 Emperor Hirohito, no longer a deity, had achieved international prestige among his scholarly colleagues.

After the accession of the Crown Prince, first to the position of regent on behalf of his mentally unbalanced father and then of Emperor in his own right in 1926, Togo gradually retired from official duties and public life. Too old now for the boar-hunting and bird-shooting that had been his pastimes in the earlier years of his retirement, he was also afflicted by internal ailments that impeded the consumption of the sake which he had previously enjoyed so much that one of his favorite non-belligerent maxims was "No teetotaler can be a really capable man."

In Japan's violent political upheavals during the 1930s, Togo took no part whatever, except on one occasion. Just after a band of young naval officers had assassinated Prime Minister Inukai, in the spring of 1932, he was asked for a comment on the Navy's proper role in national politics, and provided a characteristically Delphic reply: "All of the officers of the Imperial Navy must be prudent in speech and action." At his modest residence near the Yasakuni Shrine Togo continued, as had been his lifelong habit, to darn his own socks and sew buttons on his own shirts, played go with one or two old cronies and neighbors, and devoted much of the time to pruning the roses in his small garden with a well-burnished pair of sharp garden scissors.

In the spring of 1934 Togo was found to be suffering, in addition to his other ailments, from cancer of the throat. There was serious doubt as to whether he could survive until the anniversary of Tsushima, but he managed to do so and on May 28th, the anniversary of Nebogatov's surrender, received his elevation to the rank of Marquis. Such honors are customarily received in full regalia at the palace. Togo, unable to rise, had the appropriate uniform laid across his bed. In deference to the occasion his wife, who was also mortally ill, was carried into his room for the presentation ceremony. It was there that they bade each other the last of their many farewells. On the afternoon of

May 30th Togo spoke his final words, which were: "I am thinking of my Emperor—and of roses." Shortly thereafter he fell into a coma and died at seven o'clock the next morning. Buried with him, after the state funeral five days later, were his favorite pruning shears.

Epilogue

No less durable than Togo himself were many of the men in his fleet, and these included a score or so of his junior officers and seamen with whom I had the good fortune to be able to converse during the summer of 1967, while gathering material for this book. Two members of the group, it developed, had been not merely on the *Mikasa* but actually on the flagship's forebridge with the Commander in Chief when he sent up the Zed flag and gave the hand signal for the famous turn. They were Ensign Kiyoshi Hasegawa and Junior Lieutenant Shinjiro Imamura, both of whom subsequently became admirals and both of whom appear in Shotaro Togo's classic painting of the scene, though to a somewhat curtailed extent. In a composition obviously influenced by rank and seniority, Lieutenant Imamura is shown standing well to the rear with his features largely concealed by a pair of binoculars. Ensign Hasegawa, as the most junior of all those present, is represented, even further in the background merely by his cap, his face being entirely masked by the broad range finder through which, in accord with his duties, he can be presumed to be peering.

The first of the Tsushima veterans whom I approached —not without some diffidence, since he had reached the advanced age of ninety-four—was Rear Admiral Ichiro Fukuda, the former lieutenant on the *Sado Maru* who searched the hospital ship *Orel* for concealed submarines and was rebuked for so doing by its head nurse. When I asked over the telephone whether I could call on him at his house, Admiral Fukuda replied that he would prefer to call on me at my hotel. He explained that he took a three-mile constitutional every morning and would welcome an excuse to vary the route of his walk.

While Admiral Fukuda was the senior member of the group of officers with whom I spoke, his exuberant vitality set the pattern for the rest. Vice Admiral Toyokazu Wanami, who as a twenty-year-old midshipman on the *Fuso* had extracted the sealed orders from the bamboo pole handed up from the despatch boat, was kind enough to join me for a lunch at which, over cocktails, he told me that he had climbed Mount Fuji for the first time a few days before. Not long afterward his contemporary, Vice Admiral Kaoru Matsushita, who at Tsushima had been a gunnery lieutenant in charge of a 12-inch turret on the *Shikishima,* made light of this mountaineering accomplishment by his good friend and colleague. He explained that he had climbed Fuji on numerous occasions, most recently the year before, but found the pastime too monotonous for annual repetition. He then added that he planned to make his next ascent in 1970, to celebrate turning ninety.

Possibly the liveliest of all the Tsushima veterans I was to encounter was Vice Admiral Takeshi Terashima, who, also on the *Shikishima,* as an assistant navigating officer with the rank of ensign, was later to serve in Japan's

World War II cabinet in the capacity of Minister of Communications and Railroads. Many Japanese naval officers —unlike most of their compatriots—are confirmed whisky drinkers in a tradition doubtless dating back to the first naval cadets who were sent to England for training, but Admiral Terashima introduced me to what, so far as I was aware, was a thoroughly novel manner of splicing the main brace.

When I called at his house early one torrid afternoon, the Admiral took me into his library, where a dutiful maid promptly brought in the traditional cups of green tea. Rather to my surprise, instead of drinking his, Admiral Terashima got up from the sofa on which he was sitting, sprang onto a stool by the wall, and, from the top of a cupboard next to it, snatched down a bottle of Johnny Walker, the contents of which he splashed into our tea in generous measure. After downing two cups of this exhilarating blend during the course of an hour's chat, I deemed it best to take my leave while still able to do so unaided but, with a gesture of authority that admitted no question, the Admiral motioned me to be reseated, meanwhile himself rising again to press a service bell that set off a clangor reminiscent of the signal for general quarters on an aircraft carrier. When the maidservant re-entered the room to receive her orders a few seconds later, the admiral uttered a terse command: *"Biru, biru!"* thus causing her to vanish and return in a flash with two quart bottles of beer. Not until we had each finished off these ample chasers did our interview come to its convivial conclusion.

No less hardy than these retired admirals were such durable seamen at Seiichi Goto, the gunner's mate who had been closest of all in the Japanese fleet to the Russians when the fight began, and Signalman Jinzaemon Takizawa, who a few moments earlier had raised the famous Zed flag. Takizawa, in recalling the later events of the afternoon, omitted to say anything whatever about his own wound from a shell splinter that opened a deep cut on his hand. When questioned on this subject he dismissed it as too trifling to mention. Gunner's mate Goto, in describing the appearance of the biggest incoming shells, comparable to those that the Russian officers described as "portmanteaus" used a significantly different metaphor. "As they flew over us," he said, "the Russian shells looked as big as rice bags."

With Gunner Goto when we talked was his young grandson, who—as could be readily deduced from the intensity with which he listened—had grown up in the generation of Japanese schoolboys reared under the Occupation-induced policy of ignoring Japan's military history in its entirety. To attempt to teach the history of any nation without reference to war is surely as misleading as it would be to teach it without reference to peace; and in Japan's naval pantheon Togo clearly merits restoration to a niche analogous to that of Nelson in England's. However, the Battle of Tsushima may have received less attention than it deserves not only from the present generation of Japanese school-children but from the rest of the world as well. It was for this reason that it seemed worthwhile to try to tell the story once more in the fore-going pages.

Acknowledgments

While the author takes responsibility for all errors and omissions in this book, he wishes to express gratitude to numerous friends, colleagues, and authorities on various aspects of the subject, for their generous contributions of time and knowledge.

Most of the new material on the Battle of Tsushima—or the Battle of the Japan Sea, as Admiral Togo preferred to call it—came from the survivors who are referred to or quoted in the text. Others who are not mentioned, however, also contributed invaluable information and advice, and the author feels especially indebted to all of the following retired officers or seamen of the Imperial Japanese Navy who were serving in it at the time of the events described:

Rear Admiral Ichiro Fukuda; Vice Admiral Kaoru Matsushita; Vice Admiral Takeshi Terashima; Vice Admiral Toyokasu Wanami; Commander Takeo Yamagata; Admiral Kiyoshi Hasegawa; Admiral Shinjiro Imamura; Vice Admiral Wataru Ukawa; Vice Admiral Sueki Hayashi; Seaman First Class Jinzaemon Takizawa; Seaman First Class Seiichi Goto; and Seaman First Class Kiichi Tanaka.

In addition to these distinguished veterans of the battle itself, many other Japanese experts on various phases of naval history supplied help of various sorts. The author owes thanks especially to the following:

Vice Admiral Tsuneyoshi Sakano (Ret.), who, too young to have been on board one of the warships at Tsushima, contributed his specialized knowledge of the effects of the premature explosions caused by the overly volatile powder used in the Japanese shells; former Commander Masataka Chihaya, now Director and Editor of *Zosen* and a staff officer during World War II, whose naval experience therein enabled him to assess the influence of Tsushima on subsequent Japanese naval strategy and tactics; Former Captain Yasuji Watanabe, now Representative Director of the Komatsu-Cummins Sales Co. Ltd., who occupied during World War II a position analogous to that held by Captain Masayuki Akiyama after the Russo-Japanese War; Former Admiral Sadatoshi Tomioka, whose determined father secured the sample of Shimose gunpowder in Paris, and former Commander Hideo Sekino, who together maintain the Historical Research Institute in Tokyo, specializing in naval materials; Colonel Susumu Nishiura, Lt. Colonel Yutaka Fujita, and Lieutenant Atsushi Ebihara, of the War History Office in Tokyo; Vice Admiral (Ret.) Nobuo Fukuchi, Commandant of the *Mikasa* in its present stage of existence as a Memorial Battleship and his able Executive Officer Kaichi Mochizuki; Colonel (Ret.) Kozo Sekiguchi; Professor Kinji Shimada of Tokyo University; Mr. Masao Yamashita, Director of the Ship's Science Museum of Japan's Maritime Science Foundation; Mr. Madoka Kanai of the Historiographical Institute at the University of Tokyo; Mr. Kenichi Matsushita, of the National Diet Library; Dr. Daishiro Hidaka, of the Centenary Cultural Council and editor of *A Cultural History of the Meiji Era (1868–1912)*; and Mr. Motohiko Fujiyama-Tanaka, whose distinguished father was one of Admiral Togo's close friends.

For assistance in research, translation of documents, and editorial counsel, the author is indebted, among many others, to his good friends and colleagues in the Japan office of the *Reader's Digest,* including Mr. Seiichi Fukuoka; Mr. Roy Otaki; Mr. Sen Matsuda; Mr. Hisao Sakimura; Mrs. Kazuko Okamura,

Mrs. Yuki Kondo, and Mrs. Yoko Matsumura. Among U.S. compatriots in Japan, he wishes to express special gratitude to Captain Lawrence A. Kurtz, U.S.N. Defense Attaché, and to Mr. Walter Nichols, Cultural Attaché, of the U.S. Embassy in Tokyo. Through their kindness he was able to fly over the Strait of Tsushima and to visit the city of Kagoshima in Kyushu. For consequent valued comment on regional influences on Japanese history during the early Meiji period, he is grateful to Mr. Suetaka Hatanoka, President of the Minami-Nihon Broadcasting Television Company, and to Professor Taro Hariguchi of Kagoshima University.

In both Japan and the U.S. the author leaned heavily on the collaboration, in research generally as well as nautical research in particular, of Captain Roger Pineau, U.S.N.R., now the editor in chief of the Smithsonian Institution Press. Captain Pineau's qualifications include active duty in the Far East both during and after World War II, as well as editorial assistance to Admiral Samuel Eliot Morison. He accompanied the author to Japan in 1967 and spent two months there, as well as much time in the U.S. before and afterward working with the material made available by Colonel Nishiura, Admiral Tomioka, and others.

Deeply appreciated was the advice and assistance, especially in connection with the most appropriate spelling of Japanese, Russian, and Chinese names of persons and places, of Professor Andrew Y. Kuroda and of Professor Robert V. Allen of the Library of Congress. Professor Robert Daly of the U.S. Naval Academy at Annapolis read the manuscript in draft form and offered authoritative comment on relevant aspects of Russian naval history. Through his kindness and that of its diligent curators, Mr. George N. Taube and Mr. John Tchoulanovsky, the author was also enabled to consult the materials available at the Russian Naval History Museum at Lakewood, N.J. Professor Stefan T. Possony, Director of International Studies at the Hoover Institution of Stanford University, contributed advice on the connection between Japanese espionage efforts and Russian revolutionaries during the Russo-Japanese War. Admiral Arleigh A. Burke (Ret.), former Chief of Naval Operations, supplied insights into the psychology underlying Japanese naval policies during World War II.

Finally, the author expresses his thanks to the editors of *The Reader's Digest* in the U.S.—most specifically, Executive Editor Hobart Lewis and Senior Editor S. A. Schreiner, Jr.—for their continuing advice and encouragement.

Bibliography

Admiral Togo: A Memoir (Tokyo: Togo Gensui Hensankai, 1934).

Adler, Cyrus, *Jacob H. Schiff: His Life and Letters* (Garden City, N.Y.: Doubleday, Doran, 1929).

Alcock, Sir Rutherford, *The Capital of the Tycoon* (London: 1905).

Alexander, Grand Duke, *Once A Grand Duke* (New York: Farrar & Rinehart, 1932).

Ballard, George A., *The Influence of the Sea on the Political History of Japan* (London: Murray, 1921; New York: Dutton, 1921).

Barr, Pat, *The Coming of the Barbarians* (London: Macmillan, 1967).

Battistini, Laurence H., *Japan and America* (New York: John Day, 1954).

Bodley, R.V.C., *Admiral Togo, The Authorized Life* (London: Jarrold's, 1935).

Borton, Hugh, *Japan's Modern Century* (New York: Ronald Press, 1955).

Davis, Richard Harding; Palmer, Roderick; and others, *The Russo-Japanese War* (New York: P. F. Collier, 1905).

Dennett, Tyler, *Roosevelt and the Russo-Japanese War* (New York: Doubleday, Page, 1925).

Earle, Edward Meade, ed., *Makers of Modern Strategy: Military Thought from Machiavelli to Hitler* (Princeton, N.J.: Princeton University Press, 1943).

Eubank, Keith, *Paul Cambon, Master Diplomatist* (Norman, Oklahoma: University of Oklahoma Press, 1960).

Falk, Edwin E., *Togo and the Rise of Japanese Sea Power* (New York: Longmans, Green, 1936).

Fiske, Bradley A., *Why Togo Won* (U.S. Naval Institute Proceedings, Vol. 31, 1905).

Fraser, Mary Crawford, "Admiral Togo," *World's Work*, Vol. 12 (August 1906).

Fukuzawa, Yukichi, *Autobiography*, trans. E. Kiyuko (Tokyo: 1934).

Green, Fitzhugh, and Frost, Holloway H., *Some Famous Sea Fights* (New York: Century, 1927).

Hargreaves, Reginald, *Red Sun Rising: The Siege of Port Arthur* (Philadelphia and New York: Lippincott, 1962).

Harris, Townsend; ed. M. E. Cosenza, *The Complete Journal of Townsend Harris* (New York: Doubleday, Doran, 1930).

Hoadley, W. T., *The Battle of the Sea of Japan* (U.S. Naval Institute Proceedings, Vol. 40, 1914).

Hough, Richard, *The Fleet That Had to Die* (New York: Viking, 1958).

Kennan, George, "Admiral Togo," *Outlook,* Vol. 80 (August 12, 1905).

Kennedy, Malcolm D., *The Problem of Japan* (London: Nisbeta, 1935).

Klado, Nicholas, *The Battle of the Sea of Japan* (London: Hodder & Stoughton, 1906).

———, *The Russian Navy in the Russo-Japanese War* (London: Hurst & Blackett, 1905).

Latourette, Kenneth Scott, *The Development of Japan* (New York: Macmillan, 1938).

Lloyd, Arthur, *Admiral Togo* (Tokyo: Kinkodo, 1905).

Massie, Robert K., *Nicholas and Alexandra* (New York: Atheneum, 1967).

Mizuno, Hironori, *This One Battle* (Tokyo: Daitoa Shuppan Kabushiki Kaikau, 1944).

Morison, Samuel Eliot, *Old Bruin* (Boston: Little, Brown, 1967).

Muragaki, Awaji-no-kami, *The Diary of the First Japanese Embassy to the United States of America* (Tokyo: The Foreign Affairs Association of Japan, 1958).

Novikoff-Priboy, A., *Tsushima* (New York: Knopf, 1937).

Ogasawara, Nagayo, *Life of Admiral Togo* (Tokyo: Seito Shorin Press, 1934).

Okuma, Shigenobu, *Fifty Years of New Japan* (New York: Dutton, 1909).

Politovsky, Eugene S., *From Libau to Tsushima* (London: Murray, 1906).

Possony, Stefan Thomas, *Lenin, the Compulsive Revolutionary* (Chicago: Henry Regnery, 1964).

Potter, E. B., and Nimitz, Chester W., *Sea Power: A Naval History* (Englewood Cliffs, N.J.: Prentice-Hall, 1960).

Potter, John Deane, *Yamamoto: The Man Who Menaced America* (New York: Viking, 1965).

Reischauer, Edwin O., *Japan Past and Present* (Tokyo: Tuttle, 1946).

Rosen, Baron, *Forty Years of Diplomacy* (New York: Knopf, 1922).

Russo-Japanese War, Reports from Naval Attachés, Vol. IV, *The Battle of the Sea of Japan* (London: The Admiralty Library, 1906).

Sansom, Sir George B., *Japan: a Short Cultural History* (New York and London: 1931).

———, *The Western World and Japan* (New York: Knopf, 1950).

Semenoff, Vladimir, *The Battle of Tsushima* (London: Murray, 1906).

———, *The Price of Blood* (London: Murray, 1910).

———, *Rasplata* (London: Murray, 1909).

Thiess, Frank, *The Voyage of Forgotten Men* (Indianapolis and New York: Bobbs-Merrill, 1937).

Togo, Kichitaro, *The Naval Battles of the Russo-Japanese War* (Tokyo: Gogakukyokwai, 1907).

"Togo's Victory as Seen from his Flag-Ship," *Harper's Weekly,* Vol. 49 (August 19, 1905).

Vladimir (pseud. of Zenone Volpicelli), *The China-Japan War* (London: Sampson Low, Marston, 1896).

Wainwright, Richard, *The Battle of the Sea of Japan* (U.S. Naval Institute Proceedings, Vol. 31, 1905).

The War in the Far East 1904–1905 by the Military Correspondent of the Times (London: Murray, 1905).

Witte, Count Sergius, *Memoirs* (New York: Doubleday, Page, 1921).

Wright, H. C. Seppings, *A Life of Togo* (London: Hurst & Blackett, 1907).

Yoshida, Shigeru, *Japan's Decisive Century, 1867–1967* (New York: Praeger, 1967).

Periodicals

Collier's Weekly
Daily Mainichi (Tokyo)
Harper's Weekly
The New York Times
The Scientific American
World's Work

Index

(250) INDEX